THRIVING BEYOND DEBT

The Lived Experience of Bankruptcy and Redemption

Zach Roche

First published in Great Britain in 2024 by

Bristol University Press
University of Bristol
1-9 Old Park Hill
Bristol
BS2 8BB
UK
t: +44 (0)117 374 6645
e: bup-info@bristol.ac.uk

Details of international sales and distribution partners are available at bristoluniversitypress.co.uk

© Bristol University Press 2024

British Library Cataloguing in Publication Data
A catalogue record for this book is available from the British Library

ISBN 978-1-5292-3115-1 hardcover
ISBN 978-1-5292-3116-8 ePub
ISBN 978-1-5292-3117-5 ePdf

The right of Zach Roche to be identified as author of this work has been asserted by him in accordance with the Copyright, Designs and Patents Act 1988.

All rights reserved: no part of this publication may be reproduced, stored in a retrieval system, or transmitted in any form or by any means, electronic, mechanical, photocopying, recording, or otherwise without the prior permission of Bristol University Press.

Every reasonable effort has been made to obtain permission to reproduce copyrighted material. If, however, anyone knows of an oversight, please contact the publisher.

The statements and opinions contained within this publication are solely those of the author and not of the University of Bristol or Bristol University Press. The University of Bristol and Bristol University Press disclaim responsibility for any injury to persons or property resulting from any material published in this publication.

Bristol University Press works to counter discrimination on grounds of gender, race, disability, age and sexuality.

Cover design: Lyn Davies Design
Front cover image: alamy/Andrew Patterson

To Eugene and Maria

Contents

List of Abbreviations and Acronyms		vi
About the Author		viii
Acknowledgements		ix
1	Introduction	1
2	A Deluge of Debt	13
3	The Uncertainties of Debt	31
4	Opening the Sweatbox: Purgatory and Debt Advice	49
5	Applying for Insolvency	71
6	A Clean Slate	94
7	Coping and Surviving	114
8	Conclusion: Thriving beyond Debt	136
Notes		156
Bibliography		157
Index		192

List of Abbreviations and Acronyms

Chapter 7	Liquidation bankruptcy in the US
Chapter 13	Renegotiation or restructuring bankruptcy in the US
DRN	Debt Relief Notice: An arrangement for those with smaller amounts of unsecured debt
DSA	Debt Settlement Arrangement: An arrangement for those with very large amounts of unsecured debt
GFC	Global financial crisis
ISI	Insolvency Service of Ireland: An organization established in 2013 to help insolvent debtors become solvent
IVA	Individual Voluntary Arrangements: An official form of insolvency renegotiation in the UK
LME	Liberal market economies: A term used in the varieties of capitalism literature to describe countries with a liberal approach to welfare delivery that focuses on commodification and market engagement
MABS	Money Advice and Budgeting Service: A government-run service that provides financial advice to debtors at no cost. MABS has a strong focus on self-help (for example, budgeting) and encourages debtors to try to see their problems as having a solution, even if that solution is difficult to accept.
PC	Protective Certificate: A protective legal document applied for by a Personal Insolvency Practitioner and issued by a court. This document makes it illegal to seize the debtor's assets for nonpayment of their debts, or for a creditor to contact them for 70 days. This document can be issued once every 12 months.
PFS	Prescribed Financial Statement: An accurate financial statement submitted by a debtor applying for an insolvency arrangement. The PFS includes information about the debtor's bills, receipts, and

budget (if they have one), and should demonstrate that the debtors finances are poor enough to necessitate inclusion in an insolvency arrangement.

PIA — Personal Insolvency Arrangement: The most commonly sought insolvency arrangement offered by the ISI. This arrangement is for debtors who have secured debt and unsecured debt.

PIP — Personal Insolvency Practitioner: The frontline operators of the ISI. Each PIP holds a licence valid to administer insolvency arrangements as regulated by the ISI and the Department of Finance for three years. The licence must then be renewed.

RLEs — Reasonable living expenses: While on an insolvency arrangement, a debtor must stick to a mandatory budget, referred to as their RLEs. These expenses are technocratically determined by the PIP, in consultation with the debtor and their creditor(s) at the beginning of an insolvency arrangement, and are revised on an annual basis in response to changing circumstances.

RTB — Residential Tenancies Board: An independent board dedicated to resolving disputes between landlords and tenants

About the Author

Zach Roche is Assistant Lecturer in Management Studies at South East Technological University, Ireland. His main area of interest is debt studies with a specific focus on insolvency and bankruptcy, but he also studies welfare, the experiences of unemployment, and the labour market. He favours a lived experience approach that is faithful to representing the difficulties and challenges experienced by people who are marginalized or disadvantaged.

Acknowledgements

I thank all those who helped me to write this book with their kindness, advice, and generosity. Most of all, I wish to thank my participants, who so generously shared their time and experiences with me; without them, this book would not have been possible.

1

Introduction

What is this book about?

This book is about the lived experience of bankruptcy and the role that debt relief plays as a form of welfare protection. If you have ever wondered what it is like to go bankrupt, then this book will answer at least some of your questions. By using the lens of lived experience, we will see the process from start to finish through the eyes of people with mortgage debt – from the day they get the keys to their new house, to falling into distress, how they go about seeking advice, applying to go insolvent and what then happens afterwards. The Irish situation is offered as a case study, with comparisons made to the UK and US contexts because these countries heavily influenced the recent Irish insolvency reforms of 2012 (Spooner 2018, 2019). Indeed, while bankruptcy was once a rare phenomenon, aimed at businesses and traders, such legal reforms along with changing social attitudes have made it more common for individuals. This is also a reflection of a changed economy: a century ago, most consumer borrowing was for luxury or non-essential goods (Geisst 2013), while today you can defer payment on a £5 supermarket pizza through a buy now pay later financing scheme (Cooke 2022).

The Global Financial Crisis (GFC) of 2007/2008 ignited interest in debt and credit across society (Graeber 2011). Yet I remain surprised that comparatively few accounts of debt include a discussion of debt relief, because we are positively drowning in debt and for many people it represents the only way out. Debt distress is associated with a whole range of negative socioeconomic indicators including relationship breakdown (Porter and Thorne 2006), unemployment (or underemployment) (Ramsay 2017; Debt Collective 2020), and poor mental/physical health (Davies et al 2015; James 2022). This is not even to mention the economic drag created by growing debt burdens and higher interest rates, meaning that people in debt have less and less to spend in the consumer economy (Spooner 2019; Davis and Cartwright 2020; Pope 2021). We are also borrowing for things that were formerly either free or at least heavily subsidized by the state, a trend that has led to the term 'loans for wages' being coined (Crouch 2011; Featherstone 2020). We borrow to go to college (Zaloom 2021), for medical bills (Braucher et al 2012) and, as the rise of payday loans has demonstrated, we often borrow merely to survive (Soederberg 2014). For these reasons, I contend that debt relief has, almost by stealth, become a crucial form of welfare protection, every bit as important as unemployment support – and it has the power to change lives for the better.

There are always fears that debt relief will be exploited by dishonest and unscrupulous debtors, usually referring to 'moral hazard' (Deville 2015; Ramsay 2017). A moral hazard occurs when you know someone else will bear the costs associated with your risky behaviour (Spooner 2019). For example, if you know debt relief is easy to access, you might borrow recklessly and write down your debt rather than paying it back, transferring the risk from you to your lender. These fears nearly always exist on paper rather than in reality (Rock 2014), as it now verges on common knowledge to point out that debt is about more than just an economic transaction (Graeber 2011; Geisst 2013); it is about trust, respect and faith, and is even baked into our language.

The word 'credit' comes from the Latin 'credo', which means faith (Nietzsche 2014), with both the borrower and the lender expecting the other to act in good faith if the relationship is to be mutually beneficial. We will see throughout this book that debtors apply a moral rather than a transactional framework to their decision making. If the creditor uses threats, refuses reasonable negotiations or pushes to bankrupt the borrower, then this person will be more likely to seek debt relief. So, in order to understand debt, we need to include an understanding of debt relief, and in order to understand relief, we must go beyond seeing it as a transaction, which takes us into the world of economic theology. This perspective suggests that theological and religious ideas remain embedded in our culture and society, and continue to influence our behaviour and institutions. Throughout this book I will use theological ideas such as purgatory (Boland and Griffin 2020, 2021) and confession (Karlsen and Villadsen 2020) to explain the seemingly irrational economic choices of debtors, which have their own logics and patterns.

This book is written as an economic sociological story which charts the entire life cycle of debtor struggling to pay their mortgage debt and what they do when they are unable to meet their obligations. We begin in Chapter 2 by considering the political economy of debt, which shows just how much debt has grown across our society, before connecting this to the transformation that has taken place in debt relief. In Chapter 3 we will see the day of borrowing, animated by a dream of living a good life, and how unemployment, relationship breakdown and increasing cost of living expenses push people into over-indebtedness. The question of why debtors refuse to give up is explored in Chapter 4, which I describe as a purgatory of debt; indeed, many debtors have told me they feel that they deserve to be punished for failing to pay. In Chapter 5, we see the meeting between the debtor and the insolvency practitioner, mediated as a confession that requires the debtor to tell the truth and take responsibility for what has gone wrong. Following this, the debtor will either succeed and attain salvation (Chapter 6) or fail and be condemned to the hellish experience of endless coping and survival strategies (Chapter 7). In the conclusion (Chapter 8) I consider the implications this book has for reforming debt relief, in terms of what can or should be done.

A brief note on terms: over-indebtedness, insolvency and bankruptcy

Before going further, it is worth explaining what is meant by the terms given earlier, because they are used throughout the book. Those readers who are already familiar with the debates in this area should feel free to skip this section. For everyone else: growing household debt has led to a corresponding growth in the prevalence of what is termed over-indebtedness. This term exists to describe when debt has graduated from a bill to a problem, and anyone familiar with the area knows that no universally accepted definition of over-indebtedness exists (Combat Poverty Agency 2009; Civic Consulting 2013; Caju et al 2016). Most definitions point to an inability to pay living expenses or service debts, such as that of Stuart Stamp, which was used in Irish section of the EU Report on over-indebtedness: 'their net resources (income and realisable assets) render them persistently unable to meet essential living expenses and debt repayments as they fall due' (Stamp 2012a, p 243).

The nebulous and uncertain nature of the key word *unable* will be a recurring theme. Each person becomes unable to meet their expenses at different points: some are willing to pawn valuables, some are willing to take on a second job and some are willing to cut anything even remotely resembling entertainment. Yet they still may not consider themselves over-indebted, even if others do. More expanded definitions include the length of time the borrower has been in arrears (12 months is generally considered a breaking point), needing to borrow in order to pay essential living expenses, being unable to pay an unexpected expense of around €1,100 and so on (CSO 2012). What is often true is that people remain over-indebted for far too long before applying for an insolvency or bankruptcy programme (Porter and Thorne 2006; Hoyes 2019). The ambiguity of whether or not one is over-indebted, combined with shame and stigma, often means that debtors delay their application until long after the costs exceed the benefits (Ramsay 2017; Spooner 2019).

Moving to the arena of insolvency and bankruptcy, nearly everyone has at least heard of the latter, while few are even aware that the former exists; because of the subject matter of this book, it is worth clarifying the difference between them. Bankruptcy generally refers to what we might term liquidation, called Chapter 7 bankruptcy in the US context (Sousa 2013). When you are bankrupted, your debts are wiped out, but so are your assets, which are seized or sold by your creditors to compensate for your failure to pay (Ramsay 2017). There are few exceptions to what can be discharged in bankruptcy, though usually tax liabilities, child support arrears or criminal damages must be paid even after bankruptcy (Spooner 2019). Infamously, the US bankruptcy system prevents the discharge of student loans, which has created a huge economic drag on younger people in America (Debt Collective 2020). Aside from these exceptions, bankruptcy is generally thought of as the quick and brutal form of debt relief, which aims to bring about a fresh start where the debtor can begin a new economic life. Restrictions usually last a year (or less), though the debtor will have to declare their status as a bankrupt if they apply for credit in the future, with obvious implications in terms of stigma (Sousa 2013).

Insolvency, by contrast, is best thought of as a form of renegotiation and is less extreme than bankruptcy (Stamp 2016). Chapter 13 Bankruptcy in the US is a form of insolvency, as is the Personal Insolvency Arrangement (PIA) in Ireland and the Individual Voluntary Arrangement (IVA) in the UK. Insolvency is a legally binding restructuring of your debts, subject to your living on a reduced income for three to five years, intended to prove your financial literacy and commitment to change. If you complete your programme, some of your debt will be written down and what remains will be restructured (Ramsay 2017). Insolvency is especially appealing to mortgagors because most insolvency regimes have a programme specifically aimed at keeping the debtor in their home (Roche 2019). This book is an account of the lived experiences of the over-indebted mortgage holder who (after many trials and tribulations) wishes to apply for insolvency.

A brief note on methods

Rather than spend a lot of space and time describing my methods in detail, I will write a short note here. Readers who are interested in the full methodological details of the research that produced this book can see Chapter 5 of my doctoral dissertation (Roche 2019). Briefly, I interviewed 18 debtors and four Personal Insolvency Practitioners (PIPs) after receiving informed consent; interviews were then fully transcribed. As this is a piece of qualitative ethnographic research, I also spent time speaking with academics, journalists, policy makers, judges, debt advisors and other people interested in debt relief to build up as full a picture of the experience as I could (Bryman

2004; Corbin and Strauss 2008). It is my hope that the book will have appeal to these same people. All participant names are pseudonyms, and if a quote does not refer to a name, then that person is not one of the interviewees. Each interview lasted about an hour, and the results were analysed thematically (Creswell 2007), with these themes featuring across the various chapters of the book. It is my goal to produce an account of debt and relief that is as faithful to their lived experience as possible.

Lived experience

It is no secret that bankruptcy is an isolating and stigmatizing experience (Sousa 2013; Debt Collective 2020). Discussions about debt often relate it to abstract moral ideals such as honour and responsibility (Graeber 2011; Lazzarato 2012; Geisst 2013), so by failing to pay and opting for bankruptcy you have revealed some moral deficiency in yourself to the world. Because of this, bankruptcy is shrouded by a halo of shame and secrecy that strangles our capacity to speak about it (Walker 2011). Indeed, debtors are reluctant to even research bankruptcy because of the superstition that admitting it as a possibility would reify it, in the same way that people are reluctant to make a will because doing so would signal they are ready to die. It is precisely this reluctance to talk about it that makes lived experience such a powerful means to grapple with bankruptcy. However, the term 'lived experience' is somewhat ambiguous and contradictory (Whelan 2022); after all, what would it mean to have an experience other than one that is lived (McIntosh and Wright 2018)? This section will clarify what I mean by this term.

Lived experience is a means of articulating or expressing qualitative research, which tends to feature small sample sizes based on interviews, focus groups, case studies or participant observation with the goal of accessing the meaning, perspectives, and beliefs of the participants. Qualitative research has often tried (with varying levels of success) to elevate the perspectives of the disadvantaged or marginalized by demonstrating how discrimination and stigma impacts people in practice. Lived experience can generally be taken to mean two things. First, it should be based on the words, reflections and thoughts of the people who have actually had the experience; this is vital because it ensures the account that is produced is faithful and accurate, which forms the 'lived' component. Second, 'experience' means that we must include context, perhaps best conveyed by Clifford Geertz (1973) when he repurposed the term 'thick description'. In order for a description to be thick, we should know details about the backgrounds of the participants (what sort of people they are), and context about the community and society in which they live, going beyond a description of behaviour and actions. I offer such details about my informants in Table 1.1, to give the reader clarification and context about the kinds of people who will be discussed throughout the book.

Table 1.1: Participant profiles

Pseudonym	Occupation	Debt (approx.)	In arrears because …
Paul	Retired (formerly teacher)	€250,000	He refinanced his home to give his children money at a difficult time in their lives.
Sarah	Retail worker	€100,000	She had insecure part-time work, combined with the cost of going back to college as a mature student.
Roger	Chef	€150,000	His partner was disabled in an accident, which reduced their income and put pressure on their lives.
Michael	Self-employed	€180,000	He expanded his business shortly before the financial crash of 2008, leaving him vulnerable and over-indebted.
Amy	Freelance writer	€100,000	She applied for a mortgage when freelance writing work was better paid and more plentiful. Fewer opportunities have put pressure on her ability to make regular repayments.
Jane	Nurse	€340,000	Her mortgage was purchased by a credit management firm (also called 'vulture funds'), which has refused to negotiate and has increased both fees and interest.
Barry	Self-employed	€280,000	He was disabled in an accident, leaving him unable to work as often or efficiently.
Michelle	Customer service	€33,000	She grew up underprivileged and needed a payday loan to pay her rent and avoid eviction. She has been unable to repay this debt due to a rate of interest of ~40%.
Rachel	Manager with industry specific qualifications	€95,000	She left her job after being sexually harassed. She has been blacklisted in her industry and is unable to get another job at the same pay scale.
Aileen	Medical services	€100,000	She has student loans in addition to her mortgage debt, exacerbated by being unable to find a full-time job in her profession.

Table 1.1: Participant profiles (continued)

Pseudonym	Occupation	Debt (approx.)	In arrears because …
Mona	Part-time lecturer	€105,000	She has precarious work, leading to an irregular and unpredictable income; combined with an aggressive repayment policy from her bank, this has led her to fall into arrears.
Simon	Technical support advisor	€120,000	He purchased a mortgage at the height of the boom in 2007. The discovery of a potentially fatal health issue several years ago has put pressure on his ability to work.
Ciara	Administrator	€116,000	She refinanced her mortgage in 2007 and was able to make the higher repayments until her partner passed away a few years later.
Tara	Retail worker	€50,000	She is the only non-White participant in my project. She found that she was unable to get loans from reputable credit institutions after encountering racial abuse. Consequently, she instead had to seek payday loans at a higher level of interest.
Laura	Customer care advisor	€195,000*	*She currently has no debt, as her house was repossessed following years of legal battles. She was formerly €195,000 in debt, which she was unable to pay when her partner left her.
Sean	PhD student; part-time tutor; part-time retail worker	€120,000	His precarious work in the university sector leaves him with an irregular income. He can make his mortgage payments in some months, but not others.
Max	Technical support advisor	€105,000	He assumed responsibility for his parents' mortgage when they were hospitalized.
Rick	Administrator	€85,000	His case is unusual, in that he had a personal relationship with his PIP and bank which enabled him to easily pursue insolvency.

Lived experience gives us a certain amount of empathy for the people in question because we can imagine ourselves in their place and can also reveal problems or inconsistencies with hegemonic perspectives. Participants will have their own rationalities and reasons for doing things that may contradict or conflict with widely held viewpoints or seem irrational to an outside observer. For example, in Chapter 3 we will meet Barry, who described his budgeting technique to me – a system of hats. This involves placing three hats on his kitchen table at the beginning of each month. The bills he will pay go in one hat, the bills he might pay go in another, and the bills he will not or cannot pay go in the third. This is not a rationalized economic strategy, or anything close to double entry bookkeeping, but it does have its own internal logic and Barry is fastidious about tracking who has been paid what. He could not imagine budgeting any other way.

Theories and metaphors of debt

To augment and develop this understanding of debt and bankruptcy as a lived experience, I draw on various metaphors and theories throughout the book to help us reimagine how we think about debt. Principally I do this because debtors think of and describe their debt in metaphorical terms, and if we are to gain an understanding that is rooted in context, then we must see this experience through their gaze. Metaphors also help to spark the imagination and encourage us to think about problems in abstract and nonlinear ways (Lakoff and Johnson 2008). Metaphors have played an important role in sociological research since the inception of the discipline, with Durkheim conceptualizing social solidarity by using machinery or the body as metaphors for how social cooperation could take place (Mechtraud 1955).[1] Debt is no exception to this trend (Arrese and Vara-Miguel 2015) with over-indebtedness described using the language of war (for example, the fight against debt [Bergeron 2016]), natural disaster (for example, a debt earthquake [Holland 2010]) and biology (for example, debt is a disease that can be cured [Shipman-Roberts 2022]).

With our growing volume and intensity of debt, it is therefore not surprising that contemporary metaphors tend to describe debt as an oppressive force that possesses physical power. Debtors almost never describe themselves using technical terms like defaulted or over-indebted; rather, they are being 'crushed' or 'drowned' by debt (Montgomerie 2019). Likewise, they do not say their mortgage is in negative equity; instead, it is 'underwater' (White 2010). Something about the helplessness and isolation of drowning has struck a chord in our imaginations, and the stigma of debt often makes it a highly individual experience because people are so ashamed to speak about it (Debt Collective 2020). My favourite of these metaphors is 'deluge', which is used by Montgomerie (2019, p 5) and which I feel is the only metaphor that can properly encapsulate the sheer volume of debt that now bears down upon us as a society. It is the metaphor of the deluge that I draw upon in Chapter 2 when I discuss the political economy of indebtedness.

In the latter part of the book, the metaphorical stance pivots as the debtor moves through the relief process and we will begin to see a certain religious ethos emerge, which I situate in terms of economic theology (Schwarzkopf 2020). Once again, it is the debtors themselves who provoke this, as when they discuss what they hope to achieve through bankruptcy, they gradually come to use more salvific language. As one participant said to me when discussing why she needed to go bankrupt, "I need a miracle". Economic theology seeks to unpack the theological aspects of ostensibly secular economic behaviour, activities, or phenomena (Goodchild 2020; Karlsen and Villadsen 2020; Schwarzkopf 2020; Boland and Griffin 2021). This framework can easily be applied to debt, which so often uses the language of sin, confession, revelation, and so on, which are felt so keenly as guilt, fear, and shame by debtors (Nietzsche 2014; Sløk 2020). Indeed, how we treat debtors (and how they behave) does not make sense unless we go beyond rational choice explanations and see debt as a moral and theological trial that the debtor must undergo in order to be forgiven (Lazzarato 2012; Karlsen and Villadsen 2020).

As previously mentioned, this feeds into the moral rubric that is so important for understanding why debtors do what they do. I build on the work of Viviana Zelizer (1994, 2011), who has persuasively argued that money is imbued with moral power (for example, money received from welfare is often seen as less valuable than an equivalent amount of money from paid work) (Wilkis 2017). I similarly argue that different types of debt are seen as morally distinct by debtors, and this influences how they proceed and whether they seek relief. I identify four kinds: leisure, survival, status, and caring debts. Debt taken on for survival (to pay rent or buy groceries) is morally different from money borrowed to go on an expensive holiday (leisure debt). As we shall see, debtors are engaged in a constant tug of war with creditors, who usually try to categorize all debt as leisure, as ultimately it is spending someone else's money.

The case for debt relief

Debt relief is controversial, involving as it does the remission, forgiveness, or cancellation of part or all of a debt (Debt Collective 2020), meaning that part of the job of this book is to demonstrate why we ought to support it. In my view, the case for relief has never been stronger and can even be made on grounds that ought to appeal to creditors. Relief is a positive force for entrepreneurship and employment (Spooner 2019), as debt inflicts a considerable amount of economic drag on a debtor whose income becomes increasingly swallowed up in attempting to simply meet their minimum repayment schedule (Langley 2009). This means that they have less money to spend in the economy. In a liberal market economy (LME) such as Ireland, the UK and the US that depend so much on consumer activity to generate economic growth, this can only do damage (Hall and Soskice 2001).

Wage stagnation, combined with the withdrawal of the welfare state, has led to loans replacing wages (Featherstone 2020), where individuals now borrow privately to make up for socioeconomic shortcomings in society. In Ireland the minimum wage has increased by 13 per cent since 2011, while rents have increased by 89 per cent (Hearne 2022), the difference has to come from somewhere. Accordingly, the landscape of bankruptcy has also changed with insolvencies counted in the hundreds of thousands across the Anglosphere (Spooner 2019). This has stirred up quite the debate: is this due to greater financial hardship or less stigma surrounding the process? McClanahan (2018) says it is both, and while I agree with her, I lean more towards the former than the latter.

Building on this, while it is true that debt has a powerful disciplining effect by compelling debtors to accept work under any conditions (Soederberg 2014), research has also shown that the stress of indebtedness can be paralysing, leading to unemployment or underemployment (Ramsay 2017). Paradoxically, the only way to survive this situation is to borrow more money (typically at a higher rate of interest), solidifying the logic of the debt trap and lengthening the chain of creditors who will never get their money back (Rock 2014). By relieving people of such longstanding debts, we would generate economic activity and restore hope to people trapped in a state of financial melancholia (Davies et al 2015).

Preventing people from discharging these debts does not enable creditors to get their money back; it merely prolongs the suffering of the debtor who tends to focus their repayment efforts on those who 'shout the loudest' (Kirwan 2018). This has led to increasingly aggressive repayment strategies from collectors who know that a person with one problem debt likely has other creditors, all of whom will be clamouring for whatever they can get (Deville 2015). Indeed, at a time when household debt is exploding, debt relief systems have been made harder rather than easier to access (Ramsay 2017). Legal literature has advanced the term 'sweatbox' to describe the time spent by the debtor before they file bankruptcy (Foohey et al 2018). These same authors have found that two years is the break point where a debtor transitions into a 'long struggler' who 'lose their homes to foreclosure, sell other property, report going without food and other necessities, all while employing multiple tactics to try and make ends meet and dealing with persistent debt collection calls and lawsuits' (Foohey et al 2018, p 221). In many ways, this book is a description of what it is like to be a long struggler in the sweatbox, and the consequences this experience has on people's social and economic lives, in the full knowledge that debt relief would end this hellish experience.

With this in mind, it is not surprising that modern legislation has trended away from what we traditionally think of bankruptcy (liquidation) and towards insolvency (restructuring). While full bankruptcy can be advantageous for the creditor under certain circumstances, and the introduction of measures such as the IVA in the UK or the PIA in Ireland were initially unpopular with creditors, it is increasingly the case that creditors favour restructuring and continued negotiation over liquidation (Deville 2015; Spooner 2019). This forms part of a larger trend in finance where credit is now made available to everyone (Langley 2009) – the only question is under what terms and at what rate of interest. The most recent financial innovations push debt towards those least able to pay – what Deville (2020) has called the digital subprime, Soederberg (2014) calls the surplus population, and Ramsay (2017) refers to as NINA (no income, no asset) debtors. The new logic of financialization is to move from repayment to payment (Adkins 2020), and financial instruments are now designed with the expectation that most borrowers will never fully repay. Profit will instead be extracted through fees, commissions, penalties, and fines, but most importantly through interest (Langley 2009; Deville 2015; Montgomerie 2019; Featherstone 2020).

By the very same logic, indefinite negotiation and continuous restructuring has become a part of the framework of profitability. Restructuring was initially unpopular with creditors because it often entails a cramdown (a mandatory writing down of debt), but only if the debtor can complete the programme. Creditor strategy has been to push for longer programmes (they now typically last for five years) and to create networks of dependency between themselves and insolvency practitioners, who often prefer to take a bad deal over no deal because they are paid by the fees generated by these arrangements (Spooner 2019). Such programmes also typically feature harsh penalties even for minor mistakes, and many debtors are ejected from a Chapter 13 bankruptcy in the US for missing a single payment (Debt Collective 2020). They must then return to their original unsustainable payment plan likely resulting in Chapter 7 (liquidation) bankruptcy and the seizure of any assets that have not already been pawned or sold (Porter and Thorne 2006).

This strategy effectively increases the length of time the creditor can extract interest and fees from the debtor, and so even bankruptcy and the legal system surrounding it have been drawn into the logic of infinite repayment. Even when the debtor's resources are completely exhausted, they may be unable to file for bankruptcy because the fees are too high, resulting in people having to 'save up' to go bankrupt (Mann and Porter 2010). Thus, the strongest argument for opening up debt relief is that it will end this purgatorial cycle of infinite extraction, give debtors a meaningful fresh start, and encourage creditors to lend money at a price that reflects its true social cost.

Ireland serves as a fascinating case study for the potential of debt relief because its profile is so extreme. Like most Anglosphere countries, it featured a dramatic rise in household indebtedness during its property-driven economic boom known colloquially as the Celtic Tiger (Coulter and Nagle 2015), peaking at an astonishing 235 per cent of average household income in 2009. This was even higher than the peaks in the US (144 per cent in 2007) and the UK (174 per cent in 2007) (OECD 2023). The crash which followed the Celtic Tiger made legislative change inevitable, culminating in a modernization of the Victorian era bankruptcy laws with a framework imported from the UK and inspired by the US (Spooner 2012; Stamp 2016). The rapidity and totalizing nature of this transformation led to concerns that the new system would be too lenient on debtors. These fears were quickly allayed once the legislation was unveiled and even Christine Lagarde (then head of the International Monetary Fund [IMF]) said the laws were "exemplary" and a model for the world to follow (Spooner 2018).

This book will unpack the Irish insolvency system to explain what made it so appealing to hegemonic political actors. However, the newness that makes it novel and interesting also means that comparatively few debtors have completed an arrangement, and so the statistical data available is sparse (for now). For this reason, I make frequent comparisons to the UK and US contexts, whose systems heavily influenced Irish law makers, and which have much more established insolvency practices (Spooner 2018). We begin by considering just how over-indebted we are by looking at the situation from a political economy standpoint.

2

A Deluge of Debt

Introduction

This chapter will unravel several myths about debt relief, primarily that the growing prevalence of debt relief is due to a lessening of stigma, that is, that people are no longer ashamed to go bankrupt. Instead, I will present the case that the growth in the usage of insolvency is best explained by the vast expansion of household indebtedness over the past 50 years combined with the modernization of debt relief, both of which happened concurrently. Further, usage of debt relief is cyclical, structural, and driven by policy. From the standpoint of political economy, usage of debt relief is driven more by the booms and busts of the business cycle than by cynical debtors seeking to escape from their obligations.

The discussion in this chapter is presented in two parts. The first part argues that the ideological supremacy of neoliberalism after the 1980s led to policies that created the economic and social conditions for a deluge of debt, within which we remain trapped. The second part charts how the liberalization of lending that has led to us becoming so indebted was simultaneously accompanied by the modernization of debt relief. This means that the pivot towards debt relief was a deliberate policy decision within many Western governments and was not due to a sudden moral vacuum among borrowers.

Everywhere we look, debt seems to have grown beyond our ability to control it. Americans now owe an eye-watering $12 trillion in mortgage debt, approaching the $14 trillion record from just before the financial crisis (New York Federal Reserve 2023; De Visé 2023). Unsecured debt has likewise expanded dramatically, with the average American now having four credit cards and a grand total of a trillion dollars owed across the country (White 2022). As I write these words, student loan debt in the US has just crested over $2 trillion, which has sparked significant debate in the public sphere due to it being one of the few forms of debt that cannot be discharged in bankruptcy (Martin 2005; Haverstock 2023). One wonders how this debt could possibly ever be repaid, but of course the secret of the system is that it must constantly expand in order to survive (Featherstone 2020). The common belief is that banks have a stockpile of money, from which they lend. This is incorrect, debt in-fact creates new money at the point of borrowing, and is not based on the cash reserves possessed by the creditor. This gives banks a unique power in our society, and means that all debt cannot ever be repaid. Pettifor (2017, p xi) has put this in stark terms by citing an estimate that global GDP now stands at $77 trillion, while financial assets have grown to $225 trillion.

This is the deluge that has overwhelmed us; indeed, water metaphors have become more common in descriptions of debt. In a positive sense, these metaphors raise the potential of debt to stimulate growth in the same manner that irrigating a field is crucial to the survival of crops and agriculture (Montgomerie 2019). In the same way, credit provides liquidity and can be a generator/instigator of economic activity and innovation. Nearly all entrepreneurs engage in some sort of borrowing to start their business, which creates jobs and stimulates economic activity (Pettifor 2017, pp 6–7). There is of course a darker strain of debt/water metaphors; we often hear of people who are being 'crushed' or 'drowning' in debt, or whose mortgages are 'underwater' (White 2010; Graeber 2011; Davies et al 2015). Something about the helplessness and oppressive experience of drowning has struck a chord in our indebted imaginations and has provoked renewed conversations about the role that debt relief should play in our economy and society.

The neoliberal turn

It is worth taking a moment to unpack what I mean by neoliberalism, as the sheer volume of literature that now cites it has generated many alternative accounts and readings, so it is at risk of being overused. As Elisabeth Prügl has observed: 'Neoliberalism has become somewhat of a master variable, an explanatory hammer that fits all nails' (2015, p 3). I aim to be as specific as possible about the explanatory power of neoliberalism, while also giving space for other theoretical readings. To further expand on this, Watts (2021) in his excellent article on the uses and abuses of neoliberalism breaks the concept down into four theoretical forms. Neoliberalism can be: (1) a set of economic policies; (2) a hegemonic ideological project; (3) a political rationality (governmentality); and (4) as a specific kind of embodied subjectivity. He further observes that there is often strain in connecting neoliberalisms 1, 2, and 3 with neoliberalism 4, and that society may not be quite as overrun with neoliberal subjects as we have been led to believe. I am generally in agreement with Watts, and this chapter explores the impact that the first three neoliberalisms have had on indebtedness, while the extent to which debtors are neoliberal subjects will be explored in subsequent chapters.

If you read these kinds of books, then you are most likely familiar with a story about the decline of social democracy and the rise of neoliberalism, including its key players like Margaret Thatcher, Ronald Reagan, and Friedrich Hayek, the last of whom serves as the traditional intellectual champion of the Chicago School of Economics. Other scholars have written about this era in considerable detail, and I recommend Harvey (2007); Foucault and Senellart (2008); Mudge (2008); Streeck (2011); and Coulter and Nagle (2015) for those who are interested in a more complete version of the story. I will refer to the major features in passing, but will focus predominately on how neoliberalism encountered and transformed the field of finance, credit, lending, and debt generally – and the profound impact this has had on our social and economic lives.

In brief, neoliberalism is an ideological project dedicated to implementing and enhancing market-oriented policies (Harvey 2007), and where possible reducing the influence and impact of the state within the market. Most forms of regulation, particularly those which restrict or impede the movement of capital, are positioned by neoliberals as economically irrational – representing an intrusion of the state into an arena it simply cannot comprehend (Burchell et al 1991). Markets are made up of uncountable individual actors who make decisions based on their rational best interests, and placing restrictions on these decisions is not only economically unwise but also counter to the values of liberty and freedom (Bell 2020). In the case of markets, their sheer complexity makes a mockery of attempts to regulate it, producing an exhausting game of cat and mouse where the regulators are always chasing the latest loopholes found by the regulated (Harman 2009). In the latter case, it is suggested that attempting to tell people what is best for them is patronizing at best or tyrannical at worst – captured effectively by the British slogan 'the nanny state', which has since come to be used in many countries (Streeck 2011).

Predictably, then, the neoliberal project has set about doing exactly what it said it would do – deregulating the economy, privatizing or marketizing services that were formerly provided by the state, and reducing barriers to trade and other protectionist policies (Foucault and Senellart 2008). These were always made amenable to the electorate by appealing to some notion of freedom: a responsible state does not meddle in your life and tell you what to do, trusting you in turn to be responsible for your own wellbeing (Rose 1991). In a wider sense, the creation of healthy market conditions is also good for everyone. The change is persistent and direct: do not think of yourself as a citizen, think of yourself as a consumer (Leicht and Fitzgerald 2014a).

This ideological turn by itself was not sufficient to bring about social change; as Rose (1991) has discussed, it became essential to govern people through their freedom rather than through authoritarian or tyrannical means. This was achieved through a general embedding of finance in people's everyday lives (Langley 2009), not that they were given much of a choice. In most cases the attractiveness of finance was enhanced by the tactical withdrawal of state support that made a financialized solution the only rational course of action (Springer 2016; Gershon 2018; Zaloom 2021). Consider retirement, for example. Tax incentives were amplified for private retirement savings accounts as state-supported retirement programmes were withdrawn. State programmes would provide a flat and predictable stream of income that may (just barely) be enough to survive, though certainly not thrive. Conversely, a responsible actor who invested in private pension and got a mortgage will have two significant assets available to them upon retirement (Leicht and Fitzgerald 2014a, 2014b).

In this way, risk and investment grew to take on more positive connotations (Langley 2009), as the public were encouraged to be more speculative and daring with their money and savings. Again, this happened as the deregulation of the finance industry and collapse of interest rates made it virtually worthless to invest in a 'traditional' savings account, with interest rates so low that it was merely a place to store (rather than grow) your money.

Loans for wages

David Harvey has made the observation that capitalism does not ever truly solve its problems, but it can delay facing them by moving them around (Harvey 2007, 2017). The 'stagflation' (stagnation and inflation) crises of the 1970s and 1980s which propelled the neoliberals into power and have haunted us ever since are such a problem. The issue was 'solved' by having central banks abandon full employment as a guiding strategy, which allowed them to raise interest rates many times in the struggle against inflation. This was accompanied by deindustrialization and the movement of most primary and secondary sector activities to less developed nations, which dramatically reduced labour costs, while still ensuring developed countries would have access to the final product through inequitable trade agreements.

These changes led to shockwaves in the economy. While employment eventually stabilized, some of those whose jobs were 'outsourced' never found work again, and their communities were devastated by the sudden vacuum in their local economy with social problems that linger to this day (see Lister [2004; 2013] and Harvey [2017] for more on sinkhole estates). This led to steady increases in long-term unemployment, which in turn led to the workfare reforms of the 1990s. To compound this, for the first time in the postwar era, productivity became decoupled from hourly compensation. From 1948 to 1973, productivity increased by 96.7 per cent, while hourly compensation increased by 91.3 per cent, but from 1973 to 2014, productivity increased by 72.2 per cent and hourly compensation by just 9.2 per cent (Economic Policy Institute 2022). The jobs which replaced the old manufacturing jobs have overwhelmingly been in the service economy, which tend to be paid at minimum wage. In the US, the federal minimum wage has been $7.25 an hour since 2009, but rent has been increasing by more than 3 per cent a year since 2012. The average American can now expect to pay $1,700 a month for a 900 sq. ft. apartment (Rent Café 2023).

In Ireland the minimum wage has increased by 13 per cent since 2011 (currently €11.30 an hour), while rents have increased by 89 per cent (Hearne 2022) and now average almost €1,500 per month, with half of tenants spending more than 30 per cent of their pay on rent (Pope 2021). The gap between rising costs and stagnant income has been closed by debt (Crouch 2011; Kirwan et al 2020), with 71 per cent of the Irish population now carrying some form of debt, up significantly from 56 per cent in 2013 (Household Finance and Consumption Survey 2013, 2018, 2020). Almost 40 per cent of Irish people now have some amount of credit card debt, up from 17.5 per cent in 2013, and now carry a median debt of €1,000 (Household Finance and Consumption Survey 2013, 2018). Nonmortgage loans are also up and are now held by a little over 45 per cent of the population, with the median Irish borrower owing €7,300 (Household Finance and Consumption Survey 2020). Student loans are among the fastest-growing loan categories in Ireland, with education costs up 18 per cent in the last decade (Lajoie 2020), and are often lent to parents to pay for fees or student rental accommodation. The situation is not as extreme as other LMEs such as the UK or the US, where student loans are more financialized; however, this is how the process starts, and once borrowing for education becomes normalized, it becomes difficult to reverse as colleges price this income into their strategic plans (Zaloom 2021).

This phenomenon has been called loans for wages or privatized Keynesianism (Crouch 2011; Spooner 2019; Featherstone 2020). The latter name was coined because in traditional Keynesian macroeconomics, the state borrows to provide for citizens, while in privatized Keynesianism, it is individuals who borrow to purchase that which was formerly supplied by the state. Housing, education, health, and transport have all been identified as areas where borrowing has increased as a consequence of a reduction of state services or the imposition of fees, which has had the entirely predictable effect of hugely increasing debt loads (Davis and Cartwright 2020; Deville 2020). There remains one further aspect of the neoliberal turn to discuss: the asset economy and the mortgages which underpin it.

The asset economy

While wages have stagnated, neoliberalism offered a kind of olive branch to workers: a stake in your country. The easiest asset in which to give people a stake was, of course, housing – its security and permanency was something which people already desired (Žižek 2015; Waldron and Redmond 2016). The stagnation of wages was then simultaneously accompanied by a deliberately policy choice to tie economic growth to the inflation of assets, a tendency Adkins et al (2020) have termed the asset economy. Increasing homeownership has been a consistent political goal across many different neoliberal governments. Housing rapidly became the keystone of the neoliberal project, as it could solve many problems at once. Individuals would instead gain a secure asset that would continuously appreciate in value, providing security for them and their family, while also leaving something for the next generation (Adkins et al 2020). Banks and other creditors, by contrast, found a way to profitably extract money, while also packaging mortgage debt into financial instruments such as securities that were then traded on increasingly large scales – ultimately with disastrous results.

In principle, mortgages became more accessible than ever before, enabling many who were excluded from financial systems to acquire a very desirable little piece of their country. It was an economically sensible decision, as rent is generally thought of as 'dead money' (Hearne 2017), while a mortgage repayment is typically cheaper, and you end up with a valuable asset at the end. This facilitates wealth building and security for retirement, and gives a productive outlet for your income (as opposed to rent) (Langley 2009). Stagnating wages have only made asset ownership more desirable; however, this has introduced several paradoxes that have pushed asset-based housing to its limits.

If the purpose of the asset economy is the indefinite inflation of assets, and these assets are primarily housing, but wages do not increase relative to the value of the asset, then the number of people excluded from this system will grow (Bramall 2016a; Adkins et al 2020). It is a very attractive system if you are already a part of it: those who own assets see their value increase year on year and can even leverage these assets to acquire more properties by using them as collateral (Langley 2009), while those who do not own assets risk falling out of the system entirely (Hearne 2022) . This is particularly the case in the current crises (inflation, energy, cost of living), where larger shares of income are being spent merely to survive. Further, as asset prices have continued to swell, this means that the minimum deposit also increases, leading to further difficulties for those on limited incomes (Montgomerie 2009; Prasad 2012; Hearne 2017).

Rent is a particularly insidious culprit, as it siphons away money that would otherwise be saved and put towards a mortgage, and as housing had become more commodified and financialized, there are fewer rental properties available, leading to significant increases in rent. To add insult to injury, rent is also not considered on someone's credit report, leading to a further paradox that someone could pay €2,000 a month in rent, but be refused for a €1,250 a month mortgage (Hearne 2022). Those who are behind fall even further behind, while those who are ahead get even further ahead, able to earn so-called 'passive income' from their assets, which they rent to those who are excluded, reproducing the very inequalities that assets were meant to solve (Keohane 2013; Adkins et al 2020).

This is the very situation in which we find ourselves now. A shrinking portion of the wealthy elite can afford a mortgage, and everyone else must settle for lifelong renting. In Ireland figures from 2020 show that a median mortgage now stands at an eye-watering €260,000, up from €250,000 in 2018 and €129,000 in 2013 (Household Finance and Consumption Survey 2013, 2018, 2020), while the median age of a mortgagor has increased from 33 to 43 over the last ten years (Law Society of Ireland 2023). This has led the media to cast a critical eye over the 'lowest rates of home ownership in 50 years' (Downing 2019, p 1), which is among the most critical media coverage of government policy (Oireachtas 2023; Phelan 2023). This policy has been to provide demand-side incentives to borrowers and developers, such as the help-to-buy scheme, which gives first-time property purchasers an income tax refund up to a maximum of €30,000. Property developers then made the entirely predictable decision to increase the market price of houses by €20,000–30,000 around the time that the scheme went into effect (Hearne 2022). Once schemes and a deposit are factored in, the true median price of housing is over €300,000, far out of reach those with a median income of €46,000 (Household Finance and Consumption Survey 2020). Those who do manage to borrow are therefore acquiring more debt, at a higher rate of interest, in a situation where the housing market has once again become overheated – though for different reasons compared to 2008.

The increases we are seeing in the usage of debt relief are therefore due to the fact that people are borrowing more than they used to. In addition, the stagnation of incomes relative to inflation and rises in the cost of living have made households more vulnerable to income shocks (such as a once-in-a-lifetime recession or pandemic or energy crisis). While LME households may just about be able to make their minimum repayments, even a short illness or bout of unemployment often creates unmanageable arrears and lead a debtor down the road to eventual insolvency, which I will explore further in Chapter 3. However, while the instruments of lending were liberalized and deregulated under neoliberalism, there was a simultaneous push to reconfigure and modernize the mechanisms of debt relief.

Modernizing debt relief

This section outlines a simple but often overlooked reason why the number of bankrupts is increasing: the fact that debt relief was modernized in the postwar era. Older systems of debt relief were highly punitive and stigmatizing, positioning debtors as moral deviants who had failed to keep their word, with the creditor being the wronged party (Graeber 2011; Stamp 2016). The fingerprints of this are all over our culture and language; even the word 'credit' comes to us from the Latin 'credo', which means faith (Nietzsche 2014). Both parties entered an arrangement in good faith and by failing to repay, the debtor has erred. This implicitly assumes that the conditions under which the debt were offered were reasonable and that repayment was possible to begin with, which was often not the case. Usurious rates of interest did not stop existing simply because they were banned, with black and grey credit markets filling the lending gap when banks or other formal creditors would not lend to subprime borrowers (Zelizer 1994, 2011; Geisst 2013; Deville 2020).

In some countries, bankruptcy was so punishing that the debtor would move country, declaring that they were now a taxable resident in their new jurisdiction so that they could go bankrupt under more favourable conditions. This phenomenon, known as bankruptcy tourism, gained notoriety when Irish businessmen implicated in the financial crisis moved to the UK to take advantage of its much more lenient bankruptcy laws. Seán Quinn, once the richest person in Ireland, moved to Belfast to declare bankruptcy (McDonald 2019); though initially successful, the bankruptcy order was annulled within a year and he was forced to declare bankruptcy under much harsher conditions in the Republic of Ireland (Hourigan 2015). I begin by outlining what the typical formula of reform looks like, then move on to address the relative effectiveness of these reforms by considering who goes bankrupt and why, before finally closing by exploring popular arguments around what debt relief should do in LMEs.

What changed?

Four key changes have been made as part of modern bankruptcy reforms. First, the period spent insolvent or bankrupt was reduced, often considerably. In Ireland, for example, a period of bankruptcy could last between 12 and 16 years, but the Personal Insolvency Act (2012) reduced this to three years (Insolvency Service of Ireland 2013a). Surprisingly, though there was a brief initial spike, this did not lead to a permanent increase in the number of bankrupts, and the period was later reduced to just one year, which was more in line with international norms (Insolvency Service of Ireland 2016b, 2016c).

Second, the field of insolvency was opened through offering more options that were less extreme than bankruptcy, such as the IVA (the UK), Chapter 13 Bankruptcy (the US) or the PIA (Ireland) (Heuer 2014; Stamp 2017). These insolvency arrangements enable the insolvent person to write down some of their debt while also restructuring what remains, as long as they complete an insolvency programme where they live on a strict budget. Restructuring arrangements have existed for as long as debt and credit, but these have traditionally been an arrangement struck privately (even informally) by the debtor and the creditor without the interference of outside forces (Jones 2003; Rock 2014). Contemporary insolvency arrangements are more formalized and offer a range of legal protections to the debtor that were not present before. For example, the stipulation that creditors cannot contact the debtor while they are on an insolvency arrangement; such contact must be mediated by the insolvency institution that presides over the arrangement. Research has shown that insolvency is ultimately a mixed bag, as creditors now favour pushing debtors into long insolvency arrangements (up to six years in some cases) and then ejecting the debtor from the arrangement if they fail to make a single payment (Debt Collective 2020). Ultimately, while the rewards for completing such an arrangement are significant, many start but few finish.

Third, the restrictions the applicant was required to abide by were reduced in terms of their severity. Outside of the US, imprisonment for the nonpayment of debts is unusual, though not impossible (Graeber 2011). Likewise, attachment or garnishing of salaries has become less common, and the monitoring of the insolvent person is certainly not as extreme as it once was (Rock 2014). Efforts were also made to reduce the stigmatizing elements of going broke (Hayes 2000) – for example, until 2009, new bankrupts were still published in local newspapers in the UK, though this information is still published in the *London Gazette* (Sousa 2017). Most countries still maintain a register of people who have gone insolvent, though this is mostly for the benefit of creditors rather than the public.

Fourth, and finally, insolvency became something the debtor was encouraged to apply for themselves. While this may seem counterintuitive, it was at one time more common for a creditor to bring a bankruptcy request to the courts, and they did so when a tipping point was reached where the debtor still had assets (secured or otherwise) worth seizing or auctioning, and where they were not likely to recover to solvency in any meaningful way (Rock 2014). This tactical calculation was always weighed against the moral and reputational damage incurred by bankrupting someone (Heuer 2014; Brennan 2015). While a person could technically bring forward a request to bankrupt themselves, the requirements were so extreme that the person would have to live in the most absurd destitution for the order to be granted. Creditors have retained the ability to initiate proceedings if they deem it necessary, but it is now more conventional for a debtor to apply themselves.

There are many reasons for these transformations. Delinquent debt is, from a wide range of perspectives, quite toxic, and not just for the individual (Honohan 2009; Hodson et al 2014). Failure to repay can clog up the credit market and create backlogs where significant effort is expended to 'chase' debts that are no longer likely to be paid (Deville 2015). Clearing the market is a vital function of insolvency. Neoliberalism created a notion of good financial subjects who participate in consumer culture; the overhang of bad debt is a threat to this, potentially producing a situation where debtors are no longer able to meaningfully participate in the market. A clean slate may cause some damage to the creditor, but it also enables the debtor to better participate in the economy and society. The older systems were ineffective and were showing their age, having often been based on legislation from the Victorian era (Stamp 2016).

In each of these countries, we saw a similar story play out: debt relief lost its overtly punitive character and was replaced with a more structured, rationalized, and bureaucratic system which placed more emphasis on technicalities and rules than on moral wrongdoing. Their reinvention also happened quite close to one another in the mid to late 20th century, that is, Australia (1966), the UK (1986), the US (1978; 2005) and Canada (1985); Ireland (2012) stands as an outlier, with impetus for change being provided by the aftershock of the financial crisis (Heuer 2014; Stamp 2016; Ramsay 2017; Roche 2019; Schwartz 2022). These reforms had the simple and entirely predictable effect of increasing the number of people who availed themselves of debt relief by creating a modern administration and legal framework to govern it. Nevertheless, the stigma and moral values of the previous systems continue to have sway over who gets to go insolvent and why, and so we will now consider this question.

The survival of stigma

McClanahan (2018) has tapped into an important debate when she outlines the two major perspectives on why usage of debt relief is increasing. Is it due to a lessening of stigma or a greater prevalence of financial hardship? In this chapter I make the case for the latter, but it is important to discuss the former, because these hegemonic moral discourses profoundly influence how debt relief is implemented in practice. Goffman (1963, p 3) famously defined stigma as an 'attribute that is deeply discrediting', which can range from skin colour to criminal record and bankruptcy. In the case of bankruptcy, it is the financial and moral competence of the debtor that stands to be discredited. Stigma and debt have a long history, and the rhetoric that surrounds debt has always centred on morality and the perceived laziness of the debtor. In his book on *Character*, Samuel Smiles said the following of debtors in 1872: 'They cannot resist the temptation of living high, though it may be at the expense of others; and they gradually become reckless of debt, until it enthrals them. In all this there is great moral cowardice, pusillanimity, and want of manly independence of character' (Smiles 2009, p 51).

A person of poor moral character is attracted to debt because it enables them to live on the money of others; they are selfish, they lack self-control, and lack even the awareness to see that debt is a trap that enthrals themself to others. You may think that this quote is so antiquated that it could not possibly apply to the modern world, but consider the furore provoked among US Republicans by Joe Biden's fairly modest student loan forgiveness proposal:

> 'For our government just to say, "OK, well your debt is completely forgiven"... it's completely unfair. And taxpayers all over the country, taxpayers that never took out a student loan, taxpayers that pay their bills and maybe even never went to college and are just hardworking people, they shouldn't have to pay off the great big student loan debt for some college student that piled up massive debt going to some Ivy League school. That's not fair.' (Cohen 2022, p 1)

Remarkably little has changed. This statement was made by Republican Congresswoman Marjorie Taylor Greene, who herself had $183,504 in Paycheck Protection Program (PPP) loans completely forgiven (Cohen 2022). As in Smiles' quote, there is a contrast drawn between the responsible hardworking person and the reckless debtor who went to an expensive college without due consideration for the consequences of their actions. Everyone pays taxes to fund services they do not personally use – this is the foundation of the contemporary welfare state (Esping-Andersen 1990), and in this case the outrageous cost of tuition means that loans are unavoidable. Perhaps we might say that borrowing has lost some of its old stigma, but even a casual examination of the practice of insolvency shows that stigma has not only survived, but in many ways is also thriving.

A requirement of many bankruptcy programmes in various countries involves the debtor taking one (or more) financial literacy classes (Sousa 2013). In the US, this is applied rigidly to all applicants, regardless of the reason for their filing. This led to controversy when one woman who went bankrupt due to the medical bills accrued from her terminally ill child who died in hospital having to take a degrading financial literacy class where the meaning of the term 'APR' was explained to her (Oliver 2021). Financial literacy in general operates as a smokescreen. While debtors may struggle with the exact meanings of financial terms or fail to understand the minutiae of fiscal economics, it does not alter the fact that many now borrow simply to survive (Soederberg 2014). Debtors are often aware, for example, that payday loans are predatory and often multiply problems rather than solving them; however, if you are facing imminent eviction and homelessness, then you may have no alternative but to seek such a loan and try to figure it out later.

Even if financial literacy is not mandated, insolvency programmes generally require the debtor to live within a technocratically determined budget (called Reasonable Living Expenses in Ireland), which aims to impart good financial practices to the applicant. Once again, the applicant is stigmatized and it is taken for granted that they cannot budget by themselves. One problem with detecting moral or stigmatizing discourses is the tendency for modern insolvency organizations to cloak their activities in the language of economics, bureaucracy, and law. Exemplifying an economic or consumer-oriented approach (Heuer 2014), the US Courts website introduces bankruptcy to the reader by saying: 'Bankruptcy helps people who can no longer pay their debts get a fresh start by liquidating assets to pay their debts or by creating a repayment plan. Bankruptcy laws also protect financially troubled businesses. This section explains the bankruptcy process and laws' (US Courts 2022a).

This is an economic and legal process; bad debt is cleared from the market by liquidating assets or restructuring the arrangement if it no longer works. The words 'creditor' and 'debtor' are not used, and the language is not overtly moralistic or stigmatizing, though this breaks down once you investigate the fine print. Where is the 'fresh start' for bearers of student loans, for example? Compare this with the Insolvency Service of England, which summarizes its role by saying: 'We are a government agency that helps to deliver economic confidence by supporting those in financial distress, tackling financial wrongdoing and maximising returns to creditors' (Insolvency Service of England 2021).

This is more overtly moral, referring to 'financial wrongdoing' and 'economic confidence', which indicates broader concerns that go beyond specific debtors and creditors, while simultaneously offering an olive branch of sorts to both parties by 'supporting those in financial distress' and 'maximising returns to creditors'. This prevarication is common, and insolvency agencies are profoundly concerned with seeming to be biased in favour of one party over the other. Ireland is an interesting case study here because its laws are the newest (2012). Lorcan O'Connor, the first director of the insolvency service of Ireland, tried to please everyone when he said:

> 'We know, above all, the worry, the anxiety, and the distress that money challenges like this can cause – how they can eat up people's lives. For that reason, we have been highly conscious of putting in place, quickly, the best solutions we can, taking account of the various complex factors that need to be addressed – the rights of creditors, moral hazard, the structures that will be needed country wide to ensure we have a fair, transparent and equitable insolvency service.' (Insolvency Service of Ireland 2013a, p 1)

The asymmetry of power that exists between the lender and the borrower makes such equitability all but impossible, and in the end a decision is always made that will make one party far less happy than the other (Spooner 2019). Equitability rhetoric is also profoundly empty because when the process is examined in detail, it is creditors who are given preferential treatment at every turn. This is particularly the case through the instrument of the veto, which allows creditors to simply reject any arrangement that they believe is unfair or not in their interests (Insolvency Service of Ireland 2016a; Stamp 2016) – if this happens, then debtors are often left with no alternative but to declare bankruptcy.

It is also interesting that in Mr O'Connor's statement, debt is positioned for a debtor in terms of individual difficulties such as stress and anxiety, while for creditors, the factors are institutional, constituting their rights and the problem of moral hazard. The spectre of moral hazard is one that haunts all contemporary debt relief policy. Briefly, a moral hazard occurs when you assume a risk knowing you will not have to bear the costs associated with that risk (Jones 2003) – for example, taking out a loan knowing you could easily go bankrupt later, thereby transferring the risk of loan repayments from debtor to creditor. Evidence of this happening in practice is thin, but policy has been aligned to prevent it regardless. I discuss examples in the text that follows.

A person can only be considered insolvent if they are *unable* to pay their debts, but when precisely is this the case? Are you unable to pay after you lose your job or are made redundant? Are you unable to pay after missing one payment? Ten payments? Fifty payments? Are you only unable to pay when you sell your car and furniture? When have you done enough to have satisfied this nebulous and unclear term 'unable'? The vagueness of the application criteria generates anxiety among debtors, who tend to be highly self-critical (Mann and Porter 2010; Atwood 2012). The truth is that the definition is an eternally moving target, and the rules (such as they are) are applied inconsistently between cases (Hourigan 2015; Spooner 2019). However, there is one truism: it is always the debtor that must prove their inability to pay (see Chapter 5) in a process that seems designed to provoke shame, guilt, and anger (White 2010; Bramall 2016a, 2016b).

Indeed, stigma is alive and well, though it now assumes a different form. Older systems of debt relief were predicated on moral intimidation to discourage applicants, and though this remains the case, there is a greater emphasis on bureaucratic intimidation through greater paperwork and complexity. Knowledge of debt relief systems tends to be the purview of a handful of experts who operate predominately in the legal system, and laypeople are happy to live in blissful ignorance, that is, until the dreaded day comes when they must use these services. Returning to the original point at the start of this section, stigma has most assuredly survived, and in many respects serves as the first line of defence for wary creditors.

Who goes bankrupt and why?

While the various instruments of debt relief are theoretically available to anyone, in practice there are certain groups who are overrepresented. Single parents (especially women), those who have recently lost their jobs, or gotten divorced, and specific to the American context non-White debtors and people with medical bills (Braucher et al 2012; Sousa 2013, 2017; Spooner 2019; James 2022; Kuperberg and Mazelis 2022). There is also a tendency for people to delay bankruptcy for various reasons, which has led to the term 'sweatbox' being coined (this was briefly explored in Chapter 1). This is a concerning tendency where people who desperately need to discharge their debts are instead trapped in a pre-bankruptcy limbo. This heavily implies that stigma remains a powerful obstacle to bankrupts and insolvents achieving a truly fresh start.

A bizarre finding of sweatbox research is that many people are now delaying bankruptcy because they cannot afford it. The modernizing reforms of debt relief have conceptualized it as a service rather than as an essential component of welfare delivery, and so these services often charge their users a fee for the privilege of going bankrupt. Stigma now has a price tag. In the UK the Insolvency Service of England (2021) will charge you £680, which is justified as a payment to the Official Receiver, the officer of the court who will administer your bankruptcy. The Irish fee is justified along the same lines, but costs significantly less at €200, and while the Insolvency Service of Ireland (ISI) did initially charge a fee for the use of its services, this was waived in 2014, and this fee waiver has since been renewed every three years (Stamp 2016). Nevertheless, the fees and other costs associated with insolvency have created the puzzle of debtors having to save up to go bankrupt, which flies in the face of its potential to facilitate a fresh start (Mann and Porter 2010).

In the US, the additional paperwork and complexity of the 2005 Bankruptcy Abuse Prevention and Consumer Protection Act (BAPCPA) has created a whole industry of predatory lawyers who deliberately steer their clients towards the more costly Chapter 13 solution. This can cost anywhere from $1,000 to $4,000 and has a problematic racialized character, with one study by Braucher et al (2012) finding that Black Americans are twice as likely to file for Chapter 13 bankruptcy when compared to their White counterparts. Many of those who file for Chapter 13 bankruptcy have no meaningful assets, and so would logically be better served by Chapter 7 bankruptcy, which would wipe out their debts instead of having them enter a high-risk repayment plan. Indeed, over 90 per cent of those who do file for Chapter 7 bankruptcy have no assets to surrender to their creditors, making it the clearly superior choice for those aiming for a fresh start (Foohey et al 2018). While bankruptcy may masquerade as an economic process, success most assuredly depends on the cultural capital of the applicant and their capacity to navigate the administrative complexity of the US legal system (Bourdieu 2010).

Like any insolvency option, Chapter 13 can have a positive effect on your wellbeing and finances, but also requires very specific conditions to achieve this. An underemployed or unemployed debtor with no significant assets usually stands to gain nothing from Chapter 13 bankruptcy, as they merely delay the inevitability of liquidation. Overall, two thirds of Americans who file for bankruptcy say that they seriously struggled with their debts for more than two years before filing (Foohey et al 2018), with disastrous consequences such as foreclosure, going without food, and pawning valuables, including sentimental items like wedding rings. About 70 per cent of debtors say that they were aware that it would have been financially wiser to file at an earlier point, but that they avoided doing so out of shame. Those who say that the bankruptcy stigma is gone are not paying very close attention to the indebted experience.

While the US case raises the problematics of race in the bankruptcy system, studies also show that women have rapidly grown as users of debt relief over the last 30 years and are now as likely as men to apply, with statistics usually placing them within one or two percentage points of each other. However, examination of the statistics in detail shows that while women tend to carry smaller debt loads than men, they are nevertheless as likely to apply for insolvency of some kind (Pickford 2016; Hoyes 2019; Kanougiya et al 2021). This indicates that the average woman insolvent struggles with debt payments more than the average man, echoing the structural disadvantage of the glass ceiling and the pay gap. While married applicants are about as likely to be either men or women, divorced or single applicants are significantly more likely to be a woman; further, if the filer is a lone parent, they are, again, more likely to be a woman (Hoyes 2019).

Evidence abounds of discriminatory practices in insolvency work. In its original proposal, ISI policy specified that if a parent's income was below a given percentage of childcare costs, then they could only avail themself of a debt write-off by giving up their job to care for their children (Minihan 2013). While it was not explicitly gender-specific, women are often the primary caregiver in the home, and the requirement to leave work to care for their children during an insolvency arrangement would therefore disproportionately fall on them (National Women's Council of Ireland 2013). This clause was quickly removed due to a negative public reaction, but other research (Gazso 2009) shows that gendered discrimination can be embedded ideologically within institutions, even if they are not articulated in policy. This proposal was also likely influenced by the relatively high childcare costs in Ireland, which have often been cited as a factor that pushes women out of work (McGrath 2000).

What should the goal of relief be? Fresh starts versus dirty starts in LMEs

Insolvency legislation exists in a state of eternal compromise, which has always limited its capacity to provide debtors with a legitimate fresh start, with the balance of evidence indicating that a dirty start is far more common (Porter and Thorne 2006). This is most apparent when one looks at it through the lens of welfare. Debt relief is not generally thought of when we consider welfare provision, but why not? Modern problems require modern solutions, and debt is a pervasive and prevalent modern problem. Hegemonic discourses often situate debt as being welfare enhancing (Spooner 2019) by giving people access to a boost of money that facilitates education, employment (for example, a car loan), or, as is increasingly the case, to simply pay for rent and groceries. The rising prevalence of payday loans and high-interest credit card debt being used to pay for everyday goods and services has led Susanne Soederberg (2014) to state that we now have 'debtfare' rather than welfare, especially for the poor and the vulnerable. This makes arguments about the welfare-enhancing properties of debt harder to sustain as stigmatizing and exclusionary systems of debt relief simultaneously prevent debtors from discharging their toxic debts.

Comparative welfare frameworks usually consider Ireland, the UK, and the US as being similar enough to fall under the same rubric, namely liberal (Esping-Andersen 1990) or as LMEs (Hall and Soskice 2001; Wood 2016). Welfare in LMEs is highly commodified and tied to the market, such as the US convention of linking health insurance to employment (Atwood 2012). Welfare access is also subject to conditionality (as opposed to universality), where the claimant is expected to be responsible and abide by certain terms and conditions (that is, mandatory job search efforts while unemployed), and sanctioning, where breaking the rules will lead to a reduction or cut in forms of support (Boland and Griffin 2015). Overall welfare in LMEs is restricted and limited, both in terms of length of support given and the quality of resources that can be accessed, with a clear emphasis on re-entering the market (Hall and Soskice 2001). Bankruptcy is supposed to achieve this through flowery rhetorical metaphors like a 'clean slate' or a 'fresh start', which enables the debtor to begin again, unshackled from their debts.

If we examine modern bankruptcy legislation in LMEs from this standpoint, we can see that it has failed to achieve a fresh start that enables people to thrive beyond indebtedness and re-enter the market (Ramsay 2017). Debt relief is conditionalized through means-testing, fees, and good-faith clauses which legally compel the debtor to tell the truth in their application or risk being sanctioned by being ejected from their programme (Spooner 2018). The results of this are problematic. Porter and Thorne (2006) found that one in three American bankrupts were in a similar or worse financial situation to their pre-bankruptcy state after just one year. As we have seen, debt distress links bankruptcy with sudden income loss, which then persists, with common features being unemployment, divorce, ill health, and (specific to the US context) medical bills (Deville 2015; McClanahan 2018; Montgomerie 2019; Featherstone 2020).

Problems such as ill health do not suddenly disappear just because a person has gone bankrupt; while their debts may have been liquidated, their assets will have been given the same treatment and if the cause of their original over-indebtedness has not changed, then they can easily end up in the same situation again. In fact, they can end up in an even worse situation, because having gone bankrupt, they can now only secure new debt at a higher rate of interest, and not all debts are dischargeable, even in bankruptcy. This I term the 'dirty start', where the restrictions imposed compromise the ability of the debtor to begin a new economic life, the full consequences of this will be encountered in Chapters 6 and 7.

This leads us to one of the greatest obstacles to reforming bankruptcy: the traditional strain between the need for debt relief to provide a fresh start and to be a means for creditors to recover as much money as possible. I agree with Spooner (2019), who argues that a meaningful fresh start is only possible if the debtor is able to start over in a relatively intact state. After their time in the sweatbox, it is irrational and cruel to then squeeze the debtor for their handful of remaining assets, particularly when those assets are necessary for employment, which can cause repeat bankruptcy, the very phenomenon that restrictions are supposed to guard against. Spooner has also outlined how governments try to navigate this minefield: 'A classic response of policy makers to fears of debt relief abuse is to attribute subjective powers to decision makers under vague standards, which risks both inappropriate outcomes and inconsistency' (Spooner 2019, p 246). In Chapter 5 I chart how the new Irish PIPs have struggled in such a framework, attempting to fairly split their attention between the needs of creditors and debtors. Additionally, government is able to avert awkward conversations about bad outcomes or failures because responsibility has been delegated to a group of experts with low public visibility in an obscure system that few understand.

Following the logic of LME welfare systems, we should support a fresh start for debtors because not only will it enable them to achieve economic inclusion and re-integration more easily, but also because it would be more just. The current process evidences the worst of all possible worlds: despite imposing a huge administrative and bureaucratic burden, it is slow, stigmatizing, and those debtors who do complete a programme often achieve a dirty rather than a fresh start. The story is similar across the various LMEs which feature the changes I have described: despite the gnashing of teeth, fears of inflation, and complaints of moral hazard, the individual insolvency and bankruptcy arrangements are not used nearly as often as they ought to be. The evidence shows that the majority of people who qualify for help do not seek it, preferring to struggle on, making every effort to pay their debts (White 2010; Walker 2011; Horgan-Jones 2014; Brennan 2015). The lone exception to this trend is broad structural crisis, such as the deluge of debt that accompanied the GFC, which led to a predictable increase in the number of insolvency arrangements and bankruptcies. Otherwise, usage of insolvency instruments has increased roughly in line with population and debt growth.

Conclusion

This chapter has explained why usage of debt relief has increased by making two key points. First, more people are going bankrupt because more people are in debt, with household debt growing astronomically since the 1980s to compensate for wage stagnation and asset inflation. In Ireland, median mortgage costs were €129,000 in 2013, but in 2020 stood at €260,000 (Household Finance and Consumption Survey 2020), showing that dramatic change can happen over a relatively short period of time. This also means that assets have inflated so much that in certain parts of the country, they have even exceeded their previous highs from the economic boom. Through this political economy perspective, we can also see that usage of debt relief is heavily impacted by the business cycle, with fewer people going bankrupt during a boom and more people going bankrupt during a recession (especially the early parts of a recession). An interesting point to note here is that a sudden influx of bankruptcies during an economic boom may serve as an early warning sign of an impending crash.

Second, more people are going bankrupt because modern reforms have made it more accessible, though the US took a noteworthy step back in terms of its accessibility in its 2005 modification to bankruptcy legislation. However, in general, this growing accessibility manifested itself through institutional reform, greater advantages for debtors in the bankruptcy process, and a greater number of options for the debtor to choose from, increasing the likelihood that they will find an arrangement suitable for them. However, although insolvency has become more accessible, it is also persistently underused, with a large number of people trapped in the sweatbox of bankruptcy, in some cases for five years or longer. Some of this gap is explained by feelings of shame, but worryingly there is also a growing problem where fees and costs mean that debtors must save up to go bankrupt. This stands in opposition to hegemonic understandings of the growth of bankruptcy, which depend on individual behavioural explanations of poor morality and the reduction in the stigma of bankruptcy. This tension will be the subject of Chapter 3 as we encounter our debtors for the first time and look at individual borrowing behaviour, the impact that culture has had on indebtedness, and what people do when they fall behind their repayment schedule.

3

The Uncertainties of Debt

All borrowing begins with a utopian vision of the future. When people put their name on the dotted line (or tick the 'I agree' box on the lender's digital platform), they cannot conceive of a situation where they will fail to pay. Research from psychology has found that borrowers show certain cognitive biases, such as optimism bias (assuming that the future will be better than the present) and time inconsistency (valuing the present more than the future) (Ramsay 2017; Spooner 2019). This means that borrowers do not start out by seeing themselves as debtors, because a debtor is someone who has failed to pay their debts. Through a series of constant setbacks, they gradually adopt this mindset and begin to see the world through the lens of this subjectivity. This manifests through an obsession with budgeting, spending, and temporality – that is, how many days until I am debt-free? This chapter shows what happens when optimism meets cruel reality and builds on the work of the previous chapter by beginning to focus on culture and lived experience.

In this way it contributes to the endless debate about where, precisely, debt problems come from. Is it the result of financial illiteracy (Walker 2011)? Poor moral character (Rock 2014)? Misfortune (Atfield and Orton 2013; Atfield et al 2016)? Some combination of them all? Among scholars who have studied over-indebtedness (being unable to pay your debts), there is little debate; it is virtually a settled question. The literature[1] shows that most people slip into debt crisis due to macroeconomic or structural factors beyond the control of any given agent (Russell et al 2011, 2013; Stamp 2012a). Most prominent among these are the ongoing rolling economic crises which have characterized modernity and project powerful shockwaves into the economy and credit markets. People cannot budget their way out of a financial crisis which is exerting massive pressure on the mortgage market.

Along with this, rises in the cost of living (particularly interest rates) are a significant contributor to debt problems, as is ill health (including stress and mental illness) (Knapp et al 2011; Wahlbeck and McDaid 2012; Davies et al 2015; Braverman et al 2018). Other predictors include unemployment, particularly where that unemployment is involuntary or forced (Boland and Griffin 2015, 2021), and relationship breakdown (Johnson et al 2022), which can either be a cause or result of debt problems. The numbers of people who fall into distress or delinquency due to financial incompetence is comparatively low, and certainly does not explain why so many people fall into arrears and delinquency right as a financial crisis arrives (Walker 2011).

This chapter will shed light on this by exploring the social and cultural reasons why people assume large debts to begin with, by tapping into Lauren Berlant's (2006, 2011) framework of 'the good life', whereby our imagination has been captured by certain life milestones (such as a mortgage) that have become success symbols. Throughout the remainder of the book, this will also explain why people in debt are so reluctant to let go and give up – the so-called tendency to 'stick their heads in the sand'. It is not just a generic resource that they fear losing, but also the cultural, social, and moral impressions of success and good living that are symbolically attached to these otherwise inert objects (Bourdieu 2010).

The good life

What is the meaning of life? What does it mean to live well? How can we best achieve happiness? These questions have baffled us and have provoked a whole stream of discussion from the great philosophers of the world. Aristotle argued for a virtue-centred answer to these questions, where a good life is one where we live according to our virtues, which necessarily means that each person's good life will be a little different because we all possess and value different virtues (Skidelsky and Skidelsky 2012). Plato argued that we must achieve harmony with our sense of self, so we must achieve understanding through knowledge. Epicurus (in an echo of Buddhism) thought that anxiety and pain resulted from unfulfilled desires, and so the answer is for us to release ourselves from irrational desires (which are meaningless) and our fear of death (which cannot be avoided). Nietzsche thought that a good life was one where our authentic selves were expressed as part of the re-valuation of all values, even if this exposes us to ridicule (Nietzsche 2014), best visualized through his (possibly apocryphal) quote that 'those who were seen dancing were thought insane by those who could not hear the music'.

While philosophers usually focus on abstract moral ideas like authenticity, expression, virtue, and desire, we mere mortals tend to need more concrete answers. The psychoanalyst and cultural theorist Lauren Berlant gives us a conceptual framework that is more prosaic and modern. This may seem like a curious place to start, and yet when we confront the question of why people are so indebted, we are inevitably drawn back to the good life. Broadly speaking, Berlant's good life provides an idealized vision of what success looks like in practice, reducing complex questions around the search for meaning and good living to a relatively simple story. For Berlant (2011), this story emerges as part of the postwar consensus, an era defined by continuous improvements in socioeconomic indicators such as happiness, economic growth, income, life expectancy and so on (Streeck 2011; Krugman 2012; Stiglitz 2012).

The good life is a kind of story, and while stories can be true or false, it is its narratological components that make it so appealing – in other words, we can see ourselves in the story and imagine how it applies to our own lives. The good life tends to begin in early adulthood when we have developed enough agency to make independent decisions. The first major decision is educational – and, indeed, a good life is one that involves college, and immense stress is placed on the connection between college and success from a young age. However, this is not for your general edification, or to develop critical thinking skills, or to foment a deep sense of engagement with the world. Rather, the system of education is a kind of job training facility, and if you want a good life, you will be cautious and selective about the type of degree you get (Ladson-Billings 2006; Morrison 2014). Scientific subjects tend to be regarded as better because they provider more concrete 'hard' skills that lead to employment, which is the second element of a good life.

One cannot live well without good work, that being work which is stable, well paid, and meaningful (Bourdieu 2010; Boland and Griffin 2015). Work is vital not only because it provides income, but also because it offers a sense of meaning and many people develop a strong sense of identity which is tied to their work. People working in occupations that they perceive to be socially important report better mental health than those who struggle to find meaning in their work, and this is not necessarily connected to income (Caju et al 2016). Consider volunteers, for example, who usually work for free, but reap other benefits that are less tangible. This is not to say money is meaningless – far from it – but there are other factors at play and it will be hard for someone to feel they have lived a 'good life' without good work. In the immediate postwar era these dialogues were consumed by jobs in manufacturing or primary industries such as agriculture. This has transformed over time and it is fair to say that contemporary perceptions of good work are dominated by programming and computer science (Morrison 2014).

Around this time (if not before), several other things happen in a staggered order. While at college you should aim to find true love, and romance is a crucial part of living a good life. Someone who is successful in their career, but otherwise ends up alone is likely to be thought of as 'missing something'. Marriage and children are the inevitable result, but one needs a place to raise a family, something enabled by a home, yet the only way to have a secure home is to buy one, and the only way most people can buy a home is through a mortgage.

These messages are transmitted to us very strongly from quite a young age, and the good life is an essential part of socialization. Assuming one follows it, it can be taken for granted that many parents will endeavour to repeat the process, saving money for their children to go to college (Zaloom 2021) and laying the groundwork for the story to begin anew. In a conflicted world full of instability where the value of college, work, romance, childrearing, and homeownership are being questioned, we might ask why we continue to do this. I believe that we do not know what else to do; we live in a time when the existing template of how to do well falls further out of reach from more and more people, but we strive for it because there is nothing else.

The good life is seductive because it is alleged to bring about happiness, satisfaction, and self-actualization (Berlant 2006). Following this template will do more than just make you a productive member of society; there are other less tangible benefits to be acquired, and the good life provides a roadmap in an unstable world. This is certainly what was said to me by people who fondly remembered the day they got the keys to their new houses:

> 'Your first day in a house you have just bought is an extraordinary thing, we couldn't even sleep we were so excited. We were going into all the rooms and thinking about decorating.' (Interview with Barry)

> 'It was ours, a space to call our own. One we couldn't just be randomly evicted from. That sense of security … I have never experienced anything like it before or since.' (Interview with Aileen)

> 'I remember it like it was yesterday, I could now think that I was successful, that I had done well. I had followed the rules, I went to college, I got a great job, I got married, I had a mortgage, it was all gravy.' (Interview with Simon)

These feelings of success and empowerment are all the more tragic because this rise will be accompanied by a fall, which will come sooner than expected. In the future it will become almost impossible to recall these feelings of hope and aspiration that animated people to seek a mortgage in the first place, and so it is important to dwell on them for a moment.

The good life under attack

Naturally, the good life has flaws which encompass its social, economic, cultural, and even symbolic power to capture our imaginations. It is now obvious that access to the good life on a large scale was facilitated by the unique economic conditions which became a feature of the immediate postwar era (Streeck 2011). Convincing people that the good life remains accessible has become harder the further in the past the Second World War becomes. As economic conditions have weakened, it has become necessary for people seeking the good life to borrow larger sums of money to make it possible (Lazzarato 2014).

The imaginary of the good life takes heteronormativity for granted, assuming that families will have two parents (M+F) and a number of children. The man of the family assumed the role of the breadwinner and, indeed, in the postwar era it was possible to support a mortgage and a family on one income. This was partly enabled by continuous and regular economic growth, but also because strong unions pushed wages up and working hours down (Krugman 2012). Combined with this was the traditional view that a woman's place was in the home, dedicated to childrearing, cooking, and cleaning. Innovations in technology such as the refrigerator, washing machine, and modern stove made this job more manageable, though it has never been easy. Even in the 20th century such an image of the nuclear family, with its perfect distribution of duties, was more of an idealization than a reality (Skeggs 1997; Gayman 2011; Gane 2012). Real family life has always been messier and more negotiated than any ideal type of the family, involving queer families, blended families, one-parent families, extended families, childless families, and more. Nevertheless, the higher wages, lower working hours, and greater access to mortgages which were a feature of this era were not illusory (Langley 2009).

As house prices have increased and wages have stagnated, it has become necessary for both partners to work, which often blurs the lines of who is responsible for what household task. Despite this, socialization of women and young girls continues to emphasize childrearing, cooking, and other domestic household tasks (Crenshaw 1989; McLeod 2017). Research from the COVID-19 pandemic has shown that women working in higher education did worse than their male counterparts because after the closure of schools and childcare facilities, it was women who were expected to take care of children in the home (Kirk-Jenkins and Hughey 2021). In addition, with the withdrawal of state support, the rising costs of living, the stagnation of wages and the inflation of assets, the good life is expensive (Adkins et al 2020). In some contexts, college is now so expensive that we might think of it as a trial run to having a mortgage – if people can even qualify for a mortgage (Zaloom 2021).

Concurrently there has been a withdrawal of state support which has placed pressure on people to spend more money to end up in the same position as their predecessors (Pettifor 2017). The promise of privatization was enhanced efficiency, lower costs, less government interference in people's lives (the 'nanny state'), and greater innovation as the market develops new ways of doing things in response to competition (Burchell et al 1991; Rose

1991). Whether these benefits have ever been reaped is questionable, and the reality falls far short of the Friedman and Chicago School vision of a perfectly efficient market providing excellent services at a low cost to the consumer-citizen.

These relations are at their most intense in the United States, where 62 per cent of bankruptcies are for medical debt (Himmelstein et al 2009), and student loans (one of the few types of debt which cannot be discharged in bankruptcy) are set to exceed $2 trillion (Cohen 2022). However, the withdrawal of state support and the intensification of privatization is now common in the Western world. In Ireland, a coalition government which came to power in the aftermath of the GFC reduced the conditions under which the Student Universal Support Ireland (SUSI) grant would be offered to third-level students (Coulter and Nagle 2015). This meant that for the first time, students (especially those from disadvantaged backgrounds) would need to borrow in order to be able to go to college. Similarly, Ireland's overburdened public health service has paved the way for private insurance and hospitals to produce a two-tier healthcare service. Those without means must wait, and currently almost 900,000 people (O'Regan 2022) are on some form of waiting list, while those who can pay are enabled to skip the queue and receive quicker treatment (Hourigan 2015).

The UK faces similar issues, and the world-famous National Health Service (NHS) is now under immense pressure to privatize, as has already happened in the education system. These decisions are meeting with growing discontent, as we can see from the recent strikes in the UK higher education system. The culmination of these factors has meant that a larger (and growing) proportion of the population must borrow simply to survive (Lazzarato 2012). While medical care, education, transport, housing, and so on were once state-funded (or at least state-subsidized), these costs have now been displaced onto working people (Hodson et al 2014). These debts are also situated by those who take them on as survival debts, easily understandable for the most part, though these dialogues have even begun to permeate college. Failure to attend college would be seen as a sign of social failure and embarrassment by their peers and would also damage their future employment prospects. Debt has now fully become a form of privatized welfare.

Becoming a debtor

The previous sections have outlined why people feel compelled to take on such vast debts to begin with. There are certain life milestones that have become culturally ubiquitous (or are perceived this way) for how one leads a good life. It just so happens that these milestones are costly, and in an era of declining state support, increasing costs, and stagnating wages, the only way to afford them is through debt (Lazzarato 2014). The most substantial sum usually comes from a mortgage, which is also taken as a symbolic talisman of success (Keohane and Petersen 2013). As the person runs into more financial difficulty, there is a gradual transformation in how they think about themselves, and how they think about their own relation to political power and society more generally – a type of experience that is captured by the term 'subjectivity'.

Foucault's theory of subjectivity is appealing because it helps to explain how power impacts and transforms subjects in a manner that is both more critical and less abstract (Dean and Zamora 2021). In his early and middle career, Foucault was highly engaged with the importance of disciplinary power for subject formation (Heyes 2010). A prison creates prisoners, a school creates pupils, an asylum creates inmates, and a hospital creates patients. These institutions achieve this by the rigorous and scientific application of disciplinary power, and by compelling their subjects to adopt specific behaviours in highly controlled environments (Foucault 1989, 1995, 1996; Dwyer 1995), as echoed in Goffman's (1951) work on total institutions. Debt is intriguing in this respect because we have all but abolished the debtor's prison, favouring less institutional approaches to problem debtors. Simultaneously, it is also clear when interviewing people in financial distress that there is a difference between someone who is behind on payments and someone who thinks of themselves as a debtor (Stanley et al 2016).

People do not become debtors just by having debt; rather, being a debtor is a specific kind of subjectivity that is only brought on by persistent over-indebtedness. A person can have almost any amount of debt and not think of themselves as a debtor; so long as they continue to make their payments, a debt is just another bill. However, prolonged debt crisis will lead to a re-evaluation in priorities, and the adoption of many of the norms and mores of neoliberal finance (Rose 1999). A debtor will tend to think of their debt crisis as a 'journey' to being debtless, though not all will get there in the way that they imagined or hoped (Stanley et al 2016).

Along the way, we will see that debtors have sophisticated and highly developed understandings of finance, credit, debt, and budgeting. Choosing not to apply rationalized norms of budgeting and finance is not the same as not understanding them or knowing what they are. In this section I will explore how debtors begin to confront their debt. As I have emphasized previously, the decision to seek debt relief is a process, and this feeds into that process, as the decisions made during debt crisis govern what happens later.

Till debt do us part

Love is aspirational, but relationships can also lay the groundwork for future conflict when money becomes tighter. There is a growing literature on economic abuse and indebtedness, where the perpetrator (typically a man) will borrow money in the name of their spouse (typically a woman) (Johnson et al 2022). This is called coerced debt, and the money is borrowed recklessly and at high interest rates, with little care or concern for how it will be repaid. Economic abuse can also be taken to mean a general cultivation of economic dependency (Postmus et al 2020), where one partner is entirely reliant on the other for access to financial resources, with perceived defiance or disagreement likely leading to the vulnerable partner being deprived of money (Surviving Economic Abuse 2020). Abusers are well aware of the power and control this gives them over their victims, deliberately producing a situation where the victim cannot leave because they lack financial resources or the means to generate an income in any alternative manner. While any amount of economic abuse is a cause for serious concern, it should also be noted that as this area receives increased attention that more people are victims of such abuse than we may expect (Kanougiya et al 2021).

Debt (and money problems more generally) can produce a toxic cycle in relationships, where the absence of money creates strain and conflict, which can lead to poor or impulsive financial decisions, leading to more conflict and so on. Indeed, on occasion, even after people acquire the financial resources necessary to economically recover, the damage to the relationship may be permanent and separation can be inevitable. This can also work the other way around, where things are (initially) fine from a financial perspective, but there is an issue in the relationship, and the repeated fighting leads to a breakdown in trust and cooperation, which can easily spiral into financial crisis. Many of my participants told me about the impact that their debt crisis had on their relationships:

> 'It [debt crisis] made things that much harder. We were an ideal family at one point, but now it is hard to remember those days. We fight over money all the time, and it's incredible how you can needle each other over the little things. A lunch out can be the difference between paying the mortgage on time or not. You wonder how did it come to this?' (Interview with Roger)

> 'My marriage broke down after we got into trouble [financially]. People told us they thought we were the ideal couple, and we worked hard to maintain that image around other people, but behind closed doors? We hated each other. But we also had debts taken out jointly, so we were trapped.' (Interview with Sean)

Perhaps even more concerning is the prevalence of hidden debt – when a debt is hidden from one partner by another (Postmus et al 2020). Usually, one partner is more responsible for the finances than another and is capable of concealing minor problems for a few weeks or months (depending on how involved the other partner is in the finances):

'It was a complete shock. He just sat me down one day and said we are fucking broke. He had been trying to borrow money on credit cards to pay back overdrafts and all this kind of thing, it was almost impossible to work backwards through everything he had done. I was shocked, until he said it I had no idea that we were behind.' (Interview with Jane)

The feelings of betrayal evoked by hidden debt should not be underestimated, and any of my participants who were deceived in this way always left their partners. Some attempted reconciliation, with varying degrees of success, but there was also a feeling that it was impossible to go back to the way things were:

'He just kept saying to me, we can go back, we can go back, we can go back. I had to drill it into his brain that he had betrayed his family, and that there was no way to forget that. He never apologized, if you can believe that he just wanted to travel back in time before there was a problem, but he had broken my trust, and there was no way for me to move past that.' (Interview with Amy)

Romantic relationships between partners, much like the financial relationships that exist between creditor and debtor, are contingent on trust. Once there is a feeling that trust has been broken or that that one party has acted in bad faith by concealing information, it is almost impossible to recapture the sense of homeostasis and equilibrium that defined the relationship. Some shared their reflections with me on why they did all this to begin with: "You have this idealized vision of what family life will be like, 2 kids and a golden retriever, you know? But the reality is messy and ugly" (interview with Sarah).

What is lost is not just the relationship, but also the dream of the good life that was earnestly and sincerely believed in. This leads to uncomfortable questions on the search for meaning:

'I feel that I followed all the rules that were set out, you know? I went to school, I got a degree [in college], I married, I had kids, I got a mortgage. I did everything right, and I still got stabbed in the back. Now I'm looking at my single friends who have plenty money and freedom and I think to myself: why did I fucking bother?' (Interview with Paul)

When the good life fails, people are somewhat at a loss over what they ought to do and this leads to a re-evaluation of all the previous decisions which led them to this point. Some feel that they should have been more cautious about their choice of partner, thinking that it would have been better to have waited for longer before settling down. Others regret having children at a younger age (usually their mid-twenties), meaning that they did not have an opportunity to enjoy the end of their young adulthood. The tragedy of course is that this information could not have been known in advance and speculating often does more harm than good.

Nobody will give me a job

The economic depression which followed the GFC provoked an increased interest in unemployment and what it is like to experience unemployment (Boland and Griffin 2015, 2018, 2021). It should come as no surprise that many people were unemployed in the aftermath of the financial crisis, and so it became a common experience. Concurrently, it should also come as no surprise that debt problems become more severe after losing your job. I spoke with most of my participants for the first time in 2012 or 2016, and the memory of the financial crisis was foremost in their minds:

> 'I was scrambling after I was made redundant. They had sold me an overpriced house near the end of the Celtic Tiger [the Irish economic boom], and then I lost my job so it became ten times as hard.' (Interview with Ciara)

> 'I had never been unemployed before, the closest I ever came was a two week break when I had quit one job and was ready to start another. I am educated and have loads of experience, I never imagined a situation where I would be looking for a job and not able to find one, but the crash proved me wrong.' (Interview with Mona)

Debt is insidious in this way because you continue to owe the money regardless of changes in your circumstances, whether you are rich or poor, single or married, employed or not. It is up to the debtor to overcome any problems and make the payments on time, and the experience of being unemployed has a compounding effect which makes indebtedness even harder:

> 'It was dreadful after I was out of work. You are around the house all the time, and you're thinking I wonder will the bank send me the letter today to tell me I'm homeless?' (Interview with Laura)

> 'Being unemployed was really hard because you have nothing but time, and you're in your own head, just thinking. I looked for work every day, it made no difference.' (Interview with Max)

We all wish we had more free time, and yet the free time produced by unemployment is considered almost entirely to be a negative experience because it is characterized by waiting for work (Boland and Griffin 2021). Unemployment creates an absence of structure and activity, in addition to a loss of meaning which many associate with work. When money is borrowed, there is typically an automatic calculator that will give you an indication of how long it will take to pay the money back at a specified rate, how much interest you should expect to pay, and what the total is with the principal and interest added together. Unemployment puts immense pressure on the temporalities of indebtedness, causing a re-evaluation and recalculation as people begin to grasp how much trouble they are in. The injunction of debt is to become a rationally calculating entrepreneurial subject who is (at the minimum) financially literate, if not financially proficient (Schwartz 2022). The practice of calculating how much money you still owe and how long until it is all paid back is a common one, a procedure which evokes thoughts of prisoners counting down the days until their sentence ends (Stanley et al 2016).

If the person cannot find a job in their preferred industry, or otherwise at the rate of money they had previously earned, there are three broad responses to the experience of unemployment for debtors. They can take a job which is easier to get, which likely involves accepting a lower rate of pay, poorer working conditions, a more insecure contract and so on:

'I got two jobs actually, each worse than the other if you can believe that. The hours were abysmal and the pay was horrendous, but every time I thought about quitting I just thought about those letters the bank send you with "past due" on them and I just knew I had to stick it out.' (Interview with Roger)

'It's amazing the kind of work you'll do when you're desperate. I got a job in sanitation and maintenance, which is to say that I cleaned toilets. I don't think that kind of work is inherently degrading, but it is seen that way by other people, and I always had that in my head when I was doing it.' (Interview with Michael).

'When I lost my real job, you know, there's always a period of time where you can get by without doing anything drastic, but after six months I still had nothing and ended up having to work in a shop [as a cashier]. I felt like I was starting my career all over again.' (Interview with Amy)

Alternatively, they can borrow more money, known to us through Kipling's adaptation of the phrase 'borrowing from Peter to pay Paul'. There is a stigma around this practice because from a financial perspective it is inherently self-defeating; the new money borrowed is nearly always at a higher rate of interest because the person is unemployed and desperate. Creditors likely to take a chance on such a person will do so at a much higher rate of interest than usual, with research on payday lenders indicating that this may reach rates of 500 per cent or more (Soederberg 2014). These debts are situated by those who take them out to be survival debts, used only to ensure you can continue to get by day by day:

> 'When I lost my job I had to borrow more money, borrowing from Peter to pay Paul as the old saying goes, I knew it was a bad idea but the only other choice was to give up the house and I wasn't going to do that.' (Interview with Rachel)

> 'It's easy to say something is bad from a general point of view, or when you're not in the situation, I needed more money. I got more money. It was very bad but I made it work.' (Interview with Tara)

> 'My family had to survive, and they needed me to provide for them. I got a payday loan when I was out of work, it was the only way to keep up with the minimum repayments, but I always regretted having to do it.' (Interview with Simon)

The final option, which is always available even if it is distasteful, is to seek out insolvency or bankruptcy – at this point, most people have only been in distress for a few months and are not yet willing to concede that they need help.

Everything is so expensive these days

The rising cost of living has been situated as a key reason for over-indebtedness (Ramsay 2017). After the neoliberal era, the role of successive central banks has been to control inflation to prevent spiralling price increases from causing adverse shocks in the economy (Stiglitz 2012). The stagflation crises of the 1980s have lived long in the memory of central banks (Krugman 2012), and so concerted efforts have been made to keep interest rates artificially low (Pettifor 2017). Despite continuous asset inflation, this dedication to keeping interest rates low kept housing theoretically accessible for much of the population. High house prices combined with low interest rates ensured that although the absolute amount being repaid was rising, it was doing so at a rate which was (relatively) under control (Adkins et al 2020). Historically low interest rates made it possible for banks to borrow money from central banks at insignificant (in some cases even negative) interest rates, and these lower rates were passed along to customers. Recent developments have shown the fragility and instability of this set of relations. In the UK, for example, almost half of mortgage holders are worried about missing one or more mortgage payments (Adams 2022).

Those on variable rate mortgages are paying most severely. In Ireland the mortgage management fund Start Mortgages has increased interest rates on the vast majority of the 11,000 mortgages in its portfolio (Weston 2022). These mortgagors are facing a rise in interest rates from an average of 3.9 per cent to 5.1 per cent, a move which is likely to push many into bankruptcy at a time when energy and fuel costs are also rising to record highs. Political responses to this have been weak and have been dominated by the language of entrepreneurial freedom – people must refinance their mortgages with other lenders on more favourable terms for their own advantage. It is simply taken for granted that people with full-time jobs, families to raise, and personal struggles to navigate will be able to compare mortgage providers and enter into complex negotiations with them whenever their contract allows:

> 'I was always given the advice that you need to switch mortgages or change providers and all this. The same as with your [home] heating contract, you know, they offer the best deals for people who switch so you need to do it constantly. I just found that exhausting. At first you can keep up with all this stuff, but it does wear you down over time.' (Interview with Rick)

> 'I settled for a slightly worse deal because I didn't want to switch [mortgages], I can't be on the phone all day with these people and the savings were not so much that it seemed worth it to me.' (Interview with Mona)

Fixed-rate mortgages have become rarer, predominately because they are less profitable (Pettifor 2017). However, it is also true that negotiating for these financial instruments is harder and therefore more time-consuming. Consequently, many mortgagors are content to simply roll over their mortgage arrangement, retaining the same terms and conditions for the sake of simplicity. Financial literacy is ultimately a moving target, with many mortgagors settling not only because negotiating can be complex, but also because it can be contentious. Many are happy simply to have the mortgage and do not wish to provoke any kind of conflict with their creditors:

> 'You don't want to upset them [creditors] by asking for special deals and such things.' (Interview with Ciara)

> 'I am glad to have the mortgage and don't see any need to wheel and deal. What would I save by doing this? Maybe five grand over 35 years? I would rather pay it and keep them [creditors] happy.' (Interview with Barry)

From a strictly technical perspective, it is irrational to continue with your mortgage arrangement as it is, as this will cost you more money in the long run (Lazzarato 2012). Similar arguments can be made about energy companies, which encourage customers to switch often to get a better deal. Companies do this precisely because they know that customers dislike switching, preferring to avoid the awkwardness of re-entering negotiations. While a willingness to negotiate and seek the best deal is a fundamental feature of neoliberal subjectivity, it is also true that this is exhausting if done repeatedly. Customers can therefore be relied upon to switch, and then simply continue on their contracts after the initial 'teaser' offer has expired.

Symbolic gestures

It is popularly believed that debtors 'stick their heads in the sand' when they fall into distress (Mental Health Ireland 2018; Mind 2008). Creditors infamously find it a struggle to get in contact with the debtor who has fallen behind on their repayments, and attempt (to little avail) to extract an explanation for the late payments (Geisst 2013; Rock 2014). However, not remaining in contact with your creditor is not the same as doing nothing. I have persistently found that the sense of shame and guilt that permeates the relations of debt provokes spontaneous action in people: they want to be perceived to be doing *something*. Even if that something is not paying their debts in full, they wish to show others that they are taking action, and that they consider the situation with the seriousness it deserves. I refer to the actions taken as symbolic gestures, because they are intended to make a moral rather than a financial impact on one's debts.

In her landmark work *The Social Meaning of Money*, Viviana Zelizer (1994) argues that money has infinitely complex moral and social meanings. Money which is earned through a wage is perceived differently from an allowance or a charitable donation that is given. Zelizer argues that we earmark money for specific purposes and attach unique moral importance to these differing monies. Stealing from someone is wrong, but to steal their rent money or college savings is particularly offensive because this money has been earmarked for a noble purpose.

I was told many such stories where moral meaning was attached to different debts. Mona, a lecturer on insecure and temporary contracts, had to take out a loan to pay for childcare about a decade ago. It was her smallest loan, but also the most morally important one:

Mona: I made sure money was put aside for that [childcare loan] every month. I paid it first, before everything else.
Interviewer: Why?

Mona: It was money taken out to mind my daughter while I was working. If I gave up on that loan or didn't pay it, it would be like giving up on my daughter. I always paid it before any other bill, and always on time, I never missed a payment.

Paying bills is not a simple accounting exercise; there is also a moral rubric to contend with (Zelizer 1994, 2011; Wilkis 2018; Zaloom 2021). Mona attached potent symbolic meaning to her childcare loan because it was inseparably connected with the love and care she felt for her daughter (Montgomerie and Tepe-Belfrage 2016). An actuary would have told Mona that she had other bills which were more urgent, had higher interest rates, or worse penalties for failing to repay. Contrary to our expectations, Mona was aware of all of this, considered it, but felt that paying the childcare loan back first was the 'right thing to do'. She behaved accordingly.

Symbolic gestures extend into the realm of budgeting. Take Barry, a jeweller who fell deeply into debt distress due to a disability which made it much harder for him to do his job. He told me about a unique system he uses to organize his repayments:

Barry: I have a system of hats.
Interviewer: What do you mean?
Barry: At the start of the month I put three hats on my kitchen table. I put the bills I will pay in one hat, the bills I might pay in another hat, and the bills I can't pay in the third hat.
[Both laughing]
Barry: It works! I swear it works. And when my bank wouldn't stop calling me to harass me about paying, I said 'if ye don't stop ringing me you won't even get a fucking hat!'.

Barry's system of bill repayment would presumably make an accountant feel extreme distress. Yet these informal systems are part of the moral texture of money, and to the people who use a system of hats, they make complete sense. Barry cannot make a dent in his debt overall, but he can rank the bills by their relative importance and proceed from there. While he does not use a system of double-entry bookkeeping, he is still following many of the prescriptions of good budgeting: he itemizes his bills by their importance, taking interest rates and urgency into consideration. However, like Mona, when Barry ranks his bills, he is thinking about justice, fairness, and morality in addition to the numbers (Thompson 1971; Zelizer 1994; Wilkis 2018). Within certain limitations, the numbers are arbitrary. From Barry's perspective, he has tried all reasonable actions to pay his mortgage back, and so his bank calling him repeatedly asking for updates is an act of unfairness and aggression. His system of budgeting not only includes neoliberal rationalized financial management techniques, but also gives consideration to dignity, decency, and civility. This will also be important later on, as those who have been treated most poorly are also the most likely to pursue debt relief.

Symbolic gestures apply in other ways, and the discourses of financial literacy that define so much of what we understand about indebtedness focus on eradicating vices, both because vices are expensive and because they project a sense of poor moral character to the world. This is how discourses of financial literacy are most strongly assimilated by debtors. When a debtor first falls into debt distress, they will follow the typical prescriptive advice to budget, to itemize their debts, to analyse which debts have the highest interest rates, and to cut out unnecessary expenses. With respect to this latter aspect, the first thing to go are vices, with smoking often finding its way to the top of the list: "I couldn't pay the money back … and I couldn't do much of anything, but I could save as much money as I could by not wasting it on bad things, so I gave up smoking when I fell behind on my mortgage" (interview with Sarah).

Culturally, smoking serves as the quintessential bad habit. It is expensive, addictive, has a proven connection to many serious health issues, and its perception as a 'cool' activity has been irreparably damaged. For debtors who wish to make a symbolic gesture, it is the first, and most obvious step they can take once they have reviewed their finances. It should be noted that I refer to these as symbolic gestures because although smoking is expensive, the amount of money saved by quitting is not sufficient to make a significant difference on their ability to repay. Indeed, debtors think about it in these terms and admit that the decisions they make in the early stages of debt crisis were more about activity than achievement:

Michelle:	When you're broke [in debt distress] you feel so powerless. You are getting all these nasty letters and it's just so hard to do anything, so you want to do something. I quit smoking, just so people would see I wasn't wasting money when I was already behind.
Interviewer:	Did it help?
Michelle:	Not really [laughing]. I was still behind, only now I was dealing with nicotine withdrawal.

Conclusion

Continuing the argument from Chapter 2 that debt has become a new form of privatized welfare, I have introduced the prominence of culture and sociology to the discussion. People borrow due to a desire to acquire the trappings of a good life (Berlant 2011), and seek the affective, social, cultural, and symbolic certainty imbued by the good life. As with the transition to adulthood, homeownership is associated with independence, freedom, and personal growth, and people would do almost anything to hang on to their homes for reasons that go beyond its value as an asset. In Chapter 7 we will see that the aspirations and hopes which spurred on the search for the good life to begin with become toxic as debtors gradually become cruel optimists who justify pain and suffering on the grounds that it may one day enable them to pay off their debts (Berlant 2011). This chapter shows the beginnings of this process.

Debt research has long shown that over-indebtedness is more strongly associated with macroeconomic factors such as unemployment, relationship breakdown, and rises in interest rates than individual failings; this chapter has shone a light on the lived experience of these problems. Building on the work by Zelizer (1994), I have argued that debtors organize their debts morally, refusing to pay those creditors who are disrespectful or cruel, and focusing repayment efforts on those debts that have moral significance to them – for example, childcare loans, which are associated with the love the borrower feels for their children. In this way, the subjectivity of indebtedness is quite slippery because it alternates between neoliberal and moral economic conceptions of how to face the world. While debtors are obsessed with the temporality of their obligations, as we would expect from a neoliberal subjectivity, they are also mindful of the reasons why the money was borrowed to begin with and how they have been treated since then. Debtors strive to create a perception that they are taking their debts with the utmost seriousness, partly through making symbolic gestures such as quitting bad habits or making small but financially inconsequential payments to their creditor, which are intended to communicate that they are still actively attempting to pay.

They had no way of knowing at the time, but those people who make such efforts are looked upon fondly in the debt resolution process they will go through later (see Chapter 5). The implication of the phrase 'sticking your head in the sand' is that you are doing nothing, but as we can see, debtors are highly active in attempting to resolve their over-indebtedness. They can frustrate creditors because their willingness to remain in contact is inconsistent, and their attempts to solve their financial issues can seem irrational from a neoliberal perspective. But debtors have moral reasons for doing what they do, which can make their efforts to repay seem distant from what is desired by creditors. However, debtors are highly concerned about their debt, and the idea that they would renege on their debts does not enter their minds. From a creditor's perspective, this is quite frustrating because debtors do not always communicate their intentions, goals, actions, or desires to their creditors, which leaves creditors in the awkward position of having to reconstruct a story from limited information (Rock 2014).

Regardless, we end up in the same place, with people who are over-indebted and struggling; from here, the process of indebtedness is somewhat irregular. It is often the case that people make a partial recovery after finding work or negotiating a series of small loans from friends and family. Despite these semi-recoveries, they will never get the situation completely under control again and gradually come to inhabit the subject position of being a debtor. They will likely go through several moments of crisis before eventually conceding that they need help. How they go about seeking this help will be the subject of the next chapter.

4

Opening the Sweatbox: Purgatory and Debt Advice

Most of those who fall into debt distress ardently believe that the problem is merely a temporary setback and that time will provide the means to recover. While some get back on track, the sheer volume of debt in the modern era (see Chapter 2) means that many do not. These people may teeter between ruin and recover for years or even decades at a time, a phenomenon known as the sweatbox of bankruptcy (Foohey et al 2018). In this chapter I will unpack what it is like to live in the sweatbox through a metaphor inspired by economic theology: purgatory. Like purgatory, the sweatbox is defined by difficulties in comprehending time, where a day can feel like a year and vice versa. Further, the purgatorial sweatbox has a crucial transformative role for the debtor as it gets them psychologically and morally ready for bankruptcy. Research shows that many remain in the sweatbox due to an inability to afford the legal fees, but also due to shame, stigma, and anxiety (Porter and Thorne 2006). These latter elements are what I wish to focus on, as it is 'cheaper' to go bankrupt or insolvent in Ireland relative to the UK or the US, and so this plays less of a factor in decision making. Indeed, many Irish debtors remain in the purgatorial sweatbox even when they know insolvency is a calculatedly superior option, purely because they believe they deserve to suffer.

However, this suffering is not without purpose. As we will see in Chapter 5, the debtor will be able to present the sacrifices they have made to their insolvency practitioner as evidence of hardship, and thereby increase their chances of gaining the support of this crucial gatekeeper. My characterization of this time as purgatorial is deliberate, because while this experience is harsh, it is not the same as damnation, as we will see in Chapter 7. The difference lies in the absence of hope: at this point in the story, debtors are feeling uneasy about their prospects of recovery, but they remain in negotiations with their creditors and develop a growing awareness of what insolvency could do for them. Though they are anxious about the present, they remain cautiously optimistic about the future. By the time we get to Chapter 7, we will encounter those debtors who were rejected for an insolvency arrangement and whose homes now lie under threat of foreclosure. This leads to a change in subjectivity towards scapegoating and toxic survival strategies that are ultimately self-defeating.

One of the transformations that take place in the subjectivity of the debtor is the necessity of seeking advice on their situation. While Chapter 3 demonstrated that the early stages of debt distress are defined by isolation and fruitless attempts to conceal the scale of the problem, this chapter uncovers how debtors tentatively explore the universe of debt advice. Building on the economic theology positioning (Schwarzkopf 2020), I theorize the complexities of modern financial advice using Foucault's pastoral power (Waring and Martin 2016; Martin and Waring 2018; Waring and Latif 2018). Foucault uses the religious metaphor of the pastor tending to their flock as an analogy for contemporary governance (Burchell et al 1991). Our modern society has created many pastors and many flocks, and so there is a significant element of choice in terms of how we build and run our lives.

Each debtor has their own circumstances and their own approach to dealing with their problems, and this influences the pastor(s) they choose to listen to. Some seek the advice of friends or family, while others trust in their creditors, though most will encounter a formal debt advisor at some point. It is the very possibility of choice that creates the appeal of pastoral power, as it gives a granular explanation for how resistance can take place (Martin and Waring 2018). Debtors inevitably choose the pastors whose strategies and attitudes best reflect their own, and reject or resist agents, institutions, or discourses that do not match their worldview. In concordance with other research, the debt advisor emerges as the clear favourite, as their knowledge combined with their ethics of care give them great appeal.

The chapter closes by showing the limits of the purgatorial sweatbox and debt advice, which can only delay the inevitable for our indebted participants. Once this happens, they are forced to confront the only option that remains: insolvency. We will see that the field of insolvency relations is quite confusing, with prospective applicants unsure as to which arrangement applies to them or what they are expected to do. Indeed, this confusion and dislocation is itself a core part of the purgatorial experience of being in debt, and this is how the following discussion will start.

The purgatory of debt

The sweatbox

Debtors are spending longer in the pre-bankruptcy state known as the sweatbox. Surveys show that 66.4 per cent of new bankrupts in America struggled to pay their debts for more than two years, and a further 30 per cent struggled for five years or more (Foohey et al 2018, pp 235–236). These figures represent an increase relative to the time before the 2005 bankruptcy reforms were passed, which made filing for bankruptcy more complex and costly. In many cases a debtor will struggle on against all odds until long after the costs of bankruptcy outweigh the benefits, in defiance of the transactional view of bankruptcy put forward by industry actors (Ramsay 2017) or policy makers (Walker 2011).

Testimonials from debt relief services are replete with stories that show the same trend. Donna, a single mother who borrowed after losing her job following a difficult period of postnatal depression, offered a testimonial to the ISI saying that she worried constantly about money for several years before saying "part of me knew I couldn't go on like this forever" (Insolvency Service of Ireland 2023a, 00:20). Other testimonials offer a similar sentiment, such as those of Michael, who borrowed during a stint of unemployment (Insolvency Service of Ireland 2023b), or Josephine and Damien, who fell into mortgage arrears for years before eventually seeking help (Insolvency Service of Ireland 2023c). Foohey et al (2018) have shown that those who stay in the sweatbox for more than two years become 'long strugglers' who suffer severely with mental health difficulties, often pawn valuables, risk foreclosure, and juggle constant contact from angry creditors. The question has often been raised as to why these people do not file for bankruptcy. Shame and stigma offer a partial explanation, but even this does not go far enough. I contend that people remain in the sweatbox because it is a purifying purgatorial experience. While in the sweatbox, they retain a hope of salvation through a belief that necessary suffering will absolve them of the sin of failing to pay their debts.

The trials of purgatory: time and anxiety

The sweatbox and these long strugglers in particular have a distinctly purgatorial character. In the Christian theological tradition, purgatory is a liminal space that exists between heaven and hell, and is an area where those who died with unforgiven mortal sins are tested and tried (Bell 2020). This is a theological metaphor which enables greater understanding of the subjectivities of debt, in the same way that Boland and Griffin (2021) used it to develop a greater understanding of the experiences of unemployment. In purgatory, souls are subjected to an endless series of trials, judgements, and punishments, with the ultimate aim being to reform, purify, change, or transform the wayward soul and thereby justify their accession to heaven (Bell 2020; Boland and Griffin 2020). In purgatory, there is a feeling of timelessness because time itself is used as a punitive tool to redeem sinners. Some accounts of purgatory suggest that each day could feel like years or decades to those who have been confined (Boland and Griffin 2020, 2021), a sentiment echoed by debtors: 'you lose all track of time when you're in debt, there's just the next bill' or 'sometimes I felt that a week had gone by, that it was already Friday, but it was only the middle of Tuesday. Being behind on your bills is exhausting'.

A heavily indebted participant once told me that 'debt eats the future', a thought-provoking statement that raises the relation between debt and temporality. As soon as the money is borrowed, a debt exists simultaneously in the past, present, and future (Coleman 2016). It transforms us because while the money was borrowed in the past and is owed in the future, the only way to make repayment actionable is through changes in behaviour in the present (Walker 2011; Bramall et al 2016a). Debt alters and adjusts our actions and behaviours, albeit slowly. This is how debt eats the future: the money may be due in the future, but debtors can only ever think of the present. Debt creates a sense of urgency and impending danger which never relents, eases, or ceases. As one participant said to me, "you can only think about tomorrow, anything more than that is too far away, I will worry about other stuff later". The sense of anxiety is only ever temporarily moved or displaced, and many related to me that if they were not feeling anxious, this paradoxically produced more anxiety because they wondered what they had forgotten that they ought to be anxious about. In the purgatory of indebtedness time is elastic; most of the time, it is excruciatingly slow, but occasionally a problem arises that creates sudden and immediate urgency.

Rather than being a binary state, debt reaches out to people as a series of affects (Deville 2015), a feeling of constriction and anxiety. The experience is also peculiar because while being a debtor who is not servicing your debts makes you a deviant of sorts, you can instantly disclaim your deviant status by paying (Rock 2014), in the same way that an unemployed person can release themselves from the scrutiny of their welfare officer and the stigma of joblessness by finding a job (Boland and Griffin 2021). There is a limbo of sorts for debtors, a feeling that while you owe money, you are always so very close to getting 'back on track'.

The experience of being over-indebted is strange, because from a definitional standpoint nobody can tell you when you have become over-indebted. You become over-indebted when you are 'unable' to pay, a target that constantly shifts and moves. The experience of being in debt was related to me as a kind of ceaseless drudgery, with commonly used terms such as unending, relentless, nonstop, or endless. Due to the intrusion of bills, letters, phone calls, and other contact from creditors, combined with a loss of social and financial inclusion, these feelings of dislocation are punctuated by anxiety and humiliation.

Reform through necessary suffering

The long strugglers I have spoken to or interviewed have a habit of describing their problems as necessary or deserved. They blame themselves for everything that has happened, even when this would be irrational or self-defeating. In a particularly bad month, one participant told me she sold her bed frame to make ends meet, electing instead sleeping on a mattress on the floor. She punctuated this by saying "it's what I had to do, and better than I deserved, and I don't regret it, some people don't even have a couch to sleep on". The pawning of valuables and sentimental items is a common feature of the indebted experience, and many of those I spoke to had sold furniture, entertainment devices such as smartphones or televisions, or even sentimental valuables such as wedding rings.

The ultimate goal of purgatory is to purify the individual of their sins through trials and tests. One doesn't need to necessarily pass every test; it is much more important not to give up. In the arena of debt problems, policy makers have presented financial literacy as a universal panacea; across international boundaries, debtors are now expected to take financial literacy courses of various kinds (Ramsay 2017). Debtors are seen as cognitive delinquents (Walker 2011) who need to learn how to budget better. However, the proliferation of evidence from Chapter 2 demonstrated that most debt problems are due to macroeconomic factors beyond individuals' control: if the company you work for goes bankrupt and you cannot find another job, then no amount of financial literacy training will do any good. Research on social class has also shown that loss of money leads to stringent budgeting; it is in fact the middle and upper classes who waste their money on frivolities (Lister 2004). As one participant told me, "there is no faster way to learn budgeting than being in debt, believe me, you count every cent".

Theologically, this is apparent to us through the tension that exists in the Christian tradition of charity and grace that to give to the poor is good and virtuous. Medieval Christian societies had developed whole traditions around the giving of alms (Boland and Griffin 2021). However, this perspective undergoes a reconstruction as we enter modernity and its attendant Weberian focus on hard work and discipline (Parkin 2002). By giving freely to the poor, you become complicit in their poverty and even encourage it because they learn that they can receive something for nothing. Instead, it is necessary to give people the tools for their own salvation, meaning that true generosity would enable the poor to free themselves from their own poverty (Bell 2020). The result are the workhouses, modelled upon factories, which are themselves modelled on monasteries, which serve as total institutions for the poor (Foucault 1991a, 1995, 1996; Dean and Zamora 2021).

Institutions seek to reform the individual by inculcating in them the values (as well as the skills) of work, and while workhouses were often cruel, there was a certain a purgatorial logic to their operation. The cruelty of the environment is not done out of malice or hatred; it is done because suffering is purifying and will help the individual to see the error of their ways (Dempsey 2020; Karlsen and Villadsen 2020). As in the earlier case of sin, the dialogues of responsibility and choice so familiar to us through neoliberalism arise again. We must governmentalize the individual (Burchell et al 1991), we must make them complicit in their own remaking, in their own transformation, in their own salvation. In the same way that sin is a choice, reform and transformation are also choices, and the individual must make an active conscious choice to be different in order for the process to work.

Debtors believe that their suffering is worthwhile because through making sacrifices, they retain a hope that they will be able to remain in their homes. In Chapter 7 we will explore the implications of this through Berlant's (2011) cruel optimism, where attachment to the object of our desire is damaging to our flourishing. The more sacrifices debtors make to hold on to what they have, the less sense it makes because the image of a perfect life (see Chapter 3) becomes increasingly distant. As we will see, the purgatory of indebtedness creates a humble and guilty subject (Lazzarato 2012) who is eager to distance themselves from the stereotypical bad debtor. In doing so, they incidentally increase their chances of success in the insolvency process, which is designed in such a way to rebuff the morally hazardous 'professional debtor' (Rock 2014).

Pastoral power

Each person navigates the purgatorial sweatbox in different ways, but at a certain point it becomes inevitable that they contact someone to talk about what they are going through. Some opt to trust a friend or family member, some engage in dedicated direct negotiations with creditors, and some may even opt for a life coach or financial guru, but for the most part, the debtor will lean on a professional debt advisor. Debt advice has appeal because (at least at the beginning) it affords the debtor a level of anonymity, which gives the relationship a therapeutic character. Over time, the knowledge of the advisor combined with a nonjudgemental attitude that manifests itself through an ethics of care solidifies them as the superior choice in the minds of most debtors. Later in this chapter (and throughout Chapter 5) we will meet the most important pastor of all: the insolvency practitioner.

I theorize this decision-making process through what Foucault termed 'pastoral power', which is a mode of power that emphasizes the governance of the individual and the group must be simultaneous – that is, we must govern 'each and all' (Foucault 2000, p 1). Foucault taps into the Christian discourses and governmentalizing elements of the 'flock'. The shepherd cares for and manages their flock by seeing to their needs and keeping the wolves at bay, in the same way that a priest should watch over and care for their congregation (Foucault 2015).

In this reading, power is used not as a force of domination or coercion to brutally compel the flock into accepting the rules of the church (or factory, school, hospital, asylum, and so on); instead, power is a productive force that seeks to keep the flock healthy by watching out for signs of abnormality (echoing the focus on normalization so present in Foucault's work). This enables the shepherd to spot sheep who are ill or ailing, but the shepherd must protect against dangers such as wolves or find sheep who become lost. Naturally the Christian metaphors develop this sense of being 'lost' as a loss of faith in God, and so the good shepherd is wise and checks in regularly with their flock (Foucault 2003; Foucault and Senellart 2008; Karlsen and Villadsen 2020). The reason for the shepherd's constant intervention in the lives of their flock is that they are themselves responsible for the salvation of their charges, and that the salvation of each is the salvation of all – or, to put another way, to abandon one is to abandon all (Bell 2020). In the service of salvation, the shepherd may put up fences to enclose or protect the flock, which we might also think of as a moral or spiritual enclosure (Rose 1991).

Martin and Waring (Waring and Martin 2016; Martin and Waring 2018) have expanded on Foucault's original writings on pastoral power to make its applicability to contemporary modes of governance more actionable. We can think of society as a kind of collision between hundreds (or thousands) of flocks who are mingling and interacting. Neoliberalism facilitates the creation of an immense variety of experts and fields of expertise who promise to help us improve or change: doctors, teachers, therapists, life coaches, job coaches, financial advisors, and many more. Pastoral power helps to solve some of the problems that traditional Foucauldian visions of power have encountered. First, this vision of power creates an open space for choice and free will, which is important because Foucault's early and mid-career work on disciplinary institutions gave an impression of a relentless machine that crushes human agency (Foucault 1989, 1995, 1996). Second, it gives a more precise understanding of how abstract discourses reach agents in practice (McLeod 2017): it is the pastors who coproduce and relate the discourses to their flocks. This further reinforces agency, resistance, and free will, because the recipient of the discourse will internalize some discourses while ignoring others. For the purposes of this discussion, we will examine two types of potential pastors – creditors or debt advisors – and who the debtor listens to and why.

Creditors

Once a debtor has missed a payment, creditors will initiate contact and begin the collections process (Deville 2015). As with Rock's (2014) excellent depiction from the 20th century and Deville's (2015) similarly excellent research from the 21st century, this typically takes the form of an escalating series of threats. Ideally, creditors will be able to get the money without exercising much effort, but this is not always the case. Experience has taught them that contact must be firm and persistent to get any kind of satisfactory result, though this can backfire if their repeated attempts at contact become perceived as harassment. At first, the messages will be simple reminders to pay, as many people will miss at least one payment because there was not enough money in their account, or they simply forgot. These issues are usually rectified quickly. However, if further payments are missed, the creditor will issue contact which emphasizes the obligation that links creditor and debtor together. Further missed payments usually provoke a response that is more threatening: you risk losing the asset which secures the loan (a house, a car), which will impact your credit, which will in turn limit your capacity to borrow in the future.

As Deville (2015) has stated, the creditor seeks to get the debtor to respond by mobilizing their affect, especially through provoking the fear and anxiety outlined earlier. This is communicated in all aspects of the contact, which by now are meticulously and deliberately designed. For example, a historical development in the late-notice letter was for the debt collector to print their logo and letterhead on the envelope, meaning that the debtor's friends or neighbours may see it and deduce that they are having problems (Deville 2015). The well-known tendency for debtors to shut down and refuse contact means that creditors often feel the need to be assertive in their contact strategies, though I have always found debtors despise this:

> 'I'm suffering enough and don't need a man in an ill-fitting three-piece suit to lay the situation out for me, I know how bad it is.' (Interview with Michael)

> 'I always found them [creditors] nasty to deal with, they are so aggressive and over the top.' (Interview with Sarah)

> 'Sometimes I think the bank just needed to relax, I signed up for a 30-year mortgage, the house isn't going anywhere, can't we just talk like two mature adults?' (Interview with Paul)

Creditors find that they must 'shout the loudest' (Kirwan 2018) because a person with one problem debt is likely to have other creditors who will also be clamouring for payment, and the body of evidence shows that in a moment of crisis, debtors will prioritze. The goal of the creditor is then to ensure they rank among the prioritised debts by any means necessary. However, this can become self-defeating and lead to a reduction rather than an increase in contact if the methods used are seen as too aggressive or if attempts to use underhanded tactics such as humiliation or late-night phone calls and employed.

However, creditors (particularly in Ireland) are motivated to provide some level of pastoral care to debtors, which has manifested itself through an uneasy political consensus that the mass eviction of mortgagors is not acceptable. This is easily visible in the statistics on arrears and repossession. Ireland has around 716,000 mortgages on homes, of which around 50,000 are in arrears (roughly 14 per cent), which represents a significant improvement from the 100,000 arrears figure from a decade ago (Central Bank of Ireland 2023). Within these arrears figures are the long strugglers, with 4,600 in arrears for between two and five years, 5,600 in arrears for more than five years, and an astonishing 4,100 mortgages in arrears for more than ten years (Central Bank of Ireland 2023). Repossession in Ireland is both a costly and long process, and so creditors do not even bother to initiate the process unless they have completely lost hope in the borrower's willingness to pay. Building on the previous figures, only 5,600 mortgages are at the formal demand stage of legal proceedings where the creditor is actively seeking a legal solution to their claims. Despite the number of arrears, fewer than 400 houses are repossessed every year, though this has been increasing over time (Central Bank of Ireland 2023).

With quick repossession unavailable as an option, creditors have instead opted for the endless restructuring of failing mortgages. Indeed, some of my participants showed me contact indicating pre-approval for arrears recapitalization or interest-only arrangements with the bank and were given a number to call on a certain day at a certain time to avail themselves of this option. This has been the Irish solution to the mortgage crisis, with 62,000 mortgage accounts currently under a restructure arrangement of some kind (Central Bank of Ireland 2023). Some people I interviewed have had their mortgages restructured two, three, or even four times. I agree that the movement to restructuring arrangements has been used cynically to redefine dysfunctional cases such that they appear unproblematic (Waldron and Redmond 2015). Indeed, the solution has been to render purgatory eternal for some debtors, who end up trapped in a toxic cycle where they cannot repay, but are also unwilling to surrender their house. This has led to a significant uptick in the appeal of the debt advisor, who is believed to be a more neutral party in the negotiation and discussion process.

Debt advice

The deluge of debt, which was the subject of Chapter 2, has led to enduring changes in the structure of the welfare state, and there is a distinct transformation from service provision to advice. The street-level bureaucrats working in unemployment agencies will not give you a job, but they will help you rewrite your CV or teach you to use job search websites. Likewise, a debt advisor cannot write down your debt, but they can give you strategies on how best to proceed considering your circumstances. The field of financial advice is now dense and confusing, encompassing everything from self-help gurus, or family and friends, to professional advisors who may work for the state or in a semi-state capacity (Deville 2015; Featherstone 2020). Debtors who are embroiled in the purgatory of indebtedness must eventually reach out to one pastor or another for help, and debt advisors are often near the top of the list. At the bottom of each late notice bill, with its ominous but vague threats of escalation and doom (Deville 2015), is a bizarre request for the debtor to contact a reputable debt advice service. Such messages often come with a therapeutic or moral message, intended to show that the creditor is thinking of the mental health of the debtor. The following are some examples I saw from bills shown to me by my participants:

- 'You do not need to suffer in silence, contact the Money Advice and Budgeting Service (MABS) today.'
- 'We all struggle sometimes and talking *will* help: contact MABS today.'
- 'Sticking your head in the sand might make you feel better in the short-term, but we all need a long-term plan. Talk to us or MABS today.'

The latter of these came with a cute (but admittedly patronizing) image of an ostrich with its head literally buried in sand at a beach. There can be no doubt that creditors are aware of the emotional and psychological stress debtors experience as they fall further behind in their payments. Creditors have many tools to deploy and, despite popular belief, they often exercise considerable restraint in this process. There are many reasons for this – for example, they know that some people do recover from over-indebtedness, and it is important to preserve a good relationship wherever possible. A resentful debtor determined to fight you can cost a small fortune (see Chapter 7), and many debtors doing so can threaten the solvency of the creditor, or even the credit system itself, as we saw in the GFC when many debtors missed even their first payment (Coulter and Nagle 2015). Additionally, it is well established that leaping directly to your most severe threats and sanctions leaves you with nowhere to go (Geisst 2013; Rock 2014). If you immediately make threats you do not follow up on, then you look impotent, and if you do follow up on them, you can look unreasonable.

Debt advisors have a profound role to play in the debt resolution process. It must be admitted that the financial advice they offer tends to be mundane, but this is not their only role; they also have a pastoral and therapeutic role. Getting people to open up about their debt problems or even admitting that they have one is a Herculean feat in itself:

'I couldn't talk about it [my debt problems]. Every time I tried I just couldn't make the words come out. The shame, it was white hot, I felt it on my face, I would blush. The first time I managed to say something was to [a debt advisor], she was very understanding. It was more like talking to a priest than a finance-type person.' (Interview with a debtor)

'They are often not ready. It might take a year, it might take two years to soften them up and even get them to talk about it [debt problems]. The stigma is very strong.' (Interview with a debt advisor)

As already noted, the content of the advice tends to be what we would expect, and yet even this is revealing. As in the policy literature that surrounds insolvency, the problem is characterized as a lack of financial literacy (White 2010). Debtors are encouraged to make a budget if they have not done so already, and generally debt advice services will have budgets which have been prefilled to a certain extent. Usually this means the section headings (that is, phone costs, energy bills, rent, and mortgage) have already been inserted to help jog the person's memory in case they forget anything (Stamp 2012b ; Atfield and Orton 2013; Free Legal Advice Centre 2015; Money Advice Budgeting Service 2022).

Once this is done, debtors are further encouraged to look at their potential entitlements and investigate how they might get access to any schemes or programmes that they are not already using, particularly welfare payments. As is noted in a wide array of economic sociology literature, this is one of the least desirable suggestions a debt advisor can make to a debtor. Zelizer (1994) has identified in her work that there is an enormous difference between characterizing a one-off payment as a welfare payment and characterizing it as an earned-income tax credit payment. The former is money 'given' by the state for doing 'nothing' (Wilkis 2018), while the latter is 'earned' through working and therefore does not have the stigma that is conventionally attached to welfare. This is despite the fact that it is the same money being paid to the same group of people. It is the same here, with debtors extremely reluctant to pursue a solution that is overtly rooted in welfare and many commenting that this is due to a fear of social demotion (Whelan 2022):

'Other people might be comfortable with that, but I'm not. I wouldn't take money from the government even if the alternative is starving. I work for my money and that's it.' (Interview with Sarah)

'You would be looked down on for taking the dole [welfare]. I know if anyone found out I had done that, that it would change their perception of me.' (Interview with Michelle)

Discourses of self-worth, deservingness, work, and justification all clash here. Retaining a feeling of independence is crucial for a debtor to feel that they remain in control. While it may seem irrational for a person in financial crisis to turn down any sort of money, I wish to emphasize again here that in order for such money to be acceptable, it must be framed in the right way to the potential recipient. Debt advisors have many functions beyond the purely financial, something that extends throughout the networks of expertise that surrounds indebtedness. Debt advisors come from a wide array of backgrounds, and while expertise in financial resolution and indebtedness is a requirement, it forms only part of what is done on a day-by-day basis:

> 'I have had calls from … thousands of people over the years, and actually you would be surprised that for most of them the problem is not a lack of money. It is an abusive relationship, it is an addiction, it is a gambling problem, it is a temporary setback.' (Interview with a debt advisor)

This lends a profoundly therapeutic role to the work, and it is not surprising that the training and qualifications for debt advisors have a greater focus on vulnerability and vulnerable clients than previously – that is, on economic abuse (Postmus et al 2020; Johnson et al 2022). A recurring challenge in social care is that vulnerable and marginalized people must advocate for themselves, whether they are facing addiction issues, mental health difficulties, disability, racism, sexism, and so on (Whelan 2022). This places even more pressure on someone in an already disadvantaged position and can compound and multiply existing inequities such that they become unmanageable. One of the advantages of debt advice is that advisors are trained to advocate for debtors and are extensively trained in the language and negotiation strategies that are likely to be acceptable to creditors. As part of their pastoral function, they can also impart this to their clients, who can use these new skills to great effect:

> 'I had a great [debt] advisor, and she taught me all about delinquency and default and terms like these that I would never have used. When I got a call from the bank then I was able to say "look I'm really sorry that my debt is in delinquency, but I have the situation under control and I will not fall down into default". I think the lady on the phone was shocked that I put things in those terms, I was speaking her language … I offered to provide a payslip from my new job, and the tone was completely different, the nasty letters stopped and I had peace of mind again.' (Interview with Mona)

This resulted in the debtor being offered arrears capitalization and what essentially amounted to a clean slate because he was able to use the jargon and present his case in a way that made sense to his creditor. The strategy took the form of three phases: first, the debtor apologized, implicitly taking responsibility for failing to pay along the agreed schedule; second, they indicated that they were taking the situation seriously and that improvement could be expected in the near future; and, third, they offered to supply a payslip from their new job, providing the creditor with proof and enabling the bank employee to have a satisfying way to explain that the situation had been resolved to her superiors. Unlike insolvency, there is no pretence that the debt advisor is expected to be (or even should be) neutral; they are expected to be on the debtor's side (Stamp 2012b, 2016, 2017; Deville 2015). While this does raise the taint of bias in their negotiations, it also sets clear expectations about who is advocating for whom, and, as in the example given earlier, this does not always work against the creditor; in many cases, it can even work to their advantage by giving the debtor the jargon and confidence necessary to enter into negotiations. However, this is not always the case:

> 'I have had a mixed experience with debt advisors. If they are going to explain the situation to you and provide a solution, then I find that useful. But a lot of the time what I notice is they string you along, they make excuses for people, and they give you false hope. It can be hard to know when you can trust them and when you can't.' (Interview with a bank manager)

Sometimes creditors find debt advisors frustrating because they can give the impression that the debtor is likely to improve if they are given more time – an elastic use of the truth can erode trust and the professional working relationship between both parties. Research has persistently shown that debt advice, when offered in a nonjudgemental manner, is highly effective (Stamp 2012b; Rock 2014; Deville 2015; Money Advice Budgeting Service 2016a, 2016b; Karlsen and Villadsen 2020; Schwartz 2022). The debtor must live life in the moment, and they can easily end up in a situation where the accretion of many small problems can make the prevailing situation seem unbearable. But having a professional who has experience in the area clearly outline your income and expenses, as well as strategies or actions you can undertake to improve the existing situation can be immensely clarifying. In other words, hope is not lost. This is one of the most important functions of debt advice: it helps debtors to shake off the sense of paralysis and shock that they will have assimilated as soon as they realized they were falling behind and which is one of the most common features of the purgatorial subjectivity of indebtedness.

This also serves as a kind of trial run for debtors' interactions with insolvency practitioners and their creditors later on when they apply for insolvency. These future interactions are set to be more combative as the creditors foresee a legally binding agreement which will be imposed on them by an outside authority. They feel compelled to resist such an arrangement, as it normalizes debt relief and often results in a financial loss. The many pastors operating in the overall area of indebtedness can provide contradictory or inconsistent advice, and so it is the responsibility of the debtor to navigate this complex world and work out what action it would be most reasonable to undertake (Waring and Martin 2016; Martin and Waring 2018; Waring and Latif 2018).

Investigating insolvency

As debtors wind their way through this process, encountering the army of experts who work in and around indebtedness, they slowly gain more information about the formalized processes of insolvency through an array of pastors. This is irregular and tends to rely on word of mouth, online searches, and information from debt advisors which may be accurate, but will also be limited. Initial interactions and impressions of the service were broad, but many of my participants approached the service with a sense of cautious optimism:

> 'It [the ISI] seemed promising, but I didn't want to get my hopes up.' (Interview with Paul)

> 'I liked the idea, I needed something like this, but I went in with no expectations I'd been let down too many times before'. (Interview with Jane)

> 'Optimistic … but reserved … just in case [it didn't work out].' (Interview with Michelle)

Others were more ambitious about what could be achieved:

> 'I thought: this is it. This is what I've been waiting for. I've been suffering and help has arrived.' (Interview with Simon)

> 'It [the ISI] seemed good, I had no reasons to be suspicious.' (Interview with Rachel)

Having heard about the service on the news or through a family member, debtors were keen to identify if the service could help them and, if so, in what way. While it was apparent that some work had gone into building the ISI website, it was unclear what precisely the service was supposed to do for an applicant. This led at an early stage to a misalignment of expectations from those who believed that the service would write off all their debt without making bankruptcy necessary to those who went in with a conviction that the ISI was 'useless' or 'not for me', but still wanted to find out more.

All of my indebted participants were interviewed in the summer of 2016, but had their first experiences of the ISI before it even started taking cases in September 2013 (Croffey 2013). There were concerns variously from politicians (Oireachtas 2013), academics (Stamp 2012a, 2012b), and charitable organizations (Irish Mortgage Holders Organisation 2014a) about how the service would perform. In the media there were fears that the service represented a 'moral hazard' (Weston 2012; Paul 2018), which occurs when one party takes a risk while knowing that another party will ultimately bear the cost associated with that risk – for example, a debtor who seeks a loan they cannot pay back, knowing they can have the debt written down at a later date. Several different media organizations and opinion pieces warned or suggested that the ISI represented the beginnings of a programme of systematic debt relief, shifting the burden of debt from debtor to creditor (Croffey 2013; Mortgage Brokers 2013; Horgan-Jones 2014; Brennan and Bardon 2018; The Business Post 2013).

By contrast, my participants held to a kind of reserved optimism. They were hopeful about the possibilities that might be represented by the service, but were fearful that these hopes would be dashed. From the outset, none of them was quite sure as to what precisely the ISI was supposed to do:

'I still, I wouldn't be confident even now to tell you what it does, or who it's meant to help. Is it for me? That's the real question I was concerned with, but of course that's the real question everyone is concerned with. I thought that, you know yourself, it would just be a long waiting list and they'd give you a hard time and then you'd get you a hand [receive help].' (Interview with Michael)

'I thought it was like MABS but it's not even close to the same, it seemed like you had to push [work] a bit to get help, but it'd pay off down the road.' (Interview with Michelle)

Some, as in the preceding quotes, believed that the service would have its problems but ultimately would be helpful. Others believed that it was a "Godsend, I really needed this [debt relief]" (interview with Rachel).

Salvific language (Bell 2020) is common when debtors describe the possibilities they imagine are achievable through debt relief, and many have told me that they 'needed a miracle' or something similar (see Chapter 6 for more details). The strongest criticisms came from participants who feared that it would be like welfare organizations such as the Department of Social

Protection, and that applications were written and would take a very long time to be resolved, requiring many appeals. "[I thought] Here we go, just like the social [Department of Employment Affairs and Social Protection] apply, apply, apply then appeal, appeal, appeal. I dunno how they [the government] have the energy for it" (interview with Ciara).

Immediate first impressions of the service were therefore generally positive, and all of my participants eagerly sought out additional information. All used the ISI's website and attempted to grapple with the data presented there. Some gave up attempting to find which of the three new arrangements was appropriate for them and searched for someone they could telephone or email. They discovered that the ISI has no centralized contact details and is instead operated by independent agents who have a licence – called PIPs. This caused irritation and confusion: "I remember thinking, who were these guys [the PIPs]? Is this the government or not and what do ... what do they do?" (interview with Sarah).

Who was the PIP? What exactly did they do? Were they a government employee or not? Is this a state body or a semi-state body, a private organization or a detached NGO? The answers to these questions were unclear, and my participants were not sure how the ISI was to be differentiated from debt advice services. The ISI did not (and still does not) have centralized offices in various towns/cities where a debtor can go to acquire information or seek help. This mirrors Foucault's view of power, which is that power is multiple, transitive, and ultimately faceless (Foucault 1995). Power has no centralized point to which it can be traced back and is instead diffused throughout social relations (Mills 2000). First contact with PIPs varied, but many reported a strained and difficult conversation:

> 'He was icy. I think he was [working in the finance industry] as well, when he picked up the phone, and I even think it might have been his personal phone number it got very awkward when he figured out what I wanted. He needed to know all sorts of questions, what age was I? When did I come in debt first? Have I really tried to pay it back?' (Interview with Michelle)

> 'It [the conversation] surprised me by how tense it was. A service is a service, you use it or you don't, there's no need to be testy with me.' (Interview with Aileen)

Despite this, anyone who phoned or emailed was given a one-on-one meeting with a PIP. Even at this early stage, of my 18 participants, only 13 elected to go ahead and have a meeting with one of their local PIPs. The other five had heard stories from friends or family who discouraged them from attending the meeting:

'I heard they [the PIPs] are brutal, they bring you in and savage you [treat you badly] and there's no light at the end of the tunnel either.' (Interview with Jane)

'I couldn't go through with it John [participant's friend] told me the kind of questions they asked him. I couldn't face that humiliation.' (Interview with Paul)

At the point of first contact, the PIPs informed the prospective applicants that they were working professionals who were running their own businesses, not government employees. This meant that in order for the meeting to go ahead, my participants had to pay the PIP a fee. The amount charged varies, but between €50 and €100 is common, and five potential applicants were discouraged by this initial cost:

'€100 might not sound like much to you, but just getting to the next week was a lot for me.' (Interview with Ciara)

'I just don't have it [the fee money].' (Interview with Simon)

'I could have paid it, but just barely, and just the once. If he was charging me each time, what was I supposed to do?' (Interview with Mona)

In this telephone conversation, much of the basic structure of the ISI was revealed to the prospective applicants for the first time. As previously stated, each PIP is effectively an independent contractor who administers their own small business. The ISI delegates responsibility for administrating the various insolvency instruments to the PIPs and gives them the authority to implement and manage these arrangements. Insolvency arrangements can be appealed by the debtor or their creditor(s), but only to contest a point of law, not because one party did not like the outcome of the PIP's deliberations (Insolvency Service of Ireland 2014a, 2015a, 2015b, 2016c). The essential goal of the service is to make an applicant who is insolvent solvent again: 'You are insolvent if you are unable to pay your debts in full as they fall due' (Insolvency Service of Ireland 2016a, p 7).

The key word here is 'unable', because it implies that an attempt has been made. This certainly is how the wording has been interpreted by the PIPs who administrate and manage the operations of the service on a day-to-day basis. However, beyond this, PIPs are given few guidelines on how to implement the arrangements or how the qualifying criteria (beyond the strictly legal requirements) are to be interpreted. Each PIP therefore can determine what is allowed to count as 'unable', and while their understandings differ, they share some common themes:

'Unable means, to me at least that you have suffered. You should have sacrificed something, something you really like, that's the point when I'll take you seriously.' (Interview with PIP#4)

'If you're unable to pay your debts, that means you need to have tried and failed. Most of these ... clients, debtors just haven't. If you haven't thought about a second job then don't think about the service [ISI].' (Interview with PIP#2)

'Insolvent to me is someone who has made a good fist of it [tried their best], I wouldn't be inclined to be overly harsh but you need to keep an eye on them.' (Interview with PIP#3)

This is a key example of what Rose (1991, 1999) terms 'relays' within the framework of his conceptual device of 'governing at a distance'. Relays are a political technology which translates the goals of a given governmentality into action, and typically relays take the form of experts such as doctors. If a governmentality wished to encourage weight loss in its populace (for example), then doctors would be mobilized to begin a public health campaign, using their expertise to warn of the dangers of obesity and, in so doing, translate the goals of the governmentality into behavioural or moral changes (Rose 1991). In contemporary governmentality there is a desire to govern through freedom – in other words, to create free subjects who will govern themselves, requiring little if any intervention from the state or other governmentalizing forces (Rose 1991).

The state itself also governs thriftily and outsources or downsizes its own organizational structure to minimize its impact on the market (Foucault and Senellart 2008), in this instance the credit market. In this case we have a specific relay of the governance through freedom – the PIP. The state leaves the most important term for an application open to interpretation, which gives PIPs discretionary power over how insolvency legislation is implemented in practice. The relay is thus given a certain measure of freedom and independence in decision making, which at once frees the state from full responsibility for their actions and frees the PIPs to be decisive. Yet, while PIPs are not directly managed by the state, their independence is still limited as only individuals with a particular mindset and who will reproduce the desired neoliberal discourses around debt will be permitted to become a PIP in the first place.

Neoliberalism's strategy is to govern frugally, with minimal resources and support. This is clearly in evidence in the ISI, which does not receive a considerable amount of funding from the state; only the skeleton of its structure is paid for by the government. PIPs are licence-holding small businesspeople who must operate the service on their own, with no clerical or legal help available from the service. They are therefore incentivized to get as many distressed debtors as possible onto debt programmes, as this will maximize their income. At the same time, they have been warned that people in debt are most likely not honest and will be quick to deceive them:

> 'It was … suggested to me that people in debt are like people on welfare they want something for nothing. Those suggestions were right.' (Interview with PIP#2)

> 'They [debtors] don't mean to be tricky. I'd lie to me if I was in that bad of a situation too.' (Interview with PIP#3)

A further theme of the PIPs is sacrifice: giving up something of importance in the struggle to become solvent. For each PIP, this was represented by the surrendering or sacrificing of something of personal rather than financial significance, such as a hobby or bad habit:

> 'Hobbies. That's what I look at [when someone applies for an arrangement]. People come in here with these ridiculous hobbies, not all of them are expensive, but they're time-consuming, I'd be thinking to [myself] "what are you thinking playing soccer four times a week, going to matches and that? Do you not have enough to be getting on with?"' (Interview with PIP#2)

> 'If they're not ready to stop going down the dog track or drinking pints or going God-knows-where, then what good are they [as an applicant]?' (Interview with PIP#4)

The hobby may be relatively inexpensive, but the giving up of hobbies has a sacrificial and symbolic value in representing oneself as a purgatorial subject. These symbolic gestures are a crucial way for the debtor to show that they are taking the process seriously, and that they are genuinely repentant. Here we have two technologies of governmentality interwoven with one another: responsibilization and normalization. Responsibilization has a long history in public policy (Rose 1991, p 74), but broadly refers to the creation of moral standards to which it is the responsibility of individuals to adhere. Individuals should be healthy, fit, hygienic, well educated, have good manners, and so on, which builds a good citizenry and aids in the development of a great society. In turn, individuals take responsibility for their own moral development and are in turn held to account if they fail to meet those standards. As Rose says, responsibilization 'links public objectives for the good health and good order of the social body with the desire of individuals for personal health and well-being. A "private" ethic of good health and morality can thus be articulated on to a "public" ethic of social order and public hygiene' (Rose 1991, p 74).

In so doing, responsibilization entails constant self-improvement, self-critique, discipline, and self-monitoring, which for debtors results in an emphasis on financial wellbeing and financial health as an individual responsibility (Rose 1999). Experts (such as PIPs) are crucial in the development, justification, and maintenance of these moral standards, as they must be based on rational or scientific logic and not be arbitrary or erratic. Further, once these moral injunctions have been accepted for long enough, they become normalized, integrated into everyday behaviour in a way that becomes almost invisible; yet, in actuality, the process of normalization takes years or even decades to produce widely accepted new standards in conduct (Rose 1991, p 75). In the preceding quotes, there is a presumption that debtors are not morally fit individuals: at best they have hobbies which are 'ridiculous', but at worst they engage in morally questionable vices such as gambling or excessive alcohol consumption. Attention must be called to these vices, behaviour must be reformed, and bad habits must be corrected. As Rose elegantly sums up, "we might term this government through the calculated administration of shame" (Rose 1991, p 73).

Additionally, the sacrifice mentioned by the PIPs forms part of a wider set of discourses on scapegoating in Irish public policy. Whether they are unemployed (Boland and Griffin 2015), a lone parent (Whelan 2022), or a dissenting protestor (Power et al 2016), there is often a presumption that these groups are morally deficient in some way, which typically operates by stereotyping the whole group as possessing widely disliked characteristics, such as laziness, violence, or dependency. The PIPs assume that most (if not all) debtors not only lack frugality, but are also gambling, drinking, or abusing illegal drugs, and that this behaviour must be stopped, either through shaming them or denying them debt relief until they make the required changes in behaviour.

Even at this early stage (pre-meeting), PIPs exemplify aspects of neoliberal governmentality, beginning with the ISI's definition of insolvency. Underlying such a definition is the fear that the service will be left open to abuse, a fear shared by all of the PIPs:

> 'Obviously people will abuse it [the service]; pulling strokes and trying to get off it [get their debt discharged early]. You need, it's the checks and balances, the give and the take. We're going to give you something, some money back is what it amounts to, and you're going to give us something, but the biggest gift is honesty, and it's controversial but most people in debt and dealing with debt issues are not honest.' (Interview with PIP #4)

Neoliberal governmentality seeks to govern in this way. By characterizing social welfare, healthcare, debt relief and so on as entitlements that people must earn rather than as benefits which are universally accessible, neoliberalism creates exclusion by using market logic to design social programmes (Foucault and Senellart 2008; Boland and Griffin 2018). Under a neoliberal governmentality, the main duty of the state is to create the conditions necessary for the market to flourish. In the Irish context this means that rules and regulations pertaining to banking and lending should be limited, as people ought to have the freedom to decide if they want debt for themselves. Competition between lenders is to be encouraged and the most successful businesses will be those that offer the best rates in the most accessible manner. This produces an outcome most desirable for consumers, who should have access to a wide variety of options in the free market and be able to consume whatever there is a market for at a reasonable price.

In practice, neoliberalism is less objective than this. The government rarely simply creates the conditions necessary for a market to flourish and instead tends to favour (discreetly or openly) certain businesses or business models over others (Boland and Griffin 2015; Foucault and Senellart 2008; Foucault 2015). Neoliberals argue extensively against the minimum wage, social welfare, universal healthcare, and other social programmes, which they view as 'entitlements'. From this perspective, the market cannot compete with social welfare: if a person is receiving €300 per week in social welfare, we are told that they have no incentive to seek work for less than this amount, and even a slightly greater amount will not be sufficient because they will not want to work for a long period of time to gain only a small amount of extra money, money which they already receive for doing 'nothing' (Foucault and Senellart 2008).

Debt relief is characterized by neoliberalism in the same manner. It is seen as a problematic form of governance, as private organizations rarely write off debts (though they can be persuaded if full debt relief is an option). Neoliberal discourses on debt relief show concern that debt relief may become too common; therefore, the goal is to make debt relief difficult to access. It must be locked behind certain barriers, it must be hard to acquire information about, it must be available only to those who truly 'need' it, and it should be offered subject to terms and conditions (for example, you may only use debt relief once in your lifetime).

Conclusion

This chapter has theorized that the tendency for debtors to delay filing for insolvency or bankruptcy is due to a purgatorial belief that the problems associated with debt distress are deserved or necessary punishments. Economic theology provides a connection between the experiences of purgatory and the pre-bankruptcy sweatbox. Debtors strive to behave in a manner they hope will be perceived as virtuous by an observer, and in doing so redeem themselves from the sin of failing to pay their debts. Indeed, systems of debt relief must confront what is to be done with these indebted sinners. Do we simply destroy them, as in the old Christian belief in 'annihilationism' that sinful souls are obliterated at the same moment the body dies? As a culture and society, we have decided that the best approach is to reform, change, and transform debtors by inculcating in them appropriately neoliberal behaviours and attitudes, to be achieved through the steady application of pastoral power. The decision to manage indebtedness by managing debtors is a deliberate political and economic choice rooted in our conceptions of punishment and salvation.

This appears to the debtor as a purgatorial experience, which gives a sense that time becomes elastic or warped: because debt collapses the future into the present, the debtor must remain focused only upon the immediate future. They must work out how they will pay bills this week or month rather than making a long-term plan for self-development. Purgatory is also a highly individualizing force – theologically it is distinct from hell because it is a rigidly ordered space where each sin has a corresponding punishment intended to reform the individual. Finally, it is a cleansing, purifying, or sanctifying experience; purgatory is a prelude to judgement which will determine whether a soul belongs in heaven or hell. In this same way, the purgatorial experience of debt is highly judgmental, because the actions undertaken by the debtor will later determine if they will be successful in their insolvency applications.

As with theological representations of purgatory, the time a debtor spends in this purgatorial phase varies. Some people come to terms with what must happen relatively quickly, yet others may spend years or even decades making the minimum repayments while slowly falling further behind. Once the debtor has been appropriately transformed, and they have wholly accepted and internalized the logics of neoliberalism, including their own responsibility and efforts to make amends, then they may be suitable for insolvency. Insolvency must guard against unworthy entrants because it is an earthly representation of salvation for the debtor, the means through which they can achieve a permanent recovery and once again think about the future in positive terms.

5

Applying for Insolvency

Here we pick up right where Chapter 4 left off, with our debtors having set up a meeting with a Personal Insolvency Practitioner (PIP) to discuss their options and see if insolvency is the right choice for them. Initial contact with these experts was described using terms like 'icy' or 'standoffish', and there is confusion on the part of debtors over how insolvency works and what they are expected to do. Debtors expect a tedious process of form filling and means testing, but the reality is that success depends on a small number of micro-interactions mediated in the form of a confession. The debtor must use moral storytelling to tell the tale of their indebtedness; in doing so, they must convince the PIP and later their creditors that they are sincerely apologetic, that they take responsibility for what went wrong, and they must demonstrate that they have made a commitment to change.

This is a classed and gendered process, and middle-class men with strong access to social and cultural capital are best able to navigate the confessional interviews that determine whether one will be allowed to proceed. Working-class debtors are framed through discourses of addiction and vice, and in need of 'tough love', which will lead to painful but necessary behavioural change. It is vital that the debtor is able to advocate for themselves in this process, something that my working-class participants struggled with. They must be contrite and apologetic by accurately relating their failures and sins, while simultaneously positioning themselves as deserving of help and compassion by outlining their purgatorial suffering.

Women, by contrast, are often stereotyped as addicted to consumerism and their over-indebtedness is therefore caused by an excess of leisure debt. While immensely frustrating, many women have found that by repositioning themselves and their situations as a result of caring debts (for example, loans taken to pay for childcare), they can use misogynistic assumptions to their advantage. By shifting their confessional story from consumerist spending on shoes and makeup to caring spending on children (affirming popular gendered discourses about women and childrearing), they can create sympathy which can open up a path to insolvency.

Unbeknownst to the debtor, there is an invisible curriculum lying just beneath the surface of these interactions, and success or failure often depends on factors which lie outside of their control. In addition to offering a morally persuasive story about their indebtedness, the following are also significant: the type of debt (secured or unsecured), the quantity of debt (it is easier to discharge small debts), the category of debt (leisure, caring, symbolic, survival), the debtor's relationship with their creditors, and broader conditions in the prevailing political economy. This is a complex process involving an interplay between theology, class, gender, impression management, discourse, power, and governance. The only way to understand this process is to see it in motion, and so we begin with the first in-person meeting at the PIP's house.

A knock on the door

Debtors arrived at the meeting feeling nervous and were not sure what to expect, thoughts of delay or cancellation had been entertained and dismissed. While most had discussed their indebtedness with a financial or debt advisor, this had been done over the phone, which granted them a degree of separation and anonymity that was comforting. To describe their debt story in person was another matter entirely – as one participant put it: "How are you supposed to explain that you are a complete failure?" Most had hopes that a full explanation would not be necessary and that their assemblage of documents would speak on their behalf. In advance of the meeting, the PIP will have asked them to bring their overdue bills and other details about their debts such as mortgage statements, bank statements, examples of contact from their creditors, proof of income (such as a payslip), and any budget they may have been following. Within this bundle of documents is the debtor's whole life, and unfortunately the message is not positive or uplifting:

> 'When I got everything [the documents] all together I could see how I had fallen behind month-by-month. Failure in black and white.' (Interview with Roger)

> 'Looking back through the bank statements it is just a constant stream of money going out and nothing coming in, I tried so hard and never got anywhere.' (Interview with Jane)

These documents, combined with filling out a short form called a Prescribed Financial Statement (PFS), are as close as the ISI gets to a 'true' application form. Applicants also generally expressed surprise that an in-person meeting is mandatory and that such a meeting takes place at the PIP's home rather than in a formal office or a government building. The simple answer is that such offices are not available because PIPs are not government employees; rather, they are regulated, licensed, and supervised by the ISI, but in all other respects are essentially independent private operators who work within the legal framework provided by insolvency legislation. Unless they have the means to afford such help independently, they will not have a staff, such as clerks or secretaries, and so most practitioners maintain a small office in their homes. It is here that they meet with potential clients. This framework was copied from the UK, whose insolvency practitioners operate on the same basis, but is relatively common across the Anglosphere with similar practices in New Zealand, Canada, and Australia.

This is a favoured strategy of neoliberal governmentality (Dean 2018; Foucault 1991b), where power is dispersed across a whole field of relations rather than concentrated in institutions; this has advantages, especially if problems arise with specific practitioners. In this case, the insolvency service can say that it simply licenses and regulates these practitioners, and is not responsible for their behaviour. This provides indemnity, but also enables ignorance to be used strategically whereby the state can disclaim knowledge of what these actors do precisely because they are so far from the frontlines (Miller and Rose 1990; McGoey 2012). The independence of the practitioners also enables the state to disclaim bias: if state employees were responsible for implementing insolvency arrangements, it is likely that both creditors and debtors would level accusations of bias at the government when the outcome was unfavourable to them. Problems are therefore due to the misbehaviour of specific individuals rather than reflecting general or systemic issues. What would debtors complain about? The way they tend to be greeted will begin to give us an indication:

'It was ... I shiver thinking about it. I knocked [on his door] and as soon as he realized why I was there I could feel this atmosphere, like he was standing on the top of the temple judging me. I was some worthless failure here to be saved by him. He asked me to explain myself ... this was before I was even let into the house, I recall he said "oh you're in debt [distress] for seven years [participants emphasis] what's that about?" I could see straight away it was going to be a bumpy ride.' (Interview with Michael)

'Someone let me in, I'm still not sure who she was, could have been his wife or a secretary or something. I walked into the room, the office and he was sitting at ... like this [the participant sits at an askew angle] and reading a sheet on a clipboard. I walked in and asked him if he was the practitioner. He didn't look up at me, he pointed at the chair in front of his desk [the participant does a "you sit there" gesture] I was

there to sit and be quiet until he was ready for me. I was terrified.'
(Interview with Michelle)

Much to the surprise of the debtor, the meeting begins with awkwardness and difficulty, amplified by the fact that such meetings take place in the PIP's home. There is a feeling of intrusion and imposition that is difficult to assimilate, as many debtors will see family photographs (or even family members), children's toys, bills, letters, plates with uneaten food, clothes, and so on. Most debtors reported that the offices themselves were neat and tidy, but there is an ever-present awkwardness because the debtor knows that the PIP's family is just beyond the door. As already mentioned, each PIP is an independent contractor who has a licence from an accredited body which allows them to implement and manage insolvency arrangements; they do not receive payment from the government and are not employees. This means that all their income must be generated from clients (that is, debtors), which may cause us to wonder why they behave in this way. The answer lies in the inevitability and necessity of the confessional process.

Confessing

Once the practitioner and the debtor have moved beyond introductions, it is time for the debtor to tell their story. We have seen the indications of what they will say in Chapters 3 and 4, but now it is time for the debtor to put everything together into a coherent narrative. From the outset, the debtor will usually offer to present their bundle of documents, which may be in a folder or binder, and some elements may have been emailed to the PIP in advance. They are shocked when the PIP says no: "He told me to put the folder away and instead explain what happened to me, how it all happened, how I fell behind, I was taken off guard by this" (interview with Amy).

We likely think of confession as an activity with a fixed beginning and end, but it is better conceptualized as an ongoing process with three key elements: contrition, confession, and penance (Foucault 2015; Bell 2020; Karlsen and Villadsen 2020). Contrition girds all that comes after and was taken with the utmost seriousness by medieval scholars, as offering a false confession could result in excommunication or worse (Geisst 2013). A false confession goes beyond simply lying because deception has taken place in a forum where one has explicitly agreed to tell the truth. We will approach these one at a time and, in fact, have already seen evidence of contrition in action in the form of the vaguely hostile greeting. When explaining their rationale for such behaviour, PIPs tended to point out that debtors are untrustworthy subjects (Dean and Zamora 2021), and they are wary of 'time wasters':

'I'm not trying to be cruel, but there's a lot of tricky people out there.' (Interview with PIP#3)

'The dishonest ones are scared off [by the environment] then they try harder [to pay their debts] it's not free money.' (Interview with PIP#2)

By deliberately cultivating an environment which is affectively unpleasant, a debtor would only subject themself to this if they were legitimately remorseful. This is the essence of contrition – to confess and admit wrongdoing is not enough. It is not sufficient to simply reveal the truth (although this is crucial); the person must also feel that they have done something wrong (Foucault 2015). If you are not contrite, remorseful, or ashamed, then you cannot confess (Goodchild 2020; Karlsen and Villadsen 2020; Sløk 2020). In such an environment, the debtor is guilty until proven innocent and must demonstrate to the PIP that they are sincerely apologetic about what has transpired. PIPs told me that it is common for debtors to cry at an early stage in these interviews and that suspicion can even fall on people who do not:

'You get a sense of how the interviews go from an early stage. They are all very similar really. People are upset, they have a sob story, literally, they cry. I would say you should be wary if someone doesn't cry, they might be hiding something.' (Interview with PIP#2)

Someone who approaches the process as a scientific exercise where they feel they have read the criteria and sense that they qualify is to be held in suspicion. The emotional and psychological components of these interviews should not be understated; at all times, the PIP is attempting to gauge the sincerity and trustworthiness of the applicant, and any behaviour or attitude that does not match the PIP's expectations gives cause for doubt.

Confession is appealing because it is a powerful means to enable access to the truth (whatever that means in each given context). Historically, the confession (like many similar techniques) developed irregularly and has not always been applied consistently, with different denominations, churches, and religious traditions having their own forms of confession. While Foucault did not furnish us with a full history of the confession, he did offer a brief history and framework in the History of Sexuality Vol.1 (Foucault 2015, pp 58–73). Confession in a form that is recognizable to us emerged in the 13th century and was connected to the medieval legal traditions of avowal (a declaration of truth) and accusation (charging someone with wrongdoing) (Foucault 2015, p 58). As there were problems with geography and transportation, the expectation was that each Christian would travel once a year to their nearest church and make their full confession, with a focus on sins and a further focus on mortal sins such as lust or sloth.

For Foucault, the confession is a technology originally used to reveal the truth about sex and sexuality, which had gradually become labelled as taboo or shameful. This truth telling goes beneath the surface, then, and becomes more invested in thoughts rather than actions (Foucault and Rabinow 1984). While a sinful action might be problematic, it is also important to uncover the thought process that lies beneath it, and so confession is about revealing motivations, beliefs, desires, thoughts, and so on. Confession brings into the light those things which we find it most difficult to talk about:

> The confession has spread its effects far and wide. It plays a part in justice, medicine, education, family relationships, and love relations, in the most ordinary affairs of everyday life, and in the most solemn rites; one confesses one's crimes, one's sins, one's thoughts and desires, one's illnesses and troubles; one goes about telling, with the greatest precision, whatever is most difficult to tell. One confesses in public and in private, to one's parents, one's educators, one's doctor. (Foucault 2015, p 59)

To this list we can add debt. As seen in Chapter 4, there is a whole framework of governance and experts who operate in the general area of over-indebtedness, and the likelihood is that a debtor will confess to at least one of them before ever reaching the door of an insolvency practitioner. Debt evokes complex feelings of guilt and shame, and because of this affective framework, it strangles one's capacity to speak (Davies et al 2015; Montgomerie 2016).

Assuming you are contrite, you must appear in person and make your confession. It is crucial in the confessional process that an avowal of sorts be made. You appear in person to identify yourself, you cannot confess to something that someone else has done, and it cannot be done by proxy (Foucault 2015). Following this, you must give a thorough account of what has happened, which must be detailed and personal, you can only confess to actions you have personally undertaken or thoughts you have had. For these reasons, the PIP requires that the meeting take place in person; even in the digital age, they do not feel comfortable making a decision on the person's moral character on the phone or through a Zoom call.

How is success determined in this process? In typically Foucauldian fashion there are no universal truths; however, there are factors to which we can pay attention that definitively influence the process. Perhaps most importantly the debtor must emphasize their contrition by accepting responsibility for their problems (Gazso 2009; McLeod 2017). PIPs and even creditors to a certain extent expect the debtor to blame economic conditions, bad luck, misfortune, and bad actors who may have misled them. However, at some point and in some way, the debtor should admit (even implicitly) that they could have made better decisions and, even if it was not possible to avoid over-indebtedness, that something could have been done to reduce its severity. A debtor who exclusively blames others is not believed because they have not actually offered a confession and they have not admitted that they did anything wrong.

Next, as the tradition in sworn testimony goes – you must tell the truth, the whole truth, and nothing but the truth, so help you God. Nothing must be withheld or omitted. While it is expected that the truth will be bent slightly to tell a more convincing or elegant story (Montgomerie 2016; Kiviat 2019), vital details must not be left out or altered in a way that is fundamentally misleading. If a debtor does lie, it will almost certainly be detected at a later stage in the process and will forever lose the trust of their PIP and creditors, leaving them with little choice other than to declare bankruptcy. Then we must address the quantity of debt. As we may expect, creditors do not resist the write-downs of small quantities of debt as fiercely as they do larger sums (Rock 2014). This is not to say that there is a complete absence of resistance, only that smaller amounts draw less attention, though creditors are cautious not to normalize and publicize the write-downs of even small amounts of debt, as this could still be financially ruinous on a large enough scale.

Finally, the debtor must provide an indication that they made every reasonable effort to cooperate and work with their creditor to find a mutually beneficial resolution to the problems they faced. If a debtor falls behind, and instead of openly discussing the problem with their creditors immediately jumps to insolvency, this will be looked upon very poorly by the PIP. When embroiled in the purgatory of debt, few can face the prospect of admitting problems at first; this is normal and to be expected. However, after months or years have passed, if the debtor still has not tried to resolve things amicably, this will reflect badly upon them. Most PIPs working on an arrangement to restructure mortgage debt anticipate that the mortgage will already have been restructured in the Mortgage Arrears Resolution Process at least once (Free Legal Advice Centre 2015). In this way, the vigilance of the debtor in keeping written correspondence with their creditor can aid them immensely and can serve as a prop they can produce during their confession for dramatic effect.

The specific content of these confessions will therefore vary depending on the person's experience of indebtedness. These confessions have common features, and generally discuss the purgatorial elements outlined in Chapter 4, such as suffering and sacrifice:

> 'I started out by talking about my unemployment. I lost all my freelance work after the crash [the GFC] but kept making payments for years because I was so good at managing the money. But when it ran out and I still didn't have a job I ran into trouble.' (Interview with Amy)

'I was disabled in an accident, it was only after that that I was in trouble. It was really hard for me, and the mortgage insurance didn't do a whole lot in the end because I ended up with rehab therapy and these things and that cost even more money.' (Interview with Barry)

'Divorce was my reason, we had a complete breakdown. Then it got very messy, who gets what? Who gets to keep the house? And we were sniping at each other and that put huge pressure on the money situation.' (Interview with Laura)

From the outset, the debtor places emphasis on structural factors, bad luck, or some other aspect of life that was beyond their control. This forms part of what Kiviat (2019) calls moral storytelling and Montgomerie (2016) calls economic storytelling, aligning and subverting the expectations of the market (you must pay your debts) with moral considerations that depend on sympathy and deservingness. Kiviat (2019) points to employment and hiring processes whereby US employers try to deduce the moral salience and trustworthiness of a potential hire by reading their credit reports. However, the documents do not account for themselves, and employers rely on the candidate to provide a morally compelling explanation at their job interview. They may say, for example, that their bad credit score has been caused by medical debt, which gives a morally satisfying explanation and enables the employer to justify a hiring decision. Alternatively, a potential employee could destroy their chances by admitting that their bad credit is the result of entertainment and leisure purchases.

In the confessional interview, the debtor is under immense pressure to tell a morally persuasive story; in many respects, the PIP wants to be convinced by the person, but must restrain themself from saying so. The integrity of the process depends on this mixture of pressure and sincerity. The debtor will place weight on certain aspects of the story, while minimizing others. The most sympathetic and morally strong kinds of debt are caring (Montgomerie and Tepe-Belfrage 2016) and survival debts (Wilkis 2018), while leisure debts are seen as indulgent (Veblen 2005). Somewhere in the middle are debts taken on for status purposes (Bourdieu 2010; Zaloom 2021); mortgage debt in and of itself is seen positively because it represents an attempt to better oneself through upward social mobility. However, attempts to categorize a debt as a status debt may be challenged if the PIP senses inconsistencies in the debtor's story:

'I had a lady tell me she was very sorry to be so badly behind on payment and I pointed out she had taken on a lot of loans to send her child [for language lessons]. It all came out anyway that basically she did this because it was a trendy thing that her friends were doing. She tried to say she didn't want her child to be excluded but that didn't cut any ice with me, the amount of money was shocking, it was pure "keeping up with the Joneses". There was travel, camps, accommodation, loads of things beyond just paying the teachers, it was impossible to overlook.' (Interview with PIP#3)

In this case the debtor's attempt to categorize the debt as a caring debt (I wanted to support my children) was rejected, and the PIP instead recategorized this as a negative status debt. The PIP's remarks are close to Veblen's (2005) conspicuous consumption, and his overall point is that the debtor should have realized that she was already behind on payments and recognized that it was not responsible to continue to 'keep up with the Joneses' using the money of her creditors. In the end this debtor did get her mortgage restructured; however, she had to pay off the debt associated with the language lessons in full. While middle-class status debts are seen in an abstract sense as aspirational, it is also dangerous to spend too much money on conspicuous consumption. The 'good' kind of status debt brings about upward social mobility without necessarily entering into competition or conflict with others, while the 'bad' kind of status debt is excessive, luxurious, or used representationally – 'for bragging rights', as one PIP told me. A further example of this involved the purchase of houses that are too large:

'A client came in here, and he seemed to be ideal to get a restructure through an arrangement, but it turned out he had a four-bedroom house and it was just him, his wife and one child ... that is not reasonable. He bought a gigantic house way over the odds [market price] and was just refusing to move out. [He had] no chance.' (Interview with PIP#4)

The Irish policy (which is similar to that seen internationally) requires the debtor to be 'reasonably accommodated', and the implication hanging in the preceding quote is that this is not the case (Insolvency Service of Ireland 2013a). The house was too large for a small family and, as the PIP related to me later in the same discussion, this debtor did not take steps to address this issue by renting the rooms out, as this would have risked his local reputation and invited gossip about his status. The fear of social demotion is a powerful thing (Whelan 2022).

At all times, debtors distance themselves from leisure debts, primarily because it is almost impossible to produce a morally compelling confessional explanation that would portray them in a positive light. Where this is not possible, they interpolate using another moral device, such as positioning the debt in the context of mental health:

> 'I had a small loan that I used to pay for a holiday. It was a stupid decision, but in my debt crisis I was really struggling and felt that I needed a break. I briefly spoke about it and tried to move past it, but he [the PIP] wanted to get into it. I think he could see how mortified and embarrassed I was and didn't hold it too badly against me.' (Interview with Rick)

In this process the power rests with the person who listens and says little (if anything). As in the classical Foucauldian rubric, by confessing they gain knowledge about you, which gives them power over you (knowledge of shameful secrets or sins) (Foucault 1979, 1989, 1995; Foucault and Lotringer 1996). This process is held to have a cleansing power all of its own: by admitting what you have done wrong and telling the whole truth, you will be unburdened from the weight of your sins (Foucault 2015; Karlsen and Villadsen 2020). There is an undeniable metaphorical element here: sin and lies have weight, they are 'heavy', and there is a cost associated with keeping them concealed. Confession, by contrast, brings a lightness which is achieved by humbling yourself before an authority figure, placing yourself in their power, and willingly allowing them to judge you. Debtors related this cleansing and purgative experience – perhaps one they would not repeat, but which did give them a sense of relief:

> 'It was humiliating, but what a relief I had never talked about it [debt] out loud.' (Interview with Roger)

> 'I let out a breath afterwards [after the interview] it felt like I had been holding that breath in for five years. It was bad and good at the same time.' (Interview with Barry)

> 'I'd describe it like being unburdened. I wouldn't go through it again mind you, but it was like a weird abusive therapy session in some ways.' (Interview with Jane)

If your confession is believed, then you must make penance. It is not simply the case that you speak the truth and are forgiven instantaneously; rather, you must undertake some kind of action which will demonstrate that your contrition is legitimate. A penitent may be required to apologize or make restitution to a party who they have wronged in some way, or perhaps they must pray or offer money to the Church (Dante 2013; Boland and Griffin 2020; Sløk 2020). Penance almost universally requires a firm commitment not to repeat the behaviour that led to the confession being necessary in the first place. In this way, confession is a powerfully therapeutic process, involving the interrogation of the soul and the inner world of the sinner – and, indeed, we come closer to the political goals of confession (Rose 1991, 1999).

By giving the confessor a glimpse into the hidden motivations of each member of their flock, they gain insight into the moral and spiritual health of their congregation and are therefore enabled to correct wayward behaviour. In this way they can also observe trends, with certain sins or moral failings emerging in a pattern, which may influence how the priest chooses to deliver their sermons. By bringing the truth of individuals to light, they gain knowledge over the mass of people in a general sense and can direct them appropriately (Waring and Martin 2016). In its medieval history, confession has an uncomfortable relationship with torture, and while outright torture is not a part of contemporary confessional practices, it is fair to say people are not always forthcoming: 'One confesses – or is forced to confess. When it is not spontaneous or dictated by some internal imperative, the confession is wrung from a person by violence or threat; it is driven from its hiding place in the soul or extracted from the body' (Foucault 2015, p 59).

Regardless of the specifics, the most important aspect of penance is a pledge not to reoffend; although this promise is often unstated, it is implicitly clear that if you repeat the behaviour, then your sincerity will be cast into doubt. A debtor who seeks to go bankrupt every year will likely become seen as someone who is simply attempting to swindle their creditors out of their money. No matter how convincing their confession is or how much apparent contrition they have, their sincerity will be challenged because their actions are inconsistent with their words:

> 'Never again. Never again will I borrow money, it is just not worth it. Lesson learned.' (Interview with a debtor)

> 'I said that I would do anything, I would live on bread and water if that's what it took for me to show that I was sorry.' (Interview with a debtor)

> 'All I really wanted was to keep the house. I would have dressed in rags if I could keep the house.' (Interview with a debtor)

Fortunately, such dramatic displays as eating only bread and water or dressing in rags are not required; though the programme of reasonable living expenses outlined in Chapter 6 is not luxurious, it is also not quite so severe.

After all of this, we might append a fourth stage, absolution, where the person who has offered their confession and done their penance can be considered to have been absolved themselves of their wrongdoing. When done often enough and for enough people, this will gradually produce noticeable changes in beliefs and behaviour. In this respect Nikolas Rose explains how the confession was a kind of testing ground for contemporary governance:

'confessional churches' played a key role in the emergence of this notion of governable populations, developing a particular understanding of their role as one of reshaping the conduct of their subjects in the name of spiritual purity, deploying a range of measures for their spiritual disciplining, and thus uniting those in particular geographical areas in 'moral enclosures'. (Rose 1991, p 25)

By now the confession has been secularized and in such a way that it can be challenging to see its original theological roots, but the focus on uncovering the truth of what happened and going beyond actions has become a profound element of our justice system, medical system, the practice of psychiatry and counselling in general and more.

The general structure and practices of confession may give the illusion that it is an effective way to dispel guilt, but the opposite is the case. The very existence and universality of confession implies that we have something to be guilty about and therefore there is something that needs to be forgiven (Nietzsche 2014). The confession is a perpetual motion machine that generates rather than cures guilt (Lazzarato 2012, 2014; Nietzsche 2014). It imputes an ongoing dependency between guilt and forgiveness that never ends and seems to be ever-expanding. We are in a state of eternal apology for our sins, debts, guilty pleasures, and so on. This means that forgiveness is only ever temporary, and the confession implicitly assumes that we will return in the future if the lesson was not learned the first time. While we have outlined many of the important factors governing whether one succeeds or fails when applying for insolvency, there remain two elements that play a crucial role in the process.

Class and gender

Experience of the process varies immensely and I wish to focus on two specific aspects here: class and gender. Rumours of the death of social class have been greatly exaggerated, and it continues to exercise a powerful hold over us and influence virtually every part of everyday life. It is likely unsurprising to the reader that those who enjoy the most success in the process are middle-class men, especially those who were educated privately. The confession requires the debtor to advocate for themselves, and it is crucial that they are able to read how the interaction is proceeding and respond affirmatively to the body language, gestures, and dialogues of the PIP (Goffman 1951). In a traditional Bourdieusian (2010) sense, they are people with a great deal of social and cultural capital, who have suffered a temporary setback with respect to their economic capital and are seeking restitution. There is a sense that they have a great deal in common: "I had someone come in here who was a banker and he had fallen on hard times and I thought to myself – Gosh that could have been me!" (interview with PIP#2).

This sense that their life experiences are commensurate in some way is quite correct; it is because they share a similar class background that it is easier for the PIP to empathize with them (Lister 2004; Hourigan 2015; Whelan 2022). The PIP in the preceding quote was also a banker before he became a practitioner and was able to imagine himself in the debtor's position. He later helped this person to join a favourable insolvency arrangement. In principle a PIP can be anyone who completes the training necessary to acquire their insolvency licence, but in practice the embodied knowledge necessary to complete this training makes it more appealing to people who already have a background in law and finance. This gives PIPs a decidedly middle-class character, as they are drawn from professions that require postsecondary education and, as such, have certain embodied lived experiences which influence how they go about doing their jobs (Power 2009, 2010).

Much of class is about distinction and taste (Bourdieu 2010) – that is to say, when we select something that we find aesthetically pleasing (tasteful), that this is made in distinction to choices for other classes which we may see as tacky or ugly. These relations calcify and harden over time, such that certain sports or recreational activities are seen as classy because they are valued by middle-class people, while others are seen as lacking in such grace because they are valued by working-class people.

Another way to make this visible is through language, as the kind of words used to describe different groups of people is telling, especially in terms of how this circulates socially (that is, through the mass media). Language is important because while it may be an imperfect vessel of communication, it is also the boundary and limit of what can be thought. By repeatedly using certain kinds of language to describe certain kinds of people, we reify these speech acts and they come to inform the texture of our lives. This has important real-world consequences – consider the range of research on secondary deviance, for example, where a person labelled a deviant chooses to adopt the stereotyped behaviour and attitudes associated with that label, even though they did not behave this way before (Rock 2014). The tendency in the Irish and British mass media to describe working-class people as 'scumbags' or people battling drug addiction as 'junkies' should draw our attention (Power et al 2016; Devaney 2017). Definitionally, scum is a layer of frothy dirt lying on the surface of a liquid, while junk is anything old or discarded which is thought to be useless or have little value. Language matters.

It is telling then that the language of addiction figures extensively in the professional and legal discourses used by PIPs to describe debtors, but particularly working-class debtors:

> 'All sorts of people come to see me, but there are people of a certain background. They would have family on the dole [welfare], and may be on the dole themselves, they grew up poor … they had nothing.

For a person like that, you need to understand that debt is like a drug, they can see it as free money and you need to stamp that out right away.' (Interview with PIP#2)

Debtors who come from a 'certain background', as the PIP put it, are fully cognisant and aware of the perceptions that others may have of them, and they are in a permanent process of resisting these labels and stereotypes. The work of Beverly Skeggs (1997) can shed light on this through her discussion on the concept of 'disidentification', whereby working-class people do not seek affirmation or class recognition in the conventional sense, but rather disidentify with the perception that they are working class. For Skeggs, the dialogue of 'giving up' is a powerful example of this, where stereotypes abounded in her research about women who had stopped taking care of themselves and who began to go shopping in their pyjamas. Tellingly, it was working-class women themselves who (re)produced these dialogues and reified the power of class perception for everyday life. The strategy was to disidentify from negative classed perceptions rather than affirming a more positive connotation to what it means to be working class. In the same way, working-class debtors work hard to disidentify from the perception that they may be like the 'type' of person the PIP mentioned in the preceding quote:

'I had to try and say from the outset, I am not a beer drinking slob, I don't sit on my arse all day watching football.' (Interview with Simon)

'He asked me where I grew up. I had to think hard about if I wanted to lie, because I grew up in a rough area. In the end I told him, but had to say that I wasn't like other people from there, I had moved on and moved up.' (Interview with Michael)

It is important to disidentify from any association with vice and addiction, and it is taken for granted that if debtors fail to disidentify from it, then the assumption will be that they are not self-aware enough to understand the danger. Recurring themes include behavioural problems such as drug addiction, alcohol abuse, laziness, idleness, worklessness (sloth in a general sense), and excessive television watching. In the Bourdieusian sense, these assumptions are examples of class disgust in action. The assumed habits and behaviours of the working classes have always been under scrutiny and subject to pathologization. As one participant put it: "They [middle-class people] hate football and love tennis. What makes one better than the other?" Indeed, some debtors related experiences to me which are rooted in class disgust:

'I see them in [my local area], why are they always so fat? Just … I don't get it, you know? I don't get it? How can these fat fuckers be a fortune in debt and be out in their pyjamas all day? How do they live with the stress?' (Interview with Mona)

'Oh you'd see them alright, Zach. Look out the window there [participant points], you'll probably see [a working-class family] across the road, with their feral children, drinking cans then in the front garden letting the kids destroy the place.' (Interview with Sean)

This is the dominant strategy used by working-class debtors to secure help from their PIP: they disidentify from being working class and adopt the oppositional discursive framing by positioning the working class as being 'other' or different (Frank 2007; Jones 2011). They echo the class disgust of the PIP, even if it is used in reference to activities, behaviours, and attitudes that they themselves embody. If the PIP is a fan of tennis and hates football, then they will agree; if they love opera and hate television, then so does the debtor. By rejecting any identification with being working class, they hope to find common ground with the PIP and place themselves at an advantage as they plead their case. Those who fail to do so can find the experience quite jarring:

'As soon as I told him that I grew up in [a working-class estate] then his perspective on me … it flipped completely, it was like he was a completely different person.' (Interview with Simon)

'Once he knew that I was from … that I grew up in a [council] housing estate he … it felt colder in the room.' (Interview with Amy)

For women, the experience is governed by an overarching assumption that their debt crisis must be related to leisure debts and is particularly rooted in consumerism. The examples of makeup and shoes recurred so frequently that they serve more as symbolic or representational totems about gender than any actual reality. Perception is often every bit as important as reality; however, the belief that something is true can be enough to change one's attitudes and behaviours. For women, the defining experience of debt stereotyping is through leisure debt, rooted in the belief that women are not natural financiers. There is a certain amount of hypocrisy that enters these dialogues, as neoliberal systems crave strong economies driven by continuous consumption (Krueger and Perri 2006; Marron 2009), but when faced with subjects who are assumed to embody that assumption, the response is patronizing disgust. The fear of being labelled financially incompetent (what Carl Walker calls 'cognitively delinquent') informs and governs a great deal of behaviour:

'If they reject me, that wouldn't be the worst thing. The worst thing would be having to go bankrupt after that. I don't fear bankruptcy,

> I don't … I wouldn't worry about the consequences to my wallet, I already have nothing, what I fear is … I'd fear being socially bankrupted. Nobody would ever loan me a fiver ever again, I'd be a laughing stock.' (Interview with Tara)

The fear of being 'socially bankrupt' and its accompanying loss of legitimacy and credibility are understandable. The stigmatization of indebtedness and of seeking to have one's debt purged has led many people to try and endure their current circumstances rather than seeking help (Sousa 2017):

> 'If a lad [man] is going in there [to the ISI], you know he's turned out his pockets and it's all sad and bad. If a girl goes in there, well they nearly expect it – "ah you poor dear, you should've left running the money to the man of the house, it's no wonder this happened" – it's absurd what people will believe about you just because of your body, because of your genitals.' (Interview with Aileen)

> 'Men are supposed to be capable, managing the money, and I know by the way they [men] look at me they think I can't put 2 and 2 together.' (Interview with Michelle)

Research by scholars such as Zelizer (1994) runs counter to these gendered assumptions, as she charts how emerging gender roles in the 18th century steadily positioned men as breadwinners and women as household leaders. While this household role generally has a prominent focus on caregiving, childrearing, cleaning, cooking, and so on, it is also the case that women often became responsible for spending money in the household too, and so developed sophisticated budgeting techniques. Burgeoning industrialization meant that men often had to work at a distance, travelling to cities or to mining pits, where they would work for several weeks or months. After spending on their own subsistence, they would send what was left to their wives by post. In the absence of the man of the house, wives were responsible for spending and saving, a pattern that has repeated itself at times of migration, with men sending remittances to their families or relatives in their home countries. When enough money had been saved, the women would purchase travel and follow their partner to their host country. Recent data have indicated that this trend is reversing, as the number of women migrants are overtaking men for the first time (Titley 2015).

If working-class people disidentify from their social class, women seek to shift the conversation away from leisure debt and towards caring debt (Gallagher 2014), situating this as the most important element in their confessions:

'He [the PIP] pointed out I had taken some small loans, and he wanted to know what they were for. The implication hanging in the air was that I had gone on holidays … when I explained that the money was for childcare, he changed his tune.' (Interview with Jane)

'I had to borrow more to support my kids, it put me under huge pressure. The PIP seemed to understand that.' (Interview with Mona)

Women debtors strongly dislike the implication that they are 'naturally' worse at handling money and consequently spent without control on lifestyle expenses, clothing, and entertainment. However, they detected in the moment that it would be unwise to entirely reject their femininity and the network of assumptions existing around it. The explanation that they fell into over-indebtedness due to caring debt rather than leisure debt gives the PIP an explanation that they find both plausible and compelling. By adopting the role of the caring parent, they meet the PIP's expectations of gendered behaviour, which situates them as deserving of sympathy and help.

Contextually, indebtedness tends to be more common for women than men, with research identifying women's economic vulnerability to be a key issue (Goode 2012). This is compounded by several different interrelated problems, including occupational sex segregation, the wage gap (Atfield and Orton 2013), and the gendered division of labour within the family, whereby women often do invisible and unpaid domestic labour in the home (Attree 2005). Due to these disadvantages, women tend to require some level of debt in order to maintain the same lifestyle as men who are otherwise similar (Jackson 2009; Goode 2012). I characterize such debts as a mixture of caring and survival debts, which are by a significant margin the categories of debt that evince the most sympathy.

Several insolvency practitioners I have spoken to have raised the point that women must urgently begin an insolvency programme because the natural incapacity of women to manage money will only worsen over time:

'It's not nice and people don't like discussing it but more women than men come through that door and we all know why.' (Interview with PIP#2)

'If you let them [women] off, then the whole thing is going to get worse and worse, it'll get to the point where they'll have nothing, it'll all be gone on makeup.' (Interview with PIP#4)

Participants also raised the tendency for men in debt to be perceived as having made a handful of minor errors, but primarily it was bad luck that had been their undoing. Women in debt, by contrast, were seen as an inevitability and were perceived to be unable to understand financial instruments such as savings accounts or compound interest. On top of this, the women who fell into debt distress were perceived to be social and cultural failures, having let down their families and children by attempting to do something 'masculine' that they should have known they would not be able to do. These gendered assumptions were reported by female participants, but were also noted in interviews with both PIPs and male debtors:

> 'I would say women are worse at hanging onto cash, yes. They don't have the same brain for it that men do, they see … you know how it is, they'd see some shoes or something on sale and they'd go mad for it. That's not a solid foundation to build repayments on, or understanding interest, you see?' (Interview with Paul)

> 'How is a girl supposed to understand compound interest?' (Interview with Barry)

> 'It makes me embarrassed to say but I would say women are worse than men at managing money and I say that as a feminist.' (Interview with Mona)

My female participants were prepared to endure considerable hardship in order to disprove the stereotype that they had a fundamental inability to manage money. For most, this went beyond issues of food poverty, social exclusion, and mental health difficulties which are prevalent in debt (Mind 2008; Stanley et al 2016). One participant told me that in order to make ends meet on a particularly bad month, she had sold her bed frame, and was sleeping on a mattress in her bedroom, which was itself almost devoid of furniture. These measures were not seen as extreme by those undertaking them, as they were prepared to do anything in order to not be seen as fitting the presumed stereotype as someone who had spent all their money on wasteful consumer goods:

> 'I'd rather die than let them think the stereotypes were true.' (Interview with Tara)

> 'The shame of it has made me go further than I thought I could, a lot of charities, a lot of overtime … a lot of pain.' (Interview with Laura)

> 'They [men] think we spend all our money on makeup and shoes, it's such a joke, I hate it.' (Interview with Sarah)

This feminization of debt (Jackson 2009) and poverty (Ghate and Hazel 2002) has a tendency to create significant emotional and psychological strain for mothers in particular, as they struggle to create healthy lifestyles on a limited income, then struggle again via discrimination in debt relief organizations. In its original form, the ISI's policy specified that if a parent's income was below a given percentage of childcare costs, they could only avail themself of a debt write-off by giving up their job to care for their children (Minihan 2013). While it was not explicitly gender-specific, women are often the primary caregiver in the home, and the requirement to leave work to care for their children during an insolvency arrangement would therefore fall disproportionately on them (National Women's Council of Ireland 2013). This clause was quickly removed due to a negative public reaction, but other research (Gazso 2009) shows that gendered discrimination can be embedded ideologically within institutions, even if they are not articulated in policy.

Why do it this way?

Why should PIPs behave in this way? In a certain sense, we already know the answer: it is a mixture of path dependency and the cultural legacy of debt, combined with the legal framework of insolvency, and capped off by a simple lack of resources (Ramsay 2017; Spooner 2019). Insolvency policy documents suggest that the PIP ought to meet with prospective clients, read their documents, evaluate the case, and determine whether an application should proceed on this basis. In practice PIPs have told me that they are completely overwhelmed by their workload, and this model does not seem to be followed at all. In fact, most PIPs either leave the documents for the very end, possibly after the debtor has left, or in some cases do not read them at all:

> 'I don't have the time for that [to read the documents], I have many inquiries and every person is different, and Jesus they all have so many papers and bills and things. You can't sit down and read all that, it's not practical.' (Interview with PIP#1)

> 'You know, the Act [Personal Insolvency Act 2012] says that certain letters need to be sent by certain dates, even that is a struggle for me. I don't have a secretary to help me out, we are in the trenches here all the time.' (Interview with PIP#3)

> 'When the client [debtor] goes home, I will quickly skim their mortgage statements to make sure what they said matches up with the financial situation. But you just have to trust them, there are only 24 hours in a day and I don't have the time, the patience, or the inclination to read through ten bank statements forensically, and that is only the

start of it! There may be hundreds of bills on top of that, I am just one man.' (Interview with PIP#4)

The neoliberal strategy of dispersing power and getting work done through a web of agents has reached the edge of its limitations in the case of insolvency. Debtors are untrustworthy subjects; they must have done something wrong, otherwise they would not be sitting before the PIP. They must be made to confess in an environment that is vaguely (or openly) hostile, but not out of a cruel desire to maliciously torture the debtor. Instead, the PIP knows that creditors are against insolvency arrangements in almost all cases and they are in the exalted position of being able to veto arrangements:

> 'It's like this. I get a lot of people who inquire, and I need to figure out very fast if they're serious or not. You have to figure out if they can get past the creditors, and only the most severe cases do.' (Interview with PIP#2)

> 'If I allowed everyone to go forward and submit their application, get their PC [Protective Certificate], nearly all of them would fail and then they would hate my guts because that can set off a chain of events that results in them losing the house.' (Interview with PIP#4)

Many PIPs complained about such a system, feeling that they did not have the necessary knowledge or training to conduct such confession-oriented practices in a manner that was fair and consistent. They wondered why people with backgrounds in law and finance had been brought in to do this work:

> 'I have a background in finance, which is how I came to this business. But they didn't tell me that insolvency is not a finance business, it is a people business, this is not what I trained for. I was on the back foot in my first few meetings.' (Interview with PIP#2)

> 'The first time someone cried in a meeting … I was just not ready for that. I am not a therapist. I am not a counsellor. I am a finance person, what do I know about comforting people in that kind of situation? Their lives are in ruins, but am I really the one to help them?' (Interview with PIP#3)

Debtors echoed these sentiments, sensing from an early stage that the PIP was knowledgeable, but could also come across as aloof:

> 'He [the PIP] was not a people person, it felt like I was being dissected.' (Interview with Roger)

'[Concerning the PIP's emotional range] Cold, bare ... and hard. Not to be trifled with, very unfriendly but ... in a standoffish way, never aggressive.' (Interview with Sarah)

'A real "expert" [participant's emphasis], it was like talking to a calculator.' (Interview with Ciara)

This led to the expression of critique and dissatisfaction with the existing system of insolvency, and a feeling that it would be better to move towards a more expert-oriented bureaucratic system with specific rules. It should be recalled that this is the assumption that drives debtors when they begin the process – they assume that it is simply a matter of filling out forms and would be analogous to applying for welfare or doing your taxes. Comparisons were drawn with the Residential Tenancies Board (RTB), an independent agency that mediates between landlords and tenants to resolve disputes. Both parties submit documents and fill out forms which are evaluated by a panel of experts who then render a decision which can be appealed. This was perceived to be fairer than the extant system, which rewards those who can tell appropriately sad stories (that is, those who give the most morally and emotionally compelling confessions):

'On several occasions I have seen debtors get their arrangements approved at the Court Review, and in some ways I was unhappy with the way it happened. They basically told the judge a terrible sob story about how hard things had been for them and how unreasonable the creditors were and the judge approved the arrangement. Is that how we do things? If you tell the saddest story you get the most help? Other people had much worse hardship but did not get approved ... it makes me wonder.' (Interview with PIP#3)

The PIP here is highlighting the inequities which arise by facilitating a process that allows emotion, morals, and storytelling to play a role. The confession can be a useful way to reach the truth, but it is also ambiguous and can produce imbalances in the process if we are not careful. In their reading, it would be much fairer to formalize the process by convening panels and tribunals to make determinations, with the appropriate administrative support. While such reforms may seem fairer, we should be cautious in terms of trusting this assertion. The US system of debt resolution was modernized in 1978, but a prolonged lobbying campaign by creditor organizations led to a reform in 2005.

This more recent version is far more punitive and demanding on the debtor, featuring a Byzantine applications process, involving paperwork and, perhaps most bizarrely of all, significant application costs, leading to the paradox that many US debtors are too poor to go bankrupt (Debt Collective 2020). This is so intimidating that debtors are discouraged from applying without legal assistance, raising further points about how to find the money to pay legal costs. Systems are not necessarily better or fairer just because they require us to fill out forms. As Weber (Parkin 2002) warned us, rational-legal authority is only as strong as the framework of rules under which it operates: if the rules are informed by powerful cultural assumptions (as they always are with debt), then the bureaucratic system created by those rules will reflect these abstract cultural standards. The US reforms were driven by creditor lobbying and should ultimately be seen as a reflection of this campaign (Ramsay 2017).

Conclusion

The experience of going insolvent is a contested space: academics tend to focus on stigma, as well as the damage done to the debtor's health, life, and financial future, while policy makers often characterize it as transactional and open to manipulation. This chapter has given an alternative reading by examining the lived experience of insolvency and bankruptcy through the eyes of people who have really been there. What we find is not a starchy bureaucratic meeting, dependent on forms and documents, but rather a carefully negotiated series of micro-interactions between the insolvency practitioner and the debtor. From the moment they knock on the door, a careful back-and-forth game of impression management is taking place where the debtor is attempting to grasp the social roles and representations that are expected, so that these attitudes and behaviours can be adopted. Insolvency practitioners can see these representations as inauthentic or insincere, and so it is important that the debtor does not bend the truth too far and never outright lies or deceives the practitioner.

The most important part of this interaction is the confession. The PIP will not make their determination based on a close reading of the documents; they do not have the time or resources to do this. As an alternative, they ask the prospective applicant to relate an account of their debt through the lens of moral storytelling – the debtor must give a full and complete explanation of what has happened. The PIP will then judge if it would be appropriate for them to proceed to the application stage. Many find such a process cathartic; there is a feeling of lightness that comes from being unburdened. Some will never have discussed their debt openly before and consequently find it a relief to finally give voice to their inner pain.

Three elements must be satisfied for a confession to be legitimate. The first of these is contrition: you must be remorseful and ashamed of what you have done wrong or, seen the other way round, if you do not believe you have done anything wrong, then there is nothing to confess to. Second is the confession itself, where you sit (stand, kneel, and so on) before an authoritative judge and give a full account of your sins and what you have done wrong. The device of the confession has spread from its original theological context throughout our society: we confess to our therapists, our doctors, our gym trainers, and now to our debt advisors. The purpose of this process is to reveal the truth, to show not only our behaviour but also our hidden thoughts or motivations such that we can improve and be better people; it therefore serves a crucial role in the neoliberal governmentality matrix by making populations of guilty and governable subjects.

The final element is penance: even should you feel guilty and offer a sincere apology, this will lose its meaning unless you make restitution or commit to change. The debtor must convince the PIP that they now embody the norms of financial literacy, making them unlikely to fall into debt distress again. The content of this confession generally relates the purgatorial experience of debt from the previous chapter by outlining how the debtor has sacrificed and suffered to make it this far and emphasizing how badly they need help. Many factors influence success in this process, including the quantity of debt you seek to discharge, how cooperative you were with your creditors, the category of debt in question (leisure, caring, symbolic, survival), how you navigate the complexities of class and gender, and how effectively you represent yourself and your story through the confession. Most of all, you must take responsibility for what has happened and must accept that you could have done better. We must now consider the two possible outcomes of this process, success and salvation (Chapter 6) or failure and damnation (Chapter 7).

6

A Clean Slate

This chapter deals with those debtors who achieve that which is so desired by so many, and we shall see the final components of the struggle to join an insolvency programme, which will write down some of their debt and restructure the remainder to be more manageable. This is assuming they can complete their time on the programme, which generally lasts 3–5 years and requires the debtor to live according to their Reasonable Living Expenses (RLEs). These requirements match international standards, with the objective of RLEs (or their international equivalent) being to teach the debtor financial literacy and minimize the chance of financial recidivism (White 2010; Walker 2011; Ramsay 2017). In the US context, for example, all bankrupts must take a mandatory financial literacy course before their debts are written off. No exceptions are made to this rule, resulting in cruel absurdities, such as a woman being required to complete a financial literacy course when the reason for her bankruptcy was the death of her child and the hospital bills associated with their end-of-life care (Debt Collective 2020; Oliver 2021).

The term 'clean slate' has a convoluted history, originally coming to us from the Romans who had wax-covered tablets (tabula) which were cleared (rasa) by heating the wax and smoothing it (Geisst 2013). Usually in the social sciences and humanities the phrase 'clean slate' refers to the nature versus nurture debate over which whole libraries have been filled, with argument and counterargument presented over the relative merits of genetics and socialization (Graeber 2011). In the indebted context, we are of course talking about something quite different, where the clean slate represents a write-down of debt. Incidentally, debtors still think clean slate status has been achieved even if they only receive a partial write-down. The clean slate has a legendary, almost mythic reputation among the debtors who seek it out. It is described in hushed and reverent tones, and as debtors come closer to it, the use of salvific language increases. Phrases used include 'miracle', 'life changing', 'saved', 'lifeline', and so on.

Having gone through the purgatorial subjectification of debt characterized by suffering and penury (see Chapter 4) and then convincing the PIP to help them by offering a morally satisfactory confession (see Chapter 5), debtors now face the greatest challenge of all: convincing their creditors. In this chapter we will see what success looks like, but the reader should take it for granted that at various stages in this process, applicants fail, drop out, or are rejected. It would be reductive and tedious to deal with these unsuccessful cases every time they happen, especially because it can happen at any point, and we will instead encounter them again in the next chapter. This chapter opens with a few reflections on the theological components of capitalism more generally and how this applies to debt relief, before diving into the applications process more completely. We shall see up close how the debt relief process works, and what kinds of changes and transformations in subjectification are expected in order for the debtor to succeed. As we shall see, wiping the slate clean is hard work. We will begin by considering the dialogues of salvation which are embedded in capitalism and which have such a profound effect on the debt relief process.

Economic theology and capitalism

Economics has a habit of representing itself as the most scientific of the social sciences, imagining a relationship with the economy that is closer to physics than it is to sociology (Bell 2020). In doing this, it constantly strains against its theological and social nature, which are ill-concealed even by the language that economists choose to use. Capitalism does not produce the material conditions which eliminate poverty; it 'lifts' people out of poverty, opposition to economically liberal (or neoliberal) policies are framed as 'evil' rather than as economically and scientifically wrong (Bell 2020; Dempsey 2020). Economics is a profoundly salvific discipline: consider the dialogues of peace that suffuse the creation of the European Economic Community (EEC), the precursor to the European Union (EU). This is often framed as a collaborative effort to prevent another war in Europe by making the various member countries so economically dependent upon one another that war would be ruinous (Dempsey 2020; Goodchild 2020). Good economic policy would further save Europe from idleness, poverty, want, and so on, and the moral language that economics can save people winds its way through the books of more than one economist:

> Thus, when Milton Friedman insists that any motive in business other than pure profit must be rejected as a pernicious threat to 'the very foundation of free society' … he is not only indicating his faith in the efficiency of competitive markets, but also his belief that the greatest good can only be achieved through self- interest and competition. Traditional values of love or generosity are dismissed for unintended

consequences that are said to do more harm than good. (Dempsey 2020, p 23)

Bell (2020) has argued that economics has three gospels – efficiency, liberty, and distinction – and frames them using the terms of economic theology because these are powered more by faith and belief than by evidence. They are the axiomatic assumptions that are so taken for granted that to oppose them is not only unwise but also heretical. The gospel of efficiency says that anything which impedes or reduces market efficiency is inherently evil, because it makes saving them that much harder. When a market operates efficiently then people will have the tools necessary to 'lift' themselves out of poverty, or 'seek' a better life through economic migration, when the state interferes in the market, it impedes this, which is taken to be morally wrong.

The gospel of liberty highlights capitalism's long-held association with freedom, autonomy, and democracy. Indeed, as Rose (1991, 1999) points out, contemporary neoliberalism governs people *through* their freedom rather than subverting it or trying to command them. In a healthy economy, people are free to choose the products and services they most desire, according to nothing more complex than their own personal preferences. Thinly concealed within the gospel of liberty is the injunction that we are each responsible for our own salvation, and the discourse of choice and decision making return to us again. Jesus may have died for our sins, but it is up to us to accept him and do good works on Earth so that we may achieve salvation. Naturally this echoes Weber's Protestant Ethic, where the predestined elect could be identified because they were successful in business (Boland and Griffin 2021). Doing nothing is always an option, but salvation takes work – meaning that it must be a deliberate choice, and these choices are enabled by a well-ordered market.

The final gospel is that of distinction, perhaps better known to us through Veblen's conspicuous consumption (Bagwell and Bernheim 1996). Capitalism enables us to distinguish ourselves from others through our purchasing decisions, which acquire a symbolic or status-oriented character. Such efforts at distinction only ever reveal what is already present, apparent to us through the adage that 'money can't buy class', and so spending reveals both status and taste. Even Keynes thought that the rising productivity he observed in his time would lead to an explosion of resources which would become cheaper and cheaper as automation took hold (Skidelsky and Skidelsky 2012). This would enable us to work less and concentrate on leisure, which he imagined would be characterized by time spent with our families, on hobbies, interests, or producing art. Capitalism was destined to bring about heaven on earth. As we know, while productivity may have increased, we are working just as hard (if not harder) than ever before, as Keynes (and others) failed to consider the appeal of the cult of work (Boland and Griffin 2021).

There is a sense that without the meaning and structure provided by work, we would not be quite sure what to do.

Try as it might, capitalism cannot escape from the impact of culture and theology. This further extends into debt relief, which even in its terms of language tends to be represented as debt forgiveness, leaving the reader in no doubt as to who has done something wrong (Stamp 2016). Forgiveness is only necessary when wrongdoing has taken place after all. These gospels of efficiency, liberty, and distinction also matter immensely for understanding the process. Debtors are by their very nature inefficient actors who must be regulated and governed into being normative and acceptable neoliberal subjects. Their debts must be addressed in the most efficient manner possible by paying back the debt with the highest interest rate first because compounding interest becomes so burdensome over time. This governance must respect the gospel of liberty; however, they should not be confined in a debtor's prison. As Rock (2014) pointed out, this tended to create a situation where the debtor could never repay or have a chance to reform and transform themselves (Boland and Griffin 2021). Instead, a framework of governance should be created, where the debtor is gently coaxed into desiring the normative behaviours and attitudes, governing them through their liberty rather than against it (Rose 1991). Finally, in terms of distinction, the debtor must understand that while money can show status, it is not appropriate to use the money of others to achieve this (Sløk 2020). Once a debtor has assimilated all three of these gospels, they are showing the signs of change and transformation, which is taken as a very good sign indeed by their creditors (Bell 2020). However, there is much to do, and we will now see the process as it unfolds, one piece at a time.

The Protective Certificate

Once the PIP has considered the PFS (see Chapter 5) and has decided that they will support an application, the debtor must formally register their interest by applying for a Protective Certificate (PC). This is a huge step, because at this point their creditors will be notified (if they have not already been) that the debtor intends to seek insolvency. It represents a point of no return, and the debtor will be compelled one last time to ensure that they have hidden nothing and that the whole truth was revealed by the confession: "You always give people one last chance to turn back. Once the PC has been lodged, it starts a legal process, and your creditors will take an interest. I give them a last chance to tell me anything that did not already come up, just in case" (interview with PIP#4).

Drawing the eye (and likely ire) of your creditors can be frightening, and so you must be sure that you want to continue. Assuming they do, the PIP will lodge your PC application with the courts; they are generally granted quickly (no more than a month), and from the time they are granted, you have 70 days to submit your application for insolvency. If you fail to do so, another PC cannot be sought for a year, so you must have conviction that this is the moment you wish to apply. PCs have a short list of benefits that are nevertheless highly impactful. First, your assets are protected. Even if creditors are currently in the process of seizing your assets, they must immediately stop and wait for the PIP to contact them with the proposed arrangement. Second, creditors are forbidden from contacting a debtor under the protection of a PC; all contact must instead go through the relevant PIP. If you are successful and make it on to an insolvency arrangement, these benefits are extended throughout the life of the arrangement (which can last up to six years); the difference this makes for the affect of the debtor is significant:

> 'What a relief, no phone calls, no letters. I could watch the postman walk up the drive without a twist in my stomach.' (Interview with a debtor)

> 'Just when I had given up hope … I was a total nervous wreck. I had a massive clench in my jaw, I didn't realize what a toll it was taking on me. My phone, I turned it off in the end, why do they never stop calling? I still don't have the money on the 20th phone call of the day.' (Interview with a debtor)

> 'Sorting bills was a massive burden, but when I got the protection it was such a relief. The banks don't know the damage they do to people by harassing them.' (Interview with a debtor)

The affective components of debt are relaxed – for a time. The feeling of impending danger is temporarily suspended, and while the guilt and shame associated with debt remains, it is not quite as strong. The financial melancholia (Davies et al 2015) of debt is not as severe, with the feelings of anxiety, depression, insomnia, and loss of control being pushed back for a time. However, if this is to last, the debtor must work with their PIP to design a budget that will appeal to their creditors – no easy task.

Reasonable Living Expenses

For the debtor, this phase of the process happens so quickly that it can be overwhelming and disorienting. While they may have spent years in the purgatorial phase of indebtedness, they have a mere 70 days to work with their PIP to propose an arrangement that is possible for the debtor to manage, while simultaneously being appealing enough to their creditors for it to be acceptable. As part of this arrangement, the PIP must submit the debtor's proposed RLEs. Once again, the service introduces an ambiguous concept to the negotiations: what exactly does it mean to live reasonably? Surely this is different for each person based on their prevailing lifestyle and unique needs; this is what the guidelines state. They are to give the debtor a 'reasonable' lifestyle that does not result in 'deprivation or opulence', and results from consultation and debate between the interested parties. Once again, it is the responsibility of the debtor to plead their case and advocate for what they need:

> 'I argued with [the PIP] for 20 minutes over the RLEs. He was making me state my case that tampons could be counted as a reasonable living expense. I couldn't even believe my ears, who does he think he is?' (Interview with a debtor)

> 'For whatever reason he [the PIP] was fixated on certain things like alcohol and Sky Sports. Drink was already out of my price range and not a necessary purchase at any rate, but I never got to the bottom of the Sky Sports thing, apparently it happens a lot?' (Interview with a debtor)

> 'People do have to argue for what they need, and that is a challenge, but it is also necessary. It is an admission that you can't pay your debts after all, you shouldn't be living the high life in those kinds of circumstances.' (Interview with a PIP)

The classed and gendered components of the previous chapter return here during the negotiations for RLEs, with alcohol and entertainment under suspicion for working-class debtors. While women run into a brick wall of toxic masculinity, as most PIPs are men who can adopt an enormous amount of ignorance over the needs of their clients. But how large is this budget? According to the ISI's initial guidelines for RLEs, a couple with three children and a car would be permitted to have expenses of €2,250.65 per month. This would place such a family just barely above the poverty line, and even this amount is subject to 'transparency, consultation and debate' (Insolvency Service of Ireland 2016c), which the ISI insists works equally well for both participating groups, and that debtors can make their case for any expenses they deem reasonable, which will be fairly heard and judged by the ISI. Particular emphasis is given to cases of utterly essential expenses, such as costs to support a person with disabilities, and an entirely separate set of costs exist in cases where a car is required. The key term here is 'required', and it is necessary for a debtor to convince the PIP and their creditors that they need a car. Due to ill-funded public transport and poor urban design practices, it is likely that the debtor will indeed need a car if they are to continue working.

However, aside from cars and other necessary costs, RLEs are not open to as much consultation and debate on the debtors' behalf as the ISI implies. PIPs are inclined to offer low RLEs that are highly restrictive because they feel that this matches more with their perceptions of fairness, but also because creditors are more likely to accept an arrangement where a greater proportion of money is spent on repayment to them. The ISI may draw attention to the fact that there is meant to be consultation on this number, but the mere fact that they set the budget so low communicates to debtors that it would be improper to ask for more. The low baseline further reinforces that the debtor should feel guilty, and places them in the awkward and difficult position of having to ask for more of their own income.

In Chapter 5 we discussed the impacts and importance of social class for the insolvency process, comparing this RLE budget with a debtor with the treatment that wealthier debtors (an apparent contradiction in terms) received in Ireland. These debtors dealt with the National Assets Management Agency (NAMA) through a structured legal process, rather than being compelled to apply for insolvency or bankruptcy as was recommended to everyone else:

> Christine Connolly and her husband, developer Larry O'Mahony, took a case to the High Court over agreements they had reached with NAMA regarding outstanding loans. Under the agreement, Ms Connolly had been allocated €6500 per month in expenses for herself and her three children. In the High Court, Ms Connolly claimed she needed a further €3750 to cover the costs of renting a four-bedroom home in Dublin 4 (€3000–3500), school fees and extracurricular activities for her three children (€1644), monthly car expenses (€820) and golf club subscription (€165). Her action against NAMA was successful and she was awarded €9000 expenses per month. (Hourigan 2015, p 159)

The ISI, by contrast, involves delicate political work complicated by the fact that the proposed arrangement will also contain the PIP's own payment. This is perhaps the most bizarre feature of insolvency legislation in Ireland (copied from the Insolvency Service of England). As discussed in Chapter 5, PIPs are not employees; rather they are licenced, regulation, and supervised by the ISI, but they are not paid by the ISI – an income must be drawn from the arrangements they make for their clients. This is illustrated by the following simple example:

> Michael has successfully applied for a PC and is now on the road to getting on a PIA. His PIP has just drawn up his RLE's, based on

Michael's monthly income of €1,250 and monthly expenses of €2,500 (most of his expenses go on servicing his debts). The RLEs indicate that Michael will now have €900 per month to spend on himself (his reasonable living expenses) and the remaining €350 will pay the fees of his PIP and service his debts. Assuming that Michael completes his PIA, his unsecured debt will be written off, his mortgage debt will be reduced, his arrears will be eliminated and any remaining debt will be restructured to be more manageable. This assumes that he is capable of living on €900 per month.

The purgatorial logic has returned with a vengeance, as PIPs encourage debtors to submit the lowest possible RLEs that they believe can be justified. This is because they quietly suspect that creditors will veto the arrangement (see more on this in the next section), which will then result in a highly favourable court review. The secret then is to propose an arrangement so reasonable that creditors have no grounds to reject it. From the debtor's perspective, this is not a game: they may have to live on this budget for six years, and a punitive budget can impose significant restrictions on them. Yet this is their penance (Foucault 2015; Sløk 2020; Boland and Griffin 2021) – it is about proving that they are legitimately sorry for what has happened, an apology for having fallen behind. While creditors are inclined to accept explanations offered by the PIP as to why people have fallen into distress, they also require a show of faith, that the person is prepared to offer a meaningful penance. The amounts of money paid back to creditors while on insolvency arrangements tends to be so small that they are ultimately symbolic, and yet the most powerful symbolism comes in the form of the debtor offering to deprive themself of luxuries. This is how creditors know that the applicant is serious: "If they submit and want to keep their three cars, and their holiday home and have money put aside for quail and duck and all these other luxuries, you just know they're not serious" (interview with a bank manager).

Persuading your creditors to support you is intricate and can be quite demanding, especially because such contact must go through the PIP, who now mediates these relations and must achieve an outcome satisfactory to everyone.

Convincing your creditors: the veto

Credit reports have a long and storied history, and creditors have always struggled to identify which borrowers are trustworthy and to what extent. Nearly anyone can be lent a very small sum – the risk is low, but it also serves as a test of the borrowers' willingness to repay, enabling the lender to build a picture of the character of the debtor (Geisst 2013). The difficulty for creditors of course is the unpredictability and seemingly random behaviour of borrowers. A borrower with a perfect credit score can suddenly stop paying and cut off contact just after receiving their latest loan, while a borrower who has languished in delinquency for a decade can suddenly return to life, furnishing the creditor with both money and an explanation (Rock 2014). This of course is the problem with the widespread financialization of debt under neoliberalism: there are so many borrowers that lenders cannot possibly get to know them all, and so an algorithmic shortcut is the next best thing (Langley 2009).

The modern credit report was invented in the late 20th century, providing lenders for the first time with a universal database which would track all credit (and credit-relevant) transactions made by the applicant. This may cause us to wonder: what did lenders do before this? They certainly did not loan money at random or base their decisions on guesswork. Instead, each lender had their own systems and schemes for determining 'credit sanctioning' in the UK context (Rock 2014, p 26) and reporting in the US (Langley 2009, pp 110–112). Because there were no universal reporting systems in place, this meant that each lender had to collect their own data, and whole archives were filled with documents on current and potential borrowers. Consequently, each lender had their own independently derived formula for calculating what our modern gaze would call a credit score (Geisst 2013). They were fiercely protective of their data and the means used for decision making, which were so shrouded in mystery and styled as trade secrets. When a lender went out of business or was leaving a particular credit market, competition was fierce for exclusive access to their client records.

The lone exception to this pall of secrecy was for the so-called 'professional debtor' (Rock 2014, pp 26–27), where lenders would exchange courteous warnings with one another about severely untrustworthy debtors who were known to borrow money and skip town. Such debtors steadily developed knowledge of what was desirable to lenders, acquired through trial and error, and simply repeated back the discourses that they knew to be privileged. They would frequently masquerade as a 'stable man' (see Chapter 2) by forging mortgage papers, payslips, and marriage licences such that they could appear to be the ideal borrower (Geisst 2013). Creditors continue to live in extreme fear of this kind of debtor, who looms large in their imaginations and who will spare no effort to catch and punish them.

While lenders depended heavily on data that would be recognizable to us, such as history of repayments, frequency of loan requests, and types of debt requested, they inevitably concluded that the picture this painted was incomplete. It was necessary to get a more subjective and interpersonal sense of the applicant by inviting them to a meeting, and it was almost always this meeting that was the determining factor in the lending decision. Lenders also used more informal means, tapping into their local knowledge, paying detectives or simply inquiring in the local area to access gossip or word of mouth about how trustworthy the borrower seemed to the locals. Newcomers or other unknown quantities were undesirable because they could just as easily skip town after acquiring the money.

Why do I mention this? Because these techniques are still in use. Creditors use credit reporting and credit scoring to make decisions sporadically, because they are quite aware that this single number is frustratingly vague. Indeed, we can say that creditors do not know their clients very well in this contemporary era, a fact of which they are always cognisant. To account for this, they have created a schema for reading into the actions and behaviour of debtors, going through a continuous process of reclassifying the debtor until a final decision is made to seek legal recourse (Kiviat 2019). In this respect, merely seeking to go insolvent is likely to provoke a negative reaction, but this can be ameliorated by a long history of proven repayment and moral decency. In contemporary insolvency policy, there is a perceived need to balance the needs of creditors and debtors, who have come to be at odds with one another in the market, mediated by an expert whose independence is absolutely essential.

This is why the events covered in Chapter 5 are so important: the debtor must win over the PIP if they are to have any hope of success. While PIPs (and other agents working in the finance and credit market) believe that it is difficult to bring creditors on board with restructuring arrangements, it is also the case that the PIP's opinion can sway the process significantly. I have previously outlined the importance of social class in this process, a tendency that is repeated here, as the representatives sent by the creditor (usually bank managers and loan officers familiar with the case) will share class similarities with the PIP. This enables the creditor to trust the debtor through the proxy of the PIP, who will do the hard work of translating the decontextualized credit report information into a story that the creditor can understand and appreciate:

> 'It is so hard to get people to talk to us, but the PIPs I have found them to be very professional. They will tell you very nicely that such and such a person has fallen behind because of some temporary crisis, bereavement or injury, or unemployment, these happen often enough. But also they will tell us when the person may not make a full recovery, and that is only fair for us to know information like that.' (Interview with a bank manager)

> 'You never know what people are going through, and it is usually only when we meet the PIP that we actually find out why the hell this borrower missed 20 payments and then made 10 and then missed 20 more. I've always been baffled because there is nearly always a rational

explanation for that, we just don't know what it is until the PIP tells us.' (Interview with a bank manager)

Remarkably, those PIPs who see their role as being more 'activist' in nature, with a duty to help the debtor regardless of the damage it does to the creditor, can counterproductively destroy any chance of success:

'Most PIPs are fine, they have a mature and considered view of what has to happen, but others are just cheerleaders for the debtors. At the end of the day, we are the people being put out of pocket, we have to protect our investment and it does no harm to recognize that.' (Interview with a bank manager).

'Some PIPs when we see the emails, or letters, or get the phone calls, you just groan because you know they are going to lay it on thick. They see it as though we are just brutalizing people, and they do not represent our interests at all – which by the way the legislation says they should.' (Interview with a bank loan officer)

Creditors I spoke to told me that such PIPs become labelled as problematic, and there are a handful who are well known to every creditor, with their reputation circulating through professional networks or by word of mouth. While a PIP who champions the cause of debtors may be seen as desirable to the debtor, it can obstruct and impede their chances of succeeding. In any event, at this point the creditors must consider the proposed arrangement and perform a calculation that is both financial and moral. The legislation gives them the power to review each arrangement and decide if they wish to accept it or decline, and with the debtor still under the protection of the PC, all contact must go through the PIP. This means that they are operating based on inferences of the debtor's past behaviour:

'Look, it is actually simple when you come down to it. If someone wants to do this [go insolvent] we will look at how well they worked with us in the past. If they ignored all our letters and phone calls and just went straight to the insolvency service then obviously we will be against that – it is very unprofessional behaviour and does not reflect well on them at all.' (Interview with a bank manager)

Most creditors I spoke to told me that cooperativeness is the most important trait they look at. The legislative definition of insolvency is so elastic that almost anyone can frame their financial situation such that they are 'unable' to pay their debts (for example, by quitting their job), but to convince their creditors, it is necessary to show that they have approached the process in good faith. Creditors will consider a great deal of information here: while the debtor is mostly concerned with their own personal affairs, the creditor must take a broader view. They will consider the prevailing conditions in the economy, the overall performance of their business, the number of outstanding delinquent debtors and debtors who have already been granted insolvency arrangements, and so on. In its first incarnation, the ISI required 65 per cent of creditors to agree to an insolvency arrangement, otherwise it was rejected by default. This led to so many rejections that the service was essentially totemic or symbolic rather than practically useful, and this was reformed to require only 50 per cent of one's creditors to agree (Insolvency Service of Ireland 2016a, 2016b, 2016c).

Those people who are rejected have one final opportunity – the court review, which was introduced simultaneously with the veto change. If the debtor and their PIP feel that the proposed arrangement was reasonable, within 14 days of the rejection having taken place they can submit to have the arrangement reviewed by the courts. If the judge agrees that the arrangement was reasonable, they can compel the creditor to accept its terms. This has introduced an interesting element to the negotiations, because there is a significant loss of face and reputation associated with having arrangements imposed by the courts. It gives the impression that the creditor is unreasonable and combative, refusing to cooperate with even the most penitent of debtors. Creditors must therefore attempt to thread this needle. They still do not wish to normalize debt relief, but adopting a hostile attitude to all applicants creates bad will and may turn the public against them:

> 'It is frustrating because the public is always on the side of the debtor, no matter what they do. And repossession is an absolute nightmare, you have to avoid it because the press around it is so negative.' (Interview with a loan officer)

> 'The [Irish] banks were bailed out [after the GFC], and everyone now fancies that they are a banking and a finance expert. We are under pressure from the government to keep a good image for the public, so you can't just drop the hammer on these debtors. Softly, softly, that is the strategy.' (Interview with a bank manager)

Creditors generally prefer that the number of insolvency applicants remains low and that while they lose money on each arrangement, the overall account will remain profitable because the debtor will continue to pay even while on an arrangement. As we have already seen in Chapter 2, the greatest loss is not any write-down on the principal, but rather the interest. By adopting a longer-term view, it is still possible for them to recoup their losses.

International comparisons

While outright refusal or vetoing obviously results in failure, I will briefly mention a more covert form of disappointment for the debtor: being set up to fail. In the US system, Chapter 13 bankruptcy is equivalent to the international standard of an insolvency arrangement: the debtor (guided by a lawyer rather than a PIP) proposes a repayment plan, their creditors meet and discuss if the restructured repayment plan is appropriate, and if they agree, the debtor is placed on the agreed plan for between three and five years. However, in the US system, such plans are extraordinarily punitive and there is an emerging tendency whereby creditors allow the restructure to take place precisely because they expect the debtor to fail. In this system, missing even a single payment can result in ejection from the restructured plan. This means that the creditor is within their rights to reinitiate the old (unsustainable) repayment scheme once this happens and can simultaneously claim that they tried to work with the debtor (Debt Collective 2020). Another strategy is to use the insolvency system's 'good faith' requirement to force the debtor to submit a huge number of documents (Ramsay 2017). If a single error or inconsistency is discovered, the creditor can claim that the applicant has not acted in good faith and can apply to have them removed from their programme (Spooner 2019). Creditors also push for longer arrangements, which now trend closer to five years than to three, because the longer the insolvency arrangement, the more likely the debtor is to fail (Spooner 2019).

Offering insolvency in this way is a breach of the good faith that permeates the rest of the process and destroys the confidence of the debtor in their creditors. Just as creditors are reluctant to offer forbearance because it creates a precedent where not paying your debts is acceptable, they would be well advised not to approach the process cynically for the same reasons. Agreeing to an insolvency arrangement which has been engineered to fail likewise creates a dangerous precedent; the feelings of hatred and betrayal these practices provoke have no doubt contributed to the rising anti-debt social movements in the US (Debt Collective 2020). Creditors would be advised to avoid solutions that produce temporary short-term gains in exchange for long-term resistance. While early reports indicate that the Irish system is less punitive than its IVA or Chapter 13 equivalents, comparatively few debtors have engaged with it. This, along with the newness of the Irish system, means that we do not yet have a clear picture of success, because we do not yet have an idea of how many people finish an insolvency arrangement. However, we can say that those who do finish an arrangement reap considerable benefits, as will be discussed in the next section.

Tabula rasa

With the significant caveats of the previous section firmly in mind, both the internal reports of insolvency agencies and independently conducted research show that completing an insolvency programme works wonders (White 2010; Walker 2011; Graeber 2011; Geisst 2013; Heuer 2014; Insolvency Service of Ireland 2014a, 2014b; Stamp 2016; Debt Collective 2020; Karlsen and Villadsen 2020; Schwartz 2022). It positively impacts on mental health, keeps debtors in their homes, frees up disposable income which can then be spent in the economy, and offers the more intangible benefits of relief to the debtor. Few people ever make it this far, though the statistics collated by the relevant agencies tend to be opaque, making it difficult to give exact numbers. In the ISI, out of a grand total of 16,106 applications, 13,153 PCs have been granted, and 9,811 arrangements have been approved, the vast majority of which (6,582) are PIAs (which restructure mortgage debt). In terms of raw numbers, this would give us around a 60 per cent success rate if we consider the number of applications that make it to approval stage, which improves to an approximately 74 per cent success rate if we consider it from the standpoint of how many debtors with PCs are approved for an arrangement.

However, there is a considerable amount of uncollected data which obscures the utility of these statistics. When the ISI considers an application to have been made seems deeply arbitrary, as this depends on records given to them by PIPs, who are inconsistent in terms of what counts as an application. As a younger organization (open since 2013), the ISI is still going through a process of determining where to draw the bureaucratic lines. Its most recent statistics and application guides indicate that if a debtor completes a PFS, then that is considered to be synonymous with an application. Yet many PFSs are completed but not lodged or recorded, as the PIP recommends against an application at this time, usually because they believe creditors will not support someone in the debtor's current position. PIPs told me that there are many cases like this, and they usually do not bother to report them to the ISI. PIPs generally consider an application to have taken place if the debtor applies for a PC, as this represents a point of no return where they must take a risk and expose themselves to the creditor's attentions.

Regardless of how things appear in the statistics, it is clear that insolvency arrangements are generally positive for the debtor, and the subjective experience of being on them is always contrasted with the purgatory the debtor had to go through to get this far. Justification is the theological concept that describes how we move from a state of sin (unrighteousness) to salvation (righteousness) (Bell 2020). There are two traditional views in the Western canon: first, that justification is given by the grace of God – that is, that it does not need to be earned and that God has His own divine plan for choosing the elect. Justification can be lost through loss of faith; this is the view of Protestantism. The alternative is that justification must be earned through good works done on Earth; faith is shown through action, through which God justifies sinners. Faith remains essential, but without works or other supporting evidence, there is no way for God to justify your sin; this is the view of Catholicism. As we have seen, the salvation of insolvency must be earned, especially through suffering, trials, and tests. As reported by Davies et al (2015, p 42), a life without debt is often framed using the discursive framing of 'freedom', which is an alternative to the shackles and loss of control created by indebtedness:

> 'Some things are meant to happen, I look back at how hard things were a year ago and look now – everything is getting better.' (Interview with a debtor)

> 'I felt like I was in hell, like I had no way out. But that all happens for a reason doesn't it?' (Interview with a debtor)

> 'There was a light at the end of the tunnel, only I couldn't see it at first. It took time, and wow that time was hard but it was worth it in the end.' (Interview with a debtor)

The philosopher Slavoj Žižek (2015) points out that Western society has a similar tendency to describe love in these terms, where an event retroactively creates its own cause – for example, in films, when one person 'accidentally' spills coffee on another, which leads to an apologetic icebreaker and a conversation which turns out to be the prelude to love. Žižek points out that these accidental events are reformulated afterwards and imbued with great meaning, and eventually are even characterized as destined or fated. I met the love of my life by accidentally spilling coffee on them, which gave us a reason to talk – therefore, it was meant to happen. The suffering that the debtor went through is reformulated in these very terms after they have successfully joined an insolvency arrangement and their lives have regained a sense of stability and normalcy. They are able to look back on their suffering, selling their treasured belongings, crying as they held their bills, arguing with their loved ones over money, and see these events in a new light. They were the necessary suffering, the catalyst which had to happen to produce change:

> 'I am on track to get the clean slate, I haven't had a creditors letter in a couple of years now. You don't even realize the tension you are carrying over these things. I feel a lot better.' (Interview with a debtor)

'A second chance, I am a believer in second chances, especially now that it has happened for me. Everyone has their own struggle and crisis.' (Interview with a debtor)

'Time, I got my time back, that is the biggest change. I don't feel guilty watching TV anymore, it is finally possible to relax again.' (Interview with a debtor)

In their research on unemployment, Boland and Griffin (2021) have pointed out that unemployed people report an incapacity to enjoy the free time that is created by unemployment. Ultimately, this is because work is so aggressively normalized that its absence creates a sense of guilt that is only amplified by attempted enjoyment. Free time is a reward one gives oneself after a hard day's work; without the work, free time merely becomes time, stretching on into meaningless infinity with no graft to give it structure. In the same way, a debtor is only able to enjoy the peace and serenity of insolvency because it can be contrasted with the pain that came before. Free time must be earned. Purgatory gives salvation its meaning.

Managing salvation

As discussed previously, the arrangements we are speaking about can last up to six years (with the possibility of a 12-month extension); as they are only granted to people who are unlikely to become solvent within the next five years, creditors generally push for longer programmes. Regardless of the length, arrangements are reviewed once a year by the PIP where the same injunctions to tell the truth are repeated. As was explored in Chapter 5, PIPs do not truly have the time or resources to fully review each arrangement as they ought to. They depend on the assumed integrity of the debtor, which is proven through the confessional process, to simply tell them if there has been any change in circumstances or inform them of any relevant information: "After a certain point you have too much to do, and you have to trust people to let you know if anything is amiss" (interview with a PIP).

While subject to an insolvency arrangement, each debtor is supposed to use only a single bank account, from which they pay their bills, their creditors, and their PIP. The PIP is responsible for checking in on this account regularly to ensure that they have been spending their money responsibly. However, as we have already pointed out, the resources of the PIPs are limited and in practice they can only check in on a small fraction of their clients at any given time:

'I don't have the time or energy really to check in on people, so I just check a few every month and if the current expenses are similar to the past expenses then I close that off and don't bother checking again for a while. People are inclined to behave because if they get kicked off their programme they will lose their house.' (Interview with a PIP)

From the perspective of debtors, this lends the arrangements a panoptic gaze, where the awareness of outside actors must be assumed because the cost of getting caught is so high. The PIP will have warned them when the arrangement was first approved that they must behave in good faith, that they must follow their RLEs and that they must inform the PIP if there is any change in their circumstances. The debtor does not know when or even if the PIP checks in on their account:

> 'It is strange because you always know that your bank could check in on your account whenever they like … but there is something more personal about this. The money is mine, really, and I could spend it any way I want, but I have always just assumed they're keeping an eye on me and behaved accordingly.' (Interview with a debtor)

The lesson is clear: the debtor may have been 'saved', but salvation is conditional on continuing good behaviour. The debtors I have spoken to who have managed to get on these arrangements are dedicated and disciplined; they do not wish to do anything that would jeopardize their insolvency. The annual reviews are similarly informal in character – the PIP and debtor do not become friends exactly, but they have an established ongoing relationship and have gotten to know one another:

> 'You get to know these people, and I'm not friends with them, we're not going to a BBQ together but we are in this together. By the time you get to doing the reviews you are only doing it because the legislation says so, and because the creditors want to be sure that their circumstances haven't changed, but there are no more interrogations.' (Interview with a PIP)

The review then is a ritual to satisfy creditors that the debtor has not come into additional money and that their circumstances have not changed in a general sense. Both debtors and PIPs told me that such 'reviews' last no more than 30 minutes (most are closer to 15), most of which is filled with personal chatter, gossip, and life updates. The PIP generally reminds the debtor of their obligation to follow their RLE budget, asks if this budget needs to be updated, and if their circumstances have changed in any way. Almost always the answer to these questions is no, though occasionally minor adjustments are made. In the current context of rising energy prices and the increasing cost of living in general, it is likely that existing insolvency arrangements will need to be revised and that this should be to give the debtor more money. RLEs have always been limited and it is important that the debtor has sufficient resources to survive.

Discourses of recovery and addiction featured heavily in these discussions, and one PIP even showed me a chart with various levels of gradation, indicating how well their client was doing in the process. At the bottom level, the client is represented as an addict who gives in easily to their baser urges, but by the legal enforcement of a strict budget, the client is brought into line with 'normal' expectations and behaviour (normalization). Punishments are used in the case of disobedience, but the PIP was quick to state that these start out small and are proportionate to the level of the infraction.

Relatively minor offences, such as going overbudget by €50 on a particular month or spending an excessive amount of money on luxuries instead of necessities, would require the client to come to the PIP's office for a meeting where they would be gently but firmly told to return to the path of recovery. Larger infractions would reduce the debtor's RLE budget or involve the debtor being sent to a financial management class (which they would have to pay for themselves). In line with neoliberal market logic, a client is 'free' to refuse these terms and conditions, so long as they accept that they will be ejected from their debt programme early, subjected to the fees that this entails, and lose the legal protection they had gained from their creditors, making it not much of an option at all. As the client learns to adhere to these orthodox neoliberal norms around finance and asceticism, the PIP ascends them along the gradated scale, until they internalize the behaviour such that it becomes natural and reflexive – in other words, once their conduct has been conducted in a new way (Dean and Zamora 2021). This is the end goal of the confessional interview:

> 'Once they go along far enough [through the process] they see things differently. They [debtors] begin to understand why their negative behaviour had to be stopped. It's tough love.' (Interview with PIP)

> 'People are bad judges of how impactful ... of how serious the consequences of their own actions are, you know what I mean? You can try talking to them but that almost never works ... They all thank you in the end.' (Interview with PIP#2)

Presuming that debtors can get to the end of their arrangement, they should have been 'restored' to solvency and are once again capable of managing their own financial affairs. While the ISI is perceived to be paternalistic and intrusive, it is also seen as a good organization that helps the debtor to preserve their integrity and save face, even with disaster looming. The tangible benefits are relatively straightforward: the creditor must abide by the arrangement, which typically involves the write-down of all unsecured debt and the agreed amount of mortgage debt (the Irish average is 21 per cent). These are significant benefits; however, the sense of stability, normalcy, and peace of mind that is enjoyed by the debtor should not be underestimated and may be the most significant benefit of all.

Conclusion

With a number of important caveats, this chapter outlines what success looks like. The prospect of a second chance is enough to motivate debtors even if the terms of the arrangement are punitive and disciplinary. I have explored this as a form of justification (moving from a state of sin to righteousness) through penance. The debtor must continue to persuade all parties involved that they are serious about changing their lifestyle and habits to align more closely with the norms of neoliberalism. When they offered their confession in Chapter 5, this gives the PIP the information they require to make a compelling case to their creditors as to why they should accept the arrangement. The debtor is not only sorry; they are already used to living on a limited income and are willing to continue in this position for several more years. The suffering that has already taken place is in the past; creditors need displays of faith that apply in the present and future.

The debtor must take this display of faith seriously because creditors are in the exalted position of being able to 'veto' proposed arrangements. Perceptions vary, with debtors having an agentic, behavioural, or biographical view of what is expected, while creditors have a more structural and distant perspective. This means that while a debtor only considers their own being, status, and progress, creditors must take a broader view that considers the number of their clients who have been restructured, the prevailing conditions in the economy, and the profitability of their business. However, it would be a mistake to assume they do not think about the personal aspect at all, and they are endlessly trying to decode what the debtor's behaviour means – an immense challenge given their limited relationship with their clients. Having the support of your PIP is crucial for success, because they are a trustworthy independent professional who can translate your behaviour into terms the creditor can understand, using the appropriate financial jargon.

Those who make it on to arrangements must abide by their RLEs, which are reviewed each year. This review has a panoptic role, as there are few PIPs, and many clients, foreclosing the possibility of precisely tracking the spending habits of every client. Instead, they make the debtor aware that there will be serious consequences if they breach their RLEs. This takes advantage of the debtor's ignorance, as they are not fully aware what kind of efforts the PIPs make to observe them – essentially meaning that they internalize the gaze of the PIPs. The PIP has the theoretical capacity to observe every client account and to investigate abnormalities or unusual activity, but only the resources to check very few at a time.

For some people, we have come to the penultimate part of the process: they have been saved, and even though there are serious consequences for their future ability to borrow money and a poor standard of living relative to their incomes, they are both happy and grateful. The process is held to have a special salvific power, with many who go through it describing it as miraculous or wondrous. However, rejection is far more common, and now we must turn our attention to those people who were (for one reason or another) unable to declare themselves insolvent. The prevailing legislation states that in order to declare bankruptcy, you must first at least attempt to utilize an insolvency arrangement to resolve the problem. The majority of the people we will discuss have tried and failed, and now the prospect of bankruptcy hangs over them like a proverbial Sword of Damocles. They are unable to wipe the slate clean, but are unwilling to go bankrupt. At the very least, they are stuck in limbo – but for many, it feels more like hell.

7

Coping and Surviving

Those who have been rejected for an insolvency arrangement (or otherwise left, dropped out, or stopped their application) now have very limited options. Occasionally a person in this situation will drop out because they have returned to solvency, and their purgatorial experience of indebtedness becomes a bad memory that is eagerly forgotten. Unfortunately, recovery is rare, and we must now contend with the fates of those who are left behind. When faced with a hopeless situation, we are likely to ask why the debtor should not simply give up and 'hand back the keys', as the adage goes. Policy makers, scholars, and professionals alike continue to be astounded by the willingness of debtors to take a punishment that will have no end, when letting go should seem to be the only rational course of action (Babb 2005; White 2010; Atfield and Orton 2013; Lazzarato 2014).

In this chapter, I offer my own explanation – that the ongoing resilience of debtors is animated by cruel optimism – which occurs when what we desire is ultimately an obstacle to our flourishing (Berlant 2006, 2011). In Chapter 3 we encountered the good life, a fantasy that outlines how we can live well, and which goes beyond mere financial success and into milestones and achievements that should bring fulfilment and happiness (Forkert 2016; Bramall et al 2016a). In service of the fantasy of homeownership, debtors acquired mortgages, hoping for a place to raise their children and eventually retire before passing on an emotionally laden asset to those children (Keohane and Kuhling 2014; Szakolczai 2014). As the fantasy comes under increasing threat from mounting debts which seem to have no solution, more extreme behaviours become justifiable. Prized possessions are sold, houses are stripped bare, second jobs are sought out, and the use of charitable services becomes more common as the debtor is unable or unwilling to see the cost of holding on to their fantasy of the good life.

Concurrently, debtors begin a process of scapegoating, rejecting insolvency as illegitimate and casting blame on the political system and their creditors; however, perhaps most remarkably, the greatest hatred is reserved for other debtors. The popular neoliberal discourses of financial literacy and strategic default are adopted enthusiastically as the belief that only the most cunning and sly of debtors can use insolvency to their advantage takes hold. This is a Girardian mimetic rivalry (Girard 1965, 1987, 1989, 2013; Adams 2000), animated by competitiveness that becomes more hostile as it becomes more intense – that is, they feel that others are living the dream of the good life that should rightfully be theirs. This hostility is destabilizing and threatens to boil over into social conflict, and so the pressure is released by a sacrifice. These are stories about especially unworthy debtors who match all the expected stereotypes (lazy, ignorant, sly, irresponsible with money) who are justifiably punished through repossession. While repossession is a terrifying prospect, there is a feeling that justice has prevailed and order has been restored when such a punishment is levelled at someone who deserves it.

Facing rejection

Many of the people I have spoken to have found themselves in the difficult situation of being over-indebted, but unable to go insolvent; they must now find a way to cope with the prevailing situation, possibly indefinitely. Further, they construct new narratives and reasons as to why they are not returning to the ISI after their initial efforts failed (for whatever reason). Common themes include the applications process was so difficult they would rather remain in debt over trying again, the ISI is an organization that only helps the dishonest, and debtors are capable of coping on their own:

> 'I dread it [the ISI] much more than being in debt. I'd rather plug along how I am now than try to bow and scrape for a few quid.' (Interview with Rachel)

> 'Nobody goes back [to the ISI] ... they make you feel bad for needing help.' (Interview with Mona)

> 'It would have to be completely rechanged for me to try again, I couldn't put myself through that a second time.' (Interview with Barry)

There are many factors to consider when we examine why these debtors made the decision not to return to the ISI unless, as in the latter of the preceding quotes, it had been completely reformed. Many are married (or in long-term relationships) where the burden of paying the debt is shared, the feelings of guilt are therefore amplified as the failure becomes refracted through the gaze of others (Foucault 1995). This is further complicated by one or more children, with the attending feeling that it is essential to provide them with a stable home environment. There is more at stake for the debtor than their own bankruptcy:

'I couldn't look into the eyes of [my child] and tell [them] "we have to move, too bad about your friends but I'm sure you'll make new ones" I had to find a way to deal with this [debt distress].' (Interview with Jane)

'[My wife] is counting on me to find a way out of this mess and I owe it to her and [my children] to find a way.' (Interview with Simon)

However, with such large quantities of debt (those with mortgages each owe at least €150,000) and falling further behind on repayments over time, it became necessary for my participants to formulate new discourses for why they would not reconsider debt relief. As all of these nonapplicants had attempted to utilize the service shortly after it had been opened, and the service has been reformed several times since its inception, there was a need for them to justify why they remained distant from the ISI. These justifications did not follow a strict step-by-step process, but there are some general themes, which begin with the difficulty of the first application:

'While I don't bear [the PIP] any ill will as [they're] just doing the job, I have this feeling of fear when I think of doing it all again. For a start [my bank] really backed off [stopped contacting me] when I backed out of the application.' (Interview with Rachel)

'I heard it [the ISI] had been shaken up [reformed] a few times, but I've never seen anything that would give me the confidence that the first stages would be any easier to get through.' (Interview with Michael)

In remembering the experience they used terms such as 'hard', 'unpleasant', 'long', 'interminable', and 'pointless'. The difficulty of the first application becomes a key reason for the continued avoidance of the service in the future, not only because it was 'hard' but also because the difficulty was for nothing. The net result was that the participant ended up in the same place. In addition, there is a level of critique which evolves out of the reasons why the first application failed:

Paul:	If you really think about it, the service isn't for the likes of me, it's for quitters.
Interviewer:	How do you mean, with [regard to] quitters?
Paul:	People who aren't serious about paying their debts. If you're serious you won't get in the front door.

'This country is crawling with parasites and lazy ingrates who wouldn't work a day in their lives, that's the sort of person who goes down there [to the ISI].' (Interview with Max)

There is a sense here that the service is inherently unfair because it discriminates in favour of those who are not genuinely trying to pay their debts back. References to welfare fraud and 'nixers' (undeclared work for which no tax is paid) were also common in these discussions. There is an assumption in these discourses that the ISI is an organization that has been designed to help certain people and not others. This reflects a tendency for debtors to scapegoat the hypothetical 'other' debtor as the source of their problems. This 'other' debtor does not try to honestly pay their debts back and seeks to have their debt written down anyway. The ISI had to be made difficult to access in order to exclude this person:

> 'That's why it's hard for me, the honest man. Every fella from everywhere would abuse it if it was easy to get.' (Interview with Rachel)

> 'I wish it was more open [accessible], but it can't be. It would be used by all sorts if it was.' (Interview with Barry)

Perhaps without realizing it, they are closer to the truth than they think. The means that testing, the confessional interview, and forced confrontation with one's creditors are not exclusively to make the debtor feel uncomfortable – they are attempts to surface and unearth the truth (Foucault 1997). Despite the catharsis of revealing their vulnerability to the PIP, most of my participants were already abandoning the ISI and were constructing new discourses about how they always knew that the service would be unusable:

> 'It was never gonna work out, you know? Like it couldn't, I'd never catch a break, God really wants me to earn this house. The government would never let someone who actually gets up in the morning have something, gotta give it all to those wasters.' (Interview with Aileen)

This strategy of scapegoating was very common. Despite the mistreatment they received from the PIP, many of my participants did not have any lasting enmity towards them. Instead, they earnestly believed and argued that other debtors were at fault and strongly condemned what they saw as 'immoral' behaviour of others, and so the logic of the confession is socialized and externalized. To this end, many debtors shared anecdotes with me about individuals from their local areas who they believed were in debt and were not taking their obligation to repay their debts seriously:

> 'It's one of those weird things because I walk by that row of houses every day, there was one car outside the house, it was one of those people carrier things. It had an oil leak, I mean the guy must have been putting in €20 of oil into it every week, because there was literally a

stream of oil coming out onto the road. Then one day I noticed the oil was gone and then I noticed there was a new car there, and that there was a skip outside. The house was being done [refurbished or renovated], and then there was another skip outside. They've decided to do something else, there's sheds being built and stuff. You went from: not being able to afford to fix your leak … your oil leak in your car, to multiple home renovations in the space of … and there's only one of ye working.' (Interview with Max)

For my participants, the reason behind the indebtedness of the other was fundamentally a desire to impress those around them, rooted in pride and a fear of being perceived as 'poor' or 'working class', with many comments expressing class disgust. However, this was not the case for the speaker. Everyone who related anecdotes like the preceding one immediately followed it up with a statement that they themselves are not like this – that they do not borrow to impress other people (status debts) or to drive a car with a registration plate bearing the current year (leisure debts). Instead, they borrow for the necessities of life (survival debts), they went into debt in order to secure a family home, or they carefully examined many different used cars in order to make a responsible purchase.

Despite their vigilance and care, they are still in debt distress. However, the core of the problem is sociologically rooted in the 'other' debtor, who is scapegoated as the architect of all the problems of this individual. This echoes the psychological concept of displacement, whereby internal fears and problems are transferred onto an external source and can often become pathological (*Oxford Dictionary of Psychology* 1995, p 217). Any errors made by the participant are excused as mistakes that any person in their situation would likely have made, and they are deeply embarrassed and apologetic for those errors. However, other debtors are suspect, being likely to spend their money on luxury expenses or waste it (for example, by gambling):

'It was just a mistake and if… if you'd been in my shoes you would have done the same thing, it's all the best with hindsight you know yourself.'

[Approximately 10 minutes later in the same interview]

'She [the participant's neighbour who is also in debt] should have known better! It's one thing to take out a small bit of debt but she should have realized the property market was heating up, and I'll tell you another thing I'd bet you she has some kind of problem, there's an addiction to something there I don't like the glassy look in her eyes now these days, and now that's … that's why I can't get a debt relief thing. People like her stopped it for all of us, because they were irresponsible.' (Interview with Laura)

Stories in newspapers occasionally appear with headlines indicating that a particular debtor has not paid their mortgage in a very long time or that most debtors were not responsible people and are likely to strategically default (Gleeson 2017; Managh 2018). These stories were seized upon by my participants as proof that there are debtors in Irish society who are maliciously not paying their debts and who seek strategic default (defaulting on their mortgage despite being able to pay) (Mortgage Brokers 2013). This 'other' casts a poor light on debtors in general and is the true reason for the interrogative nature of the meeting with the PIP. The PIP is not a 'bad' person; they are simply doing their jobs and trying to distinguish those who are really attempting to repay their debts from those who are not – in the same manner that the confessional priest was not a 'bad' person; he was simply trying to get to the root of your problems so that you could be forgiven (Foucault 2015).

By the time I met my participants several years after their PIP meeting, a reconstruction of the ISI has taken place in their minds. For most, there was a small sliver of hope that they were holding on to up until they had their confessional interview with the PIP. While many initially resented the PIP, in time they came to respect that they were doing a difficult job and probably did not enjoy asking difficult questions. However, the ISI is now altered from a potential aid to a misleading farce; the service is reconstructed as a salve for the dishonest.

My participants told me that those who are truly serious about paying their debts do not need a government service to help them; they deal with the problem on their own, using their own abilities, creativity, and skills. This is a highly neoliberal viewpoint predicated on a natural state of fairness present in the world (Dean and Zamora 2021). Debt relief is reimagined; it is no longer for those who are struggling and in need of restoration or salvation, it is for the morally bankrupt 'quitter' who does not want to give it all to pay their debts. Consequently, any strategy that avoids going back to this broken service is justified, leading to participants accepting a degradation in their standard of living that they thought would never happen:

'I've had to start doing stuff I'm really ashamed of, I'm going around to bakeries in the [local area], and at night they usually throw away all the stuff they couldn't sell, so I go through the bins some nights and pick up the stale food, muffins, bread and other stuff they'd throw away.' (Interview with Paul)

'I'm in a place I never figured I'd be, the first time I went to a food charity I was so embarrassed.' (Interview with Michael)

'It's, what do they say? "Existing not living"? That's me. I'm just trying to focus on the next day, the next hour, the next minute, thinking long-term is awful.' (Interview with Sean)

This is how the technologies of governmentality discussed previously are translated (Rose 1991, 1999, 2000) from broad policy to operationalized changes in behaviour and conduct at the level of the subject. The debtor has become individualized, as all problems are atomically reduced to the level of the individual subject (Rose 1999), responsibilized into discourses of the risk-taking entrepreneur of the self which have now become normalized. This takes the character of governance at a distance (Rose 1999): the state (nor creditors for that matter) does not send letters to each individual debtor telling them that they ought to mistrust other debtors. Instead, this is a dispersed process, involving many different interlocking agents of governance, from creditors to debtors themselves, media organizations, experts such as PIPs or financiers, charities, and so on.

Cruel optimism

So far I have made the case that indebtedness is subject to a particular style of neoliberal governmentality, one which places the burden of proof on the debtor to demonstrate that they are genuinely seeking help, and not simply trying to take advantage of their creditors. The discourses around debt promote the idea that there is a widespread possibility of 'strategic default' (Walker 2011; Insolvency Service of Ireland 2014a; Waldron and Redmond 2015, 2016), where debtors who can pay their debts will choose not to do so. These strategic defaulters are eager to take advantage of generous debt relief services, which consequently have designed their debt assistance programmes to prevent this person from receiving help. Insolvency styles itself as a rehabilitative disciplinary institution, which can get debtors to live on their technocratically defined 'reasonable living expenses' (Insolvency Service of Ireland 2016a), which ensures recovery from present debts and prevents financial recidivism. The governmentality of indebtedness is therefore conceived as a misallocation of scarce resources by the debtor, and if they budgeted and spent their money responsibly, then they would recover (Walker 2011; Stamp 2012a).

Debtors, for their part, seem to believe in this narrative, and they engage with the process of proving their sincerity to pay their debt back in good faith. However, there is an unanswered question: if it is so unpleasant, then why do debtors go through this process? I argue here that the reason debtors respect and cooperate with the governmentality is because they have come to inhabit a state of subjectification which is called 'cruel optimism' (Berlant 2011). A situation of cruel optimism arises when 'something you desire is actually an obstacle to your flourishing' (Berlant 2011, p 2). This can manifest itself in many ways – for example, a desire to eat unhealthy food because it tastes good or to maintain contact with a friend whose presence we enjoy, but who is ultimately a bad influence on us. Berlant argues that optimism is about attachment to particular objects or scenes of desire, be it a love for a person or an attachment to a particular view of how the world works.

Our optimistic attachments to what we desire are therefore also deeply rooted in fantasy, and our desire to possess or remain in the orbit of a given object is more motivated by our ideas about what that object is like (Berlant 2011) rather than the way it actually is (as much as its objective status can actually be determined). As our optimism becomes more cruel and the cost of maintaining our attachments becomes higher, there is a tendency for subjects, rather than surrendering their attachment, to work even harder to remain in possession of it (Berlant 2006, 2011). As a result, our fantasy becomes even more fantastic in an effort to justify why we are working so hard to maintain these attachments.

Berlant (2011) argues that the tendency to desire something which is an obstacle to our flourishing is becoming more common in the context of modern neoliberal capitalism. Berlant's theory is situated in the history of the postwar consensus, which brought about the construction of the modern welfare state (see Chapter 2). In an environment of rising incomes, universal healthcare, and other social safety nets, Berlant argues that a particular narrative of 'the good life' became so common and pervasive that it has fully entered our social subconscious. The good life, according to this narrative, follows a particular trajectory, which allows for some deviation, but there is a general outline which remains consistent. Berlant offers the example of the standard expected life trajectory for an adult (so commonly understood that it is the entire premise behind several popular television shows and other media – for example, the sitcom *Friends*): first you go to college, at college you meet your life partner, then you get a full-time, secure, well-paid job, then you buy a house, then you have children. Once these milestones have been acquired, you work until retirement, and then your children repeat the process (Berlant 2006).

As was seen earlier, this mythos of what it means to live a 'good life' generally obliges individuals to acquire certain material resources (a home) or have access to particular socially important status symbols (marriage) at certain life stages. Berlant's argument is that in our fervour to preserve this fantasy of the good life, we have begun to behave in a way that is self-destructive: 'some scenes of optimism are crueler [sic] than others: where cruel optimism operates, the very vitalizing or animating potency of an object/scene contributes to the attrition of the very thriving that is supposed to be made possible in the work of attachment in the first place' (Berlant 2006, p 21).

My core theoretical argument is that debtors have come to accept the scrutiny of governmentality because they inhabit the subject position of being cruelly optimistic. Their attachment is to their houses, which has come to represent a whole series of complex emotional, social, and economic attachments. The home is related by my participants to stability, thriving, love, family, community, and happiness, yet the cost of maintaining their attachment to their homes (their mortgage) has paradoxically led them to sacrifice virtually all of these things. The home is a solid structure, having the quality of being relatively indestructible (Keohane and Kuhling 2014), offering the possibility of family and community, yet debtors enjoy few if any of these things. Having budgeted away much of what is considered frivolous, they cannot afford to maintain the social engagements that would enable them to be members of the community. Likewise, family life suffers, as parents finding themselves confronted by food poverty and social exclusion (Nagle 2015) must go to charitable organizations to attempt to acquire food (Combat Poverty Agency 2009). Many go without food or entertainment to provide for their children, but regardless, their children can tell that something is wrong, and that their vision of the good life has become distorted.

Cruel optimism channels related psychoanalytic theories such as displacement which occurs when the emotions about some object, person, or event are displaced onto a different object, person, or event – a typical example being an angry person punching a cushion to relieve their frustration (Freud and Gay 1995). In the case of debt, the cruel optimism of maintaining an attachment to the distorted vision of the good life leads to myriad problems: anxiety, depression, and suicide are chief among them, financial melancholia as Davies et al (2015) term it. The various promises of the good life come under strain, the job is not as fulfilling and secure as was promised, the love is not as enduring as first appearances suggested, and the home may even be under threat of repossession. The anger and hurt of this cruel optimism are often displaced onto a third party: other debtors. This fictitious 'other' is blamed when the dream promised by cruel optimism is not realized. Common stereotypes include the immigrant, the unemployed, the lazy and so on. Whoever they are, they are an obstacle to our flourishing. Media stories about lazy debtors are common, with a recent example being 'Couple to lose home after mortgage not paid for five years' (Managh 2018, p 1), but there are many other examples (Mortgage Brokers 2013; *Broadsheet* 2017; Weston 2018; Murray 2018a; Breaking News 2018). When looking for a source of blame, it is these 'other' dishonest or workshy debtors who are blamed for the problem(s) at hand. Once again, this tells us something about the moral foundations of debt: problematic relations of debt are not merely financial, but are also caused by individuals who lack good moral character. If those 'other' debtors would pay their mortgages, then my bank would not pursue me so harshly – the displacement is almost always externalized (Freud and Gay 1995).

A vague sense of optimism about the future has manifested itself in an acceptance of a cruel and harsh present, where the future is evacuated and only exists in a state of ambiguous generalities that one day things will be better. However, for many subjects, the debt-free day will most likely never arrive. The governmentality of indebtedness is such that once one falls behind, then the possibility of recovery and access to the good life becomes increasingly challenging (Walker 2011; Stamp 2012a). Cruel optimism is cruel because the tempting possibility of recovery always seems to be just about to arrive, leading them to believe that they should endure for just a little bit longer, and then they will be able to enjoy genuine happiness. It is because of this that debtors accept and even enthusiastically follow the requirements of institutions such as the ISI.

Mimesis, scapegoating, and sacrifice

But how is it that 'the good life' identified by Berlant (2011) became so important to begin with? I propose that neoliberalism's idealized vision of the good life became saturated throughout society through a process of mimetic desire and imitation (Girard 1989, 2013). As the mimesis built, it steadily grew from individuals imitating each other's desires to own a home to imitating each other's antagonisms from being unable to have their 'dream home', transforming the relationship from imitative to rivalry. As the rivalry for the object of desire becomes hostile and threatens to become violent, the participants in the mimetic process turn to someone who can be blamed for the toxic struggle for the object – a scapegoat, in this case the strategic defaulter. This scapegoat is then sacrificed, though we speak of a more symbolic sacrifice here, which happens through repossession rather than actual murder.

Generally, this is done by money management funds, which are more widely known by the pejorative nickname 'vulture funds' (Hearne 2017). These funds buy property and debt, and then leverage immense pressure on the debtor or market, seeking to squeeze as much money as possible as quickly as possible. In the contemporary Irish market, there is a shortage of housing, which has led to massively inflated rents and mortgages, making the house a significant and valuable asset. These funds operate in a grey area of the law and so are not subject to the same rules and regulations which apply to traditional creditors, such as banks (Coulter and Nagle 2015; Hearne 2017). This means they can adopt more aggressive strategies, which have occasionally been so hostile that the consequences for the debtor's mental health have been severe. The sacrifice is then made actionable by a vulture fund, which brings about the final element of the process – the curious sacralization of the sacrifice (Girard 2013). In Girard's (2013) view, there is a perceived need to punish the guilty. This grows over time until there is a risk of a violent social outburst. Once the punishment has been administered to the sacrifice, these feelings diminish.

According to Girard, mimesis in general and mimetic rivalry specifically have intensified in the modern era due to a flattening of hierarchical structures and a loss of religion, ritual, and meaning. In other words, our mimetic rivalry is a kind of compensation mechanism for the lack of consistency in the contemporary world, but this problematically implies that rivalry is less common in more hierarchical societies and that our society is itself less hierarchical than it was previously. For Girard (2013), the rivalry of our society has become problematic because we have a need to find or uncover models, limits, or the 'Truth'. Bauman (2000) is broadly in agreement with this conclusion, but his premise (that the world has become liquid and unstable due to the processes of capitalism) is different. Adams (2000) also points out that Girard's discussions, which fixate on violence, sacrifice, and scapegoating, undermine the possibility of positive mimesis, seen in Mauss' (2002) arguments about gift giving and reciprocal exchange. Adams (2000) further argues that this positive mimesis is a scapegoat within Girard's own theory, as he reduces all desire to hostile rivalries. While I think that Girard's theory is powerful and helpful for explaining certain aspects of the social world, it is important to remember that all theories (particularly those that claim to explain everything) have their limitations.

For Girard (1965, 2013), desire exists in a triangular relationship: our desire for a given object is provoked by the desire of another person (the model) for the same object. The relationship is: us (the subject); the other person (the model); and the object. Both people cannot possess the same object (at least not completely) and so they enter into a kind of contest with one another. Their desire for the object is therefore imitative; they imitate one another's reasons for wanting the object. In Celtic Tiger Ireland, the object of mimetic desire was (and remains) the house (Keohane and Kuhling 2014). Houses are sites of unique cultural importance: they are relatively indestructible, a place where families are raised, where communities are built, something which will remain after we are gone, a legacy of sorts (Keohane and Kuhling 2014). Fundamentally, however, Girard (1965, 1987) proposes that we desire these things because we know that others desire them.

Houses became located within a whole matrix of complex interlayered mimetic relationships; the price of the house was nothing compared to its potential future value. If one purchased a house in a suburban paradise, then one's children could be educated at a high-quality local school, one could live where one always dreamed, and one could be proud of one's achievement. This is the seductive nature of mimesis – the object as well as the model is not actually a real thing or person; the model is an ambitious imagining of a person who possesses that which we most desire (Keohane and Kuhling 2014, p 44). It is here that we see the links between cruel optimism (when what we desire is an obstacle to our flourishing) and mimesis (what we desire is based on an ideal type that may never have even existed).

At this stage, the mimesis goes beyond being merely imitative and transforms into a kind of rivalry. At first, two people desire an object, but then it is three, then ten, and so on. But only one of these people can actually possess the object of their desire; everyone else must settle for their second (or worse) choice. There is a curious strain here between the quantitative and qualitative. Ostensibly the house is desired for its qualitative properties – it is in a nice area, it is a 'dream' home, it is a place where family and community can be built – but this qualitative character can only be represented quantitatively by its price (Keohane and Kuhling 2014). And the rivalry created by mimetic desire caused a rapid increase in the price of the houses; as the laws of supply and demand dictate, when the supply is low and demand is high, the price will increase. And demand was very high.

Eventually the subject and the model are no longer imitating one another's desires, but rather one another's antagonisms. The relationship, which may originally have taken the form of a friendly rivalry, now becomes toxic and threatens to boil over into violence. Both groups continue in their struggle to possess the same object, and the hostility and resentment builds to a critical mass. Girard (2013) says at this point that if this struggle happens for long enough for an object that is mutually desired by everyone, it could lead to the destruction of society itself. A solution must be found; for Girard (1989, 2013), that solution is the scapegoat, a third party who can be blamed for the antagonisms caused by the mimetic rivalry of the subject and the model. Historically, a scapegoat was literally a goat that was ritually blamed for the sins of the Jewish people and then sent into the desert to die as a means of atonement (Girard 1989). The death of the goat by dehydration is a kind of metaphysical apology for the sins of the people which have been transferred onto the goat. Lazzarato (2012, 2014) proposes that in the metatheoretical sense, the Greeks have been the scapegoat for the problems of Europe and the European Union since the great financial crash. The lazy Greeks who refuse to pay their taxes took all the money loaned to them in good faith and squandered it, and now the whole European ideal is in danger (Lazzarato 2012, 2014). Scapegoating therefore provides unity through a common enemy (Girard 2013).

Scapegoating is easily identified by examining who is blamed for a problem, a sin, a crisis, an emergency, and in Ireland it is taken to be the case that all Irish people are to blame for the financial crisis. Blame is thus democratized (O'Flynn et al 2014) through rhetoric such as 'we all partied' (Murray 2010, p 1) or Coulter's (2015) three tropes of an Ireland under austerity. The corrupt political elite or banking system are not blamed; instead, it is the average Irish person who is said to have lived beyond their means and now must be contrite. Other scapegoats include the (allegedly) overpaid and underworked public sector workers, who are compared with the heroic and downtrodden private sector workforce unfavourably (O'Flynn et al 2014).

However, in the aftermath of the debt crisis, we have the scapegoat figure of the strategic defaulter, a debtor who 'partied' during the boom and now wishes to write down their debts at the expense of others. The burden of these debts would be shouldered by the bank of the defaulter or, more accurately, by the taxpayer as many Irish banks are part-owned by the Irish government. Media stories abound concerning the strategic defaulter, a person who has not paid their mortgage in five, six or perhaps even ten years (Waldron and Redmond 2016; Managh 2018). Such a person is represented and framed as contemptible, lazy, and lacking in moral character; in other words, they do not share our values, creating a demarcation between 'us' and 'them'. As in mimetic desire where the model is a fictive creation of our ideal desires, this scapegoat defaulter is similarly a creation of our antagonisms resulting from the mimetic rivalry. Where the model represents all the positive elements of desire we wish to possess, the scapegoat represents the negative perceptions of ourselves and general society that we wish to purge or remove.

Girard (2013) demonstrates that as antagonism builds and the ritual blaming of the scapegoat subjects reaches a crescendo, there is then a sacrifice. Unlike in scapegoating, the sacrifice cannot be an abstracted generality – it cannot be anybody, it must be someone or something in particular. Additionally, how and by whom the scapegoat is sacrificed is just as important as why, and historically a sacrifice is carried out by a king, a priest, or some other subject who is a valued and important member of society in a ritually ordained manner. In the contemporary Irish context, I hold that the sacrifice of the strategic defaulter is being carried out by the vulture fund. These international money funds are buying up large tranches of 'nonperforming' mortgages: those who will not or cannot pay their debts (*Broadsheet* 2017; Fegan 2018; Finn 2018). The fund then evicts the nonpaying debtor and sells the house for a profit. It is through these funds that the legacy debts of the Celtic Tiger are being dealt with, and the scapegoats are being sacrificed. In an Ireland under austerity, it is possible (perhaps even likely) that the debtors being evicted in this process will end up homeless. The rent crisis across Ireland is now very serious, with average rents in Dublin having crested over €2,000 a month from the start of 2018 (Reddan 2018). Mortgages are similarly overpriced; as was the case in the boom, there are too few houses and too many buyers (Reddan 2017), with analysis by Murray (2018b) finding that a first-time buyer needs at least a €50,000 deposit and average borrowings of €185,939 to buy a home – the average income of this group was €67,287 (in the top 10 per cent of income in Ireland). In the UK, data from the Land Registry (2023) show that the average house price is now £237,834, while the average income for someone in their twenties is £37,100, pushing homeownership out of reach for many.

Those who are sacrificed will therefore find themselves in a difficult position: rising rents, a low availability of housing and huge mortgage costs mean that they will likely have to settle for poor-quality housing or may even end up homeless. It is here that the curious sacralization of the sacrificial subject can be seen. Girard (1989, 2013) tells us that the sacrifice becomes sacred: they were the reason that the mimetic rivalry almost transformed into widespread violence, but having been sacrificed, they are also the reason why such violence has been prevented. This contradictory dualism gives the sacrifice the halo of the sacred, and the sacrifice is never remembered as a celebrated event, only as a necessary one (Girard 2013). While those who are evicted or whose houses are repossessed become the object of a kind of sacred pity, the vulture fund becomes feared and held in contempt. Even those who defend them only regard them as a necessary evil, using the argument that a vulture feeds on the carcasses of the dead, providing a vital role in the ecosystem of which it is a part (*Broadsheet* 2017). For the mortgage holder, the vulture fund becomes the source of ultimate fear; the funds come after the scapegoats, those who are suspected of strategic default, of lacking in good moral character, who did not make every effort to pay their debts. Becoming the sacrificial subject is to be avoided at all costs, and debtors will borrow money from friends and family, acquire a second job, work despite a serious injury, use charities, and more in order to keep the funds at bay.

While debtors do not like vulture funds, they are also critical of the 'bad' debtor the vulture funds are attacking, and this 'bad' debtor is the source of much stereotyping. They are said to be lazy, financially illiterate, stupid, and typically come from broken families or 'bad areas'; the 'bad' debtor is thus the object of gendered and classed discourses of disgust and stigma.

Mimetic rivalry becomes more damaging over time and will eventually lead to an outburst of violence unless a means of expression is found (Girard 1965, 2013). Typically, these take the form of the scapegoat and the sacrifice (Girard 2013). For my participants, the discourses around the punishment and pathologizing of the irresponsible debtor is a type of scapegoating used to rationalize their continued avoidance of the ISI, even if it would be financially rational to engage with the process (difficult and demeaning as it may be). The service is constructed in many different (often mutually contradictory) ways.

The service is both too difficult and too easy to engage with: the participant argues that they simply didn't try hard enough to apply, which they could do if they really wanted to, but never will. The ISI is also too restrictive and too open: it is kept restrictive and exclusive to prevent it from being overused by the untruthful debtor, but at the same time my participants believe that there are hordes of these untruthful subjects using the ISI. The service is for 'quitters' (those who have given up), but in a bizarre sense is also for those who take their debts seriously, as those people are the only ones responsible enough to admit they have a problem. The PIP is shrewd and discerning, capable of finding the most carefully concealed lie, but at the same time is easily tricked by the strategic defaulter who the PIP allows to use debt arrangements.

While these beliefs may seem irrational, they serve a purpose. They anchor my participants to their houses, the objects of their cruel optimism, and they justify the continued existence of their nonuse of the ISI and simultaneously diffuse the mimetic rivalry they feel with other debtors. The 'other', while dishonest, is more tolerable if my participants believe that justice is being done, and that the irresponsible 'other' is not able to acquire debt relief. My participants variously sought out extra work or overtime hours from their employer, got a second job, began using charities, gave up hobbies and socializing, and began to budget much more carefully, both to cope with their indebtedness but also to 'prove' their honesty. The gaze of neoliberal subjectification has now been internalized.

However, if the scapegoating of the moral hazard and the strategic defaulter does not work, then there is the sacrifice, which in the contemporary moment of Irish debt neoliberalism takes the form of the vulture fund – or, as they are otherwise known, international money management funds which purchase large tranches of 'poorly performing' mortgages, evict those living in the houses, and then sell the houses for large profits. The mere possibility of a vulture fund purchasing their house made my participants fearful. While any repossession would be bad, a repossession by a vulture fund would be a sign that they had been judged and found wanting; that they were in the group of 'nonperforming' loans which is representative of a lack of determination to cope with their debt problems. There is simultaneously here a hate and fear of vulture funds: nobody wishes themselves to be the sacrificial victim which restores the mortgage market to a healthy state. However, those 'other' dishonest debtors will get what they deserve, though my participants could never quite bring themselves to 'support' vulture funds in any meaningful way; a sacrifice, unlike scapegoating is permanent and is always difficult to look at (Girard 1965, 1989).

Resisting neoliberalism

Exploring the question of indebted subjectivities has occupied many scholars writing on debt today (Langley 2009; Graeber 2011; Deville 2015; McClanahan 2018; Montgomerie 2019; Adkins et al 2020), and it is fair to say that Lazzarato's (2012) account has proved influential with good reason. Channelling Foucault, Marx, and Nietzsche, he constructs a neoliberal analysis of indebted subjectivity that unifies a very complex field of literature to create a portrayal of an eternally guilty subject who has internalized the neoliberal logics of responsibilization and risk taking to become *homo economicus*. However, as McClanahan (2018, pp 124–126) observes, Lazzarato never fully draws on the real conditions of the economy in his account; in other words, we do not borrow because we are all entrepreneurial risk takers, we borrow because we have no other choice. Wages are stagnating or even declining in value relative to the cost of consumer goods, many cities and countries face housing crises, and the ongoing march of privatization and marketization means we have to pay for goods or services that were formerly funded through tax or were free at the point of use. Finally, while debtors are certainly mobilized and impacted by affect (Deville 2015), they also pay their debts because of the very real material consequences of failing to do so. Foreclosure, a summons to court, unemployment, and imprisonment are real physical and material consequences which give the debtor a profoundly immediate reason for paying that goes somewhat deeper than Nietzsche's 'bad conscience'.

The popular belief by creditors that most debtors are untrustworthy finds some credence here, as some debtors paradoxically reverse their earlier efforts to repay. Rock (2014) characterizes this as secondary deviance (where you internalize the label of 'deviant' and behave as such a deviant would be expected to behave). Creditors are reasonably free in asserting their belief that most debtors are bad actors who seek to cheat the creditor out of their money (Graeber 2011). I am certain that such people exist, especially because I have encountered them, but I should also say that most people do not fall into this category until after their creditors reject an attempt at reconciliation. Rejection from an insolvency arrangement was a catalyst for many of my participants, who develop a determination to fight the creditor at any cost.

Thus far, we have seen that the debtor tends to be a highly overgovernmentalized subject. While the push and pull of neoliberal subjectification is strong, and especially so for debtors, there are those who reject the authority of neoliberalism to govern them, who refuse to allow their debts to govern them through their affect. This is a rare but important part of the process, where debtors actively take on the mantle of the strategic defaulter, believing they are justified in refusing to pay because the relations of debt are inherently unfair:

'I don't think of myself as a debtor anymore. The money that was borrowed? I paid that back, I have actually paid enough to pay this house off, interest is a scam.' (Interview with a debtor)

'The banks hold all the cards. I tried my absolute best to pay back what I owed, but it's a sham, and a scam. I have paid them over €95,000 in the last 12 years, and then there's my deposit on top of that. After all that I should end up with nothing?' (Interview with a debtor)

'Debt culture is just a way to make you feel bad, I don't go in for that anymore.' (Interview with a debtor)

Debtors point to the fact that they have already made sufficient repayments and approached the process genuinely and in good faith, which was not reciprocated by their creditor. They suspect (either quietly or openly) that the creditor behaved in this fashion because they always simply wanted to evict the debtor and end up in possession of the house. In Skeggs' (1997) work, relations of class and gender are driven by the fear of 'giving up' and being perceived in this way by others. To give up means you have stopped disidentifying from your working classness and have adopted the traits and behaviours associated with the working class, such as idleness, laziness, or a lack of regard for self-care and bodily maintenance. For these people, it is an active rejection of the norms of neoliberalism, which our other debtors have worked so hard to internalize. This includes rejecting the very label of 'debtor', which is taken to have a negative connotation:

'I don't think of myself as a debtor, a debtor is a sucker who lies awake at night worrying about pleasing people determined to screw them.' (Interview with a debtor)

'I am not a debtor. I am a free man; a debtor is a slave.' (Interview with a debtor)

'Everyone told me to be really worried about strategic default, but let me tell you, it's better than being a debtor.' (Interview with a debtor)

The new mode of subjectification, then, is the active embrace of the identity of the strategic defaulter, which is reclassified from its negative roots (laziness, maliciousness, deception) and given more positive qualities (rebellious, maverick, intelligent, strong). For the creditor, this deterioration of relations is an absolute disaster: once the debtor has decided to resist, they can make things extraordinarily painful and expensive (Rock 2014). Between legal fees and the costs in time, effort, and resources from staff, the creditor can expect to spend a small fortune on removing the debtor. Irish creditors are frustrated here by having to continue to exercise restraint due to the Mortgage Arrears Resolution Process (Central Bank of Ireland 2012), which defines how contact between the lender and the borrower must take place, and what creditors must do before they can advance the process. Part of the problem is time lag, which is a general issue for understanding whether any debtor is legitimate or fraudulent. The recency effect tells us that more recent information occupies more cognitive space than less recent information.

Creditors are always attempting to gauge whether a debtor is cooperative or not (Rock 2014), and the most recent efforts of such debtors in seeking an insolvency arrangement show that while there is a misalignment of expectations, the debtor is still committed. The fact that the debtor has given up and become an adversary may not be apparent for months, during which time the creditor can do nothing but continue to send letters or contact the debtor by phone for an explanation. Lack of contact is so normal that it will not attract attention for several months, during which time the debtor has ceased to even think about their debt. Even should the creditor become able to successfully repossess the house, they may find that it is so ill-maintained and damaged that by the time it is repaired, it will cost significantly more than can be gained by selling it:

'A pipe burst last winter, and there was some minor or I suppose some modest water damage, and [the wooden] floor warped. In the old days I would have been scrambling about that, but now I left it. I got a quote that it would cost €10,000 to fix, which I found very funny. Once upon a time I would have borrowed even more money from them [creditors] to fix it, now they can pay for it themselves.' (Interview with a debtor)

The debtors are no longer animated by their cruel optimism because they no longer believe that they will be able to maintain ownership of the house indefinitely. The calculative logic and skills they learned during their time as a debtor are now used for the opposite of their intended purpose. They are on a ticking clock until the turgid mechanisms of the law catch up with them. The pride taken in the ongoing maintenance of the house is now perceived to be unnecessary and burdensome:

'I'm not going to be here forever. Once I made my peace with that I actually started to feel a lot better.' (Interview with a debtor)

'They said to me "a lot of people say to us that we'll take our chances with the courts, now you don't want to be that sort of person do you?" For a very long time I didn't, but now? Yeah, fuck it, I'll take my chances with the courts.' (Interview with a debtor)

As foregrounded by Davies et al (2015), this is the regaining of control that is so sought-after by debtors, who often feel that they have lost control of their lives and finances permanently. For creditors, the spectre of the strategic defaulter is a nightmare come to life. They do themselves few favours by pretending that such behaviour is common. However, when it does happen, the results are devastating. The strategic defaulter uses every tactic they can think of to place themselves at an advantage should they wish to go bankrupt in the future: "My job [previously] paid to my account directly. Now I work for cash in hand, there aren't always payslips. Who's to say how much money I made last year?" (interview with a debtor).

The defaulter is aware that in going bankrupt, their efforts to repay are likely to be scrutinized, and they seek to create ambiguity and fuzziness in this regard. In addition to taking cash in hand, they sporadically respond to their creditors, continuing to (falsely) claim that they are cooperative, and seeking to find additional sources of income. This can even stretch into a full monthly payment, which carries significant costs, but also creates a positive impression in the mind of the creditor that gives the debtor more time:

> 'We'll be kicked outta here eventually, but you can string them [creditors] along, you can make the odd payment, that keeps them sweet. They think they have you by the balls, but they really don't.' (Interview with a debtor)

> 'I am not paying another cent. They will get the house eventually; of that you can be sure. What condition will it be in? Who knows.' (Interview with a debtor)

This has a character that veers from dangerous to irresponsible and even improvisational. Many of these people told me that they do not really have a long-term plan; they are simply figuring things out in the moment. This means that at least some traits common to the subjectivity of indebtedness are preserved – that is, the sense that the future is collapsed into the present:

> 'We wanted to raise our son here, when we fell behind we put our plans for more kids on hold. Now my wife is pregnant again, we will figure it out as we go.' (Interview with a debtor)

> '[I am] making it up as I go. Don't really know what I'm doing and don't care either.' (Interview with a debtor)

As mentioned in Chapter 4, there are many pastors who offer advice, counsel, and expertise in the field of indebtedness, ranging from debt advisors to family members. Strategic defaulters pivot away from more traditional experts and towards more informal networks, such as friends and family. The shame, anxiety, guilt, depression, and insomnia that are so prevalent in the subjectivity of indebtedness disappear almost completely. The defaulter uses moral storytelling to relate the unfairness of their creditors to these new pastors, who almost always advise resistance:

> 'I finally told my family that I had been struggling and that I was going to lose the house because the bank wouldn't give me more time and that I didn't know what to do. My brother told me that it sounded like it didn't really matter what I did, so I should just relax and enjoy the time I have left. A bit like dying I suppose. I thought about that for weeks afterwards and I realized he was right. They are going to take the house, but I can keep living here rent free for a few months, maybe even years, so let's party.' (Interview with Rachel)

The defaulter must place importance on the fact that they have been reasonable and cooperative up to this point, as it is this earnest and sincere behaviour that justifies the 'party' which comes later. The scapegoating dialogues return here again, as they point to the belief that such activities are widespread with statements like 'everyone is doing it', thereby excusing their own behaviour. There is a sense of E.P. Thompson's (1971) moral economy here, which originated with 18th-century English peasants, caught between the norms of feudalism and capitalism. As they faced the privatization of lands which had always been held in common, and the market began to displace them from rural areas and into urban areas to work in the factories that would define the era of industrialization, these peasants would often apply moral norms, frustrating the market logic of traders and merchants, especially in times of crisis. Thompson wrote extensively about the supposed 'food riots' of the 18th century, which he deduced were often not riots at all, but rather a refusal to pay the market price for goods.

Instead, these peasants applied their own conception of justice, fairness, and ethics to transactions, seeing the market price as something for the commercial classes. When traders attempted to justify high prices for food during a shortage, the peasantry would counter with the 'just price' – the sum they felt was fair considering the circumstances. These defaulters similarly apply ideas of fairness and justice to their transactions and ongoing relationship with their creditors. Feeling that they have no obligation to pay the market price (that is, principal + interest) on their mortgaged houses, countering that they have already paid a sufficient amount (an amount they consider 'fair'). They never contend that such relations are illegal or that they did not sign the contract in good faith, but rather that the series of relations created by such contracts is morally wrong. They are therefore legitimized in rejecting these relations and supplementing them by a framework which perceives the economy through a moral rather than a purely material lens.

Even those who do not 'give up' and occupy the subject position of being a strategic defaulter can begin to see their debt in these terms, using phrases such as 'fair is fair' or 'where is the justice in all this?', or emphasizing that negotiations should be 'open and honest', with the implication that creditors may lack these traits. It is important to say again here and to strongly emphasize that these cases of strategic default are rare. Of the hundreds of debtors I have spoken to, only a handful have indicated that they have used such strategies, and only in cases where they felt that the moral economy of indebtedness was not respected. They pay their debts as best they can, they make sacrifices, they budget, scrimp, save, deny themselves pleasure, and are then rejected for insolvency and for ongoing cooperation by their creditor. This is perceived as a declaration of war, and the response sits somewhere between contempt and malice.

Conclusion

We have now come full circle through seeing the engagement and non-engagement with the applications process. My participants, having had negative initial experiences with the ISI, reconstruct it as a service for the lazy or dishonest; contradictorily, the service was also designed to exclude these same people. However, my participants believe that the shrewd and dishonest debtor who wishes to strategically default is able to gain access to the service, while honest hardworking debtors are excluded. Consequently, there is little point in revisiting the service, as the result would be a lot of effort in attempting to persuade the PIP that they are honest applicants, but the PIP would not believe them. The debtor then feels a need to take control of their life: if they cannot utilize debt relief, then they must find a way to deal with the situation on their own. This justifies extremes of budgeting and a (dis)engagement from general society due to a lack of money and the stigma that exists around indebtedness.

However, behind this governmentality is a focus on what Berlant (2011) calls 'the good life'. In essence, the good life describes a type of fantasy specific to contemporary Western liberal democracies. In effect, there are life 'milestones' that Western subjects are encouraged to meet, such as going to college, meeting a life partner, getting married, and owning a home. Homeownership is particularly important for this discussion, as homes and houses become invested with all manner of emotional and cultural debris (Keohane and Kuhling 2014). Attachment to these notions of the good life, while understandable, can also be damaging, and Berlant elaborates on what she calls cruel optimism: 'A relation of cruel optimism exists when something you desire is actually an obstacle to your flourishing' (Berlant 2011, p 1).

I argue that my participants now exist in a state of cruel optimism with respect to their houses, which helps to explain why they are so hostile to the debt relief offered by the ISI. The insolvency arrangements of the ISI represent a chance for the debtor to lose that which they have sacrificed for, as 10 per cent of applicants end up losing their houses (Insolvency Service of Ireland 2018, p 4) and a further 21 per cent move from a normal mortgage to a mortgage-to-rent scheme (Insolvency Service of Ireland 2018, p 5). My participants have a strong sense of attachment to their houses, and Berlant (2011, pp 4–6) explains that the more our object of cruel optimism comes under threat, the more grasping our attachment to it becomes. As the possibility of losing that which we desire becomes crystallized, more extreme measures first become justified and are then normalized (Berlant 2006, 2011).

Concurrently, debtors become suspicious and judgemental of other debtors, in what I argue is a kind of mimetic rivalry (Girard 1987, 1989, 2013), which centres on the house as an object for which there is a struggle for possession. Debtors are confronted with the difficulties of debt distress, and they must (at some point) explain how and why they came to be in this place, which leads to accusations and critiques of other debtors, who are the irresponsible subject par excellence. Each of these debtors is trying to own a home, yet there is a sense that they are all in competition with each other, because the irresponsible behaviour of one sabotages the debt relief chances of another. The policy will be amended to exclude the irresponsible subject, which has a knock-on effect or unintentionally damages the application chances of the responsible subject in the process. Thus, the competition for debt relief is a kind of mimetic rivalry, which, as we have seen from previous quotes from my participants, can be highly toxic. Neighbours become hidden enemies, communities break down as my participants do not want to associate with 'those' kinds of people, and former friends are suspicious as they examine the renovation works of those who are supposed to be struggling.

8

Conclusion: Thriving beyond Debt

A debtor once told me that avoiding bankruptcy was like an intricate chess game you play with your creditors. As the reader well knows, chess can only have two outcomes: checkmate or stalemate. Throughout this book, we have seen the elaborate measures undertaken by debtors to bring about a permanent stalemate between them and their lenders. The costs of this are severe and only grow worse with time. This book has sought to go beyond traditional academic accounts of indebtedness, which do not usually include the lived experience of seeking debt relief. I hope by now that the reader is convinced of the utility of this approach and that we have a better understanding of why debtors do what they do. This conclusion will summarize the main takeaways and will consider the limitations of this framework, before ending by arguing that we must push for a new jubilee of mass debt cancellation, but also that debt relief must be reformed.

The takeaways

Morality matters

The moral landscape of debt is vast and complex, and my principal argument throughout this book has been that the calculations behind whether we accept debt relief are moral, not economic. It depends on the perceived moral character of the debtor, how they have handled their debts, and even the type of debt they possess. If we begin with the latter, it is readily apparent that more sympathy is shown to those who are the victims of predatory loan schemes or who borrowed for survival, with so-called payday loans growing in popularity. Similarly, those who take out a loan for medical purposes or childcare are viewed more sympathetically; they have a morally valid reason for taking out the loan and their defaulting on it is usually not seen in a negative light.

On the other end of the spectrum, there are those who borrow for naked consumerism, who are perhaps the most stigmatized of all. Those who are lent money for televisions, smartphones, laptops, or to maintain an unsustainably lavish lifestyle are seen as terribly irresponsible, having bought something they did not need with money that was not theirs. I have always found it peculiar that such aspersions are always cast upon the debtor first and not the creditor, as it was they who had to investigate the purpose of the loan and could always have refused to grant it. How someone has handled their debts is just as important, and you must be seen to have 'made an effort' to repay – a profound demarcation exists between those who can't pay and those who won't pay.

We are always in a contiguous process of social, gender, and class analysis when we meet someone, judging them based on their attire, accent, clothing, mannerisms, and much more (Bourdieu 2010). This analysis is being revised, reviewed, and reconsidered all the time. The same is true of debt, and indeed not all debt is created equal. An analysis of discourse shows that we are inclined to be very hard on the so-called professional debtor (Rock 2014, p 26), those who maliciously seek to extract as much money from creditors as possible before declaring insolvency. The processes of debt relief have been designed specifically with this person in mind, though the political language is different in each country and context where debt relief is practised (Insolvency Service of Ireland 2013a; Heuer 2014; Stamp 2016).

Contrary to the expectations of policy makers and the devotees of neoliberalism, debt relief is not perceived as transactional by the debtors who go through it. Instead, they see it as a process of purification that only the worthy can access, and the metaphors used here indicate this – paying debt back is often likened to a journey or pilgrimage, on which you may suffer setbacks or detours, but where ultimately you get to your destination and are all the better for it (Stanley et al 2016; Debt Collective 2020). This is as poetic as it is false, and our world is full of people who have been left hollowed-out wrecks by a mixture of their indebtedness, supplemented by the callous disregard paid to them by journalists and politicians. There is an eternal fear and suspicion that each person in debt has secretly hidden a briefcase full of money under their bed and they are just waiting for the foolish creditor to give up before they reveal their ruse.

Living through over-indebtedness

To understand debt relief, we ought to take the moral logic that is so often applied to debt and simply apply this same logic to relief. When we do this, we see that the landscape of debt relief is immensely complex and depends on many overlapping factors, a field that the debtor must navigate if they are to be successful. I have told the story of how Irish debtors go through this process, but the themes presented should be familiar to readers everywhere: a man who intended to retire young, but then lost his job after the financial crisis, a woman who thought she had found true love until she discovered her partner had lost their savings through gambling, a man with an excellent job who was injured in an accident and cannot work again. When glimpsed from a distance abstractly, the temptation is always to decry debt relief, and yet when we look more closely, we find the stories of people who could be us, but for a twist of fate. This is the power of the qualitative, person-centred approach to research: to show that these stories, while they are certainly individual and parochial, also evince an element of the universal.

Each author who encounters debt must contend with the longstanding question of why debtors often fail to take action – why do they 'stick their heads in the sand', to use a commonly recurring phrase? The short answer is that the affect cultivated by indebtedness is powerful: debtors fail to act at first because they believe that they will be subject to a karmic stroke of good luck, that some good event will undo what has happened. Yet, this is not to be, which leads to a complex array of emotions, fear, anger, regret, guilt, and shame, but most of all there is anxiety, which seems to paralyse and stun debtors into inaction. When they finally do take action, it is to make symbolic gestures. They have already calculated that they cannot repay in terms of getting back on track with their repayment schedule, but they can create a kind of moral tapestry showing that they continue to take their debts seriously. In service of this, they behave in a manner that would be recognizable to Max Weber in his Protestant Ethic: they adopt an attitude of asceticism. They quit smoking, they stop consuming alcohol, they cancel their television packages, they renounce their memberships of clubs and societies – all in all, they make an active decision to deny themselves pleasure.

What is remarkable is that they know before they ever do this that this will make no difference to their fortunes – even if they should quit these bad habits or indulge in this asceticism, it will not return them to solvency. Yet they do not do it for this reason; they do it because they feel intense guilt, because they want to punish themselves, and because they feel that they do not deserve to feel pleasure. If we adopted a cynical view, we might note that the decision is tactical, as they are creating a portrayal of suffering which will make their plight all the more compelling to their creditors (and others) later on. This progressively creates a change in the subjectivity of the borrower, as they come to inhabit the subject position of the *debtor*. As in the Foucauldian tradition, we might compare these with the prisoner, inmate, pupil, and son on as a particular way of being, a certain relation of the self to the world.

Being a debtor means accepting guilt and shame as a way of being and conducting yourself accordingly. Following on from this, symbolic gestures are eventually not enough, and the debtor must begin to explore the patchwork quilt of expertise surrounding indebtedness and discover which (if any) body of expertise operating in this area they would like to follow. Some choose life coaches, others look to financial advisors, many choose debt advisors, and most (initially) reject their creditors as an authoritative source. This is facilitated by a Foucauldian neoliberal pastoral power, where each expert (pastor) is concerned about the salvation of their flock (population). While the process is different for each person, they eventually admit that they need help, even if they do not quite seek it out. We might see this as pointless, and yet for the debtor it is not so. The purgatorial elements of being indebted are crucial such that the debtor can justify the decision to seek out debt relief for themselves. If they feel that they do not deserve debt relief, then they will not even attempt an application, and they must feel that they have done everything possible to solve the problem without outside help.

When they do encounter the insolvency practitioner (or international equivalent), they must persuade this person to help them, even if they do not entirely understand the process they are participating in. The definition of insolvency is that you must be unable to pay your debts, which is nebulous and ambiguous enough that almost anyone can qualify, but there are further requirements that indicate that the debtor must have made sacrifices – not just anyone can qualify for debt relief. It must be restricted, lest the unworthy come forth in their droves to claim that which they do not deserve. For these reasons, securing the help of such professionals depends on your capacity to represent yourself as an appropriately moral subject through a confession. Confession has obvious theological roots, but has spread throughout the matrix of our social bureaucracy, being used in everything from therapy to justice to encourage or induce truth telling.

There is a peculiar game played here in the field of insolvency relations. The state-of-the-art science around insolvency dictates that the state should not meddle directly in these affairs and should instead outsource this work to trained professionals who have experience in finance and law. These professionals are distant enough that the state cannot be accused of meddling in the market; it merely gives them licences and permission to operate in the resolution of bad debts within the credit market. The support of a practitioner is crucial if they are to convince their creditors. At this point, we see the purpose of the purgatorial suffering and symbolic gestures from earlier – they show the practitioner and creditors that the debtor has taken their debt seriously. Why else would they do something so pointless according to the laws of calculability?

Debtors accepted for this process see it as a kind of salvation, which gives them hope for the future. Those who are rejected feel unspeakable anger and shame, as they are condemned to live eternally in indebtedness, unable to recover and unwilling to surrender their assets. This is because they have become emotionally and morally attached to a particular vision of the good life, a view of what success means through the achieving of specific life milestones. The house has become invested with too much personal value to be surrendered voluntarily, and so debtors languish in suffering. As a society, we seem content to allow this state of affairs to continue, as the prevailing situation suits all parties from a certain point of view. The politics of debt would be destabilized by mass debt forgiveness (which would threaten the credit market) or mass evictions (which would threaten social stability). It is therefore preferable to allow the debtors to remain in their houses, continuing to pay small amounts, and always leaving open the opportunity that they may recover one day.

Processing debtors

I have argued throughout this book that debt relief is a process that starts at borrowing and ends with insolvency or bankruptcy. The reader may be tempted to believe that some parts of it are unnecessary, that they ought to be truncated, or even removed entirely – to people with this view, I would advise caution. The debtors I have spoken to nearly always believe that they deserve to suffer in some way for failing to pay their debts, and while it may be possible to cut the length of time spent in the purgatory of indebtedness a little, I think this is impossible to remove entirely without substantial changes to our systems of lending and relief. On some level, debtors want to endure a time of difficulty because they believe they deserve it. However, this can irrationally defeat itself by exhausting the debtors' financial and emotional resources, leaving them hollowed out and depleted.

We have created a system for processing debts, which by necessity is bureaucratic. If we look at the numbers of debtors and compare this to the resources available in such systems, we would find that they are wholly inadequate and would take hundreds of years simply to get through those who are currently in debt, not to mention those who become indebted as these cases are processed. Yet despite the fact that there is immense pressure on the resources of legal systems of various countries and there are a great number of debtors who technically qualify, the systems remain stable. How can this be? The answer is simple: debtors simply do not apply en masse for these arrangements. While creditors may sound the alarm constantly, especially when the public eye turns towards debt relief, there is never any real danger of debtors applying as a mass group for relief – they feel too much guilt.

A downpour of debt

The world is awash with debt. With interest rates growing and incomes shrinking (most recently due to inflation), the question of how we deal with excess debt on a large scale is becoming increasingly urgent. If debt were a purely financial construct, then we would have few issues with resolving it. The invisible hand of the market would determine when a debt was unpayable, and then calculate how much more money could be extracted and write down the remainder. Borrowers would tell lenders as soon as they began to fall behind and would declare bankruptcy as soon as they had calculated that they could no longer repay. Of course, debt is not a purely financial construct, and is so riddled with moral and social considerations that it is almost equal parts law and custom.

Until the middle (and, for many countries, the late) 20th century, the outstanding policy approach was to represent debt relief as morally wrong. It represents a transfer of wealth from lender to borrower, but more significantly creates a precedent that it is acceptable not to pay one's debts. The solution was therefore to make debt relief so punitive that only the most destitute and desperate of borrowers would pursue it. Instead of outright debt relief, policy makers encouraged lenders and borrowers to negotiate, aiming to resolve over-indebtedness privately rather than publicly. This relationship has a massive power asymmetry and the predictable result was that debtors were at a disadvantage in any such negotiations.

The rise of neoliberalism was accompanied by financial deregulation, and a corresponding push to make finance and its instruments a part of everyday life (Langley 2009). We were to be made responsible for our own insurance plans, health coverage, retirement planning, housing, education, and more as the state began its tactical retreat from the market. This required new standards of financial literacy, in addition to the renegotiation of old mores and ideas, especially around investment. Investing acquired a more positive connotation through its association with bold entrepreneurship rather than as an elaborate form of gambling. In this way, investing was made popular because it became seen as the most rational form of saving (Langley 2009, pp 46–47).

It is fair to assume that neoliberalism is hostile to debt relief, as its more liberal predecessors were for many of the same reasons. However, one of the injunctions of neoliberalism is that while the state ought to have low-level involvement in the market, it must still create the conditions necessary for markets to flourish. Indeed, it is acceptable for the state to initially create such markets in instances where they have not previously existed. The vast (and ever-growing) debts represented a potential drag on the credit market and the economy. Such debts could lead to the exclusion of many in the burgeoning consumer class from participation in the market and consumer economy more generally as their entire incomes would be spent on servicing their debts. This echoes Graeber's (2011) observation that new kings would hold debt jubilees to prevent their subjects from ending up in debt slavery to creditors, leaving them with nobody to tax or govern.

Toxic debts are also costly and time-consuming for creditors who do not wish to have large numbers of delinquent debtors on their books whom they need to continuously 'chase' for money. In this sense, while creditors may oppose debt relief, it is in their own best interests for debtors to have a structured means to resolve and discharge their excessive debts. Neoliberals may similarly complain of the perceived unfairness and injustice of social welfare, but history has shown us that the absence of welfare leads to crime, poverty, misery, and even uprisings (Ewald 1991). In this way, social welfare is an anti-revolutionary tool, intended to give subsistence to the poor while simultaneously quelling dissent (Boland and Griffin 2021). Debt relief is the very same and serves as a stabilizing mechanism for the credit market; indeed, even without debt relief, it is unlikely that creditors would get any more money from their debtors as it is overwhelmingly a tool used by those who cannot pay.

The primary goal of the reformation of debt relief has been to distinguish between those who cannot pay and those who will not pay. The former can be judged on a case-by-case basis, while the latter must be detected and rejected at all costs. This comes from a fear that debt relief is transactional and that debtors see it as a way to balance their books – nothing could be further from the truth. There is a profound sense of moral economy and economic theology running through contemporary indebtedness. This is woven into the fabric of capitalism, which 'lifts' people out of poverty rather than using more scientific language – that is, reducing inequality. The devotees of capitalism also tend to frame market interference by the state as wrong or evil rather than as economically irrational (Bell 2020; Dempsey 2020).

Debt itself (and indeed many debtors) is described using the language of guilt and sin, and the subjective experience of being indebted is purgatorial. From a chronological perspective, over-indebtedness should seem to be an unending punishment. Debt relief in turn is described as salvific and miraculous, and it is difficult to overstate the impact that debt relief has on the lives of the indebted. Indeed, it is the salvation that they had hoped for, even though it was difficult to obtain. In fact, we might say that it is the very fact that it is difficult to obtain that makes it worth having. The journey on which the debtor has gone is now reimagined, as they look back upon struggles which were once seen as pointless or arduous, and these experiences are invested with new meaning. A similar example can be seen in welfare research (Boland and Griffin 2021), where, despite our assumptions, unemployed people are unable to enjoy the free time created by a lack of work. By going to work, we are enabled to feel productive and useful, which allows us to enjoy our free time because it has been 'earned'. A debtor who had their debts purged with no effort would feel that they had cheated their creditors out of their money, but the hardship and difficulties encountered while attempting to repay give the experience its meaning (Wilkis 2018). The journey only makes sense once you have reached the destination.

How then are we to distinguish between those who cannot pay and those who will not pay? By examining their files, budgets, and documents? There are significant obstacles to doing things in this way. The first is that it is extremely time-consuming and difficult to reconstruct a life story from such documents. They are useful for identifying crisis points, such as where the debtor first fell behind, but they can reveal little else. In any event, neoliberalism seeks to govern frugally, with the minimum of effort, and hiring an army of forensic accountants to examine every individual debt relief application would cost more than it would save. The solution is to compel the debtor to make an economic confession (Foucault 2015) where they explain how and why they have fallen into debt distress. In this confession many things tumble out: relationship breakdown, unemployment, rises in the cost of living, bereavement, bad investments, vices (such as smoking and gambling), and more.

The confession must be morally convincing and therefore relies on the debtor to appropriately advocate for themself. In most countries it is possible to opt for legal counsel, but this would raise uncomfortable questions as to how they are able to afford this expense. More abstractly, a confession only works if you are the one giving it; someone else cannot confess for you. This self-advocacy requires the debtor to walk a fine line. On the one hand, they must show that they earnestly and sincerely take responsibility for all that has happened, that they are to blame, that they fell into distress for understandable reasons, and that they did not stop paying intentionally. On the other hand, they must simultaneously endeavour to show that they are good economic subjects. If they represent themself as an incompetent buffoon who lost all their money gambling or on bad investments, then it will be hard for the legal authorities to have sympathy for them. The desired representation is of a good but imperfect moral and economic subject, and it is important to be able to point to one or more vices because these enable the debtor to disclaim these irrational behaviours and show change.

This is a purgatorial process where the debtor must openly display their suffering, and because some people are very uncomfortable with this, they never get to the stage where they can offer a confession. Some of my participants told me that there is a voyeuristic element to applying for debt relief, a sense that telling these financial professionals about their personal and private lives evinces a discomfort that is hard to articulate. The moral barrier to debt relief is and always has been greater than the bureaucratic barrier.

A political economy of obligations

We appear to be reaching a breaking point, as the rising tide of debt threatens to place more and more debtors into functional peonage to their creditors (Lazzarato 2012). Younger debtors are assuming more debt than their parents did (adjusting for inflation); as they age, this will begin to cause more problems, both for them personally and for society as a whole (Pettifor 2017; Adkins et al 2020). They will struggle to engage with the consumer economy as a large portion of their incomes is spent to service their outstanding debts, and yet the stagnation of incomes may preclude them from ever catching up, trapping them in an endless cycle of revolving debt.

Creating new growth after the crises of the 1970s was a challenge, but was eventually assured by the financialization of the economy and, more specifically, of housing (Adkins et al 2020). At this point, assets inflate, but remain relatively accessible (at least at first), leading to a renewed social contract and social stability. As we now know (and some knew at the time), this financialized asset economy required indefinite growth in housing prices for the system of revolving debt to be stable. The GFC of 2008 and the subsequent eviction of tens of thousands of subprime borrowers is proof that the situation could not last. It should be noted that the original problem of a stagnating economy was not actually solved; the symptom of the stagnation (expensive union jobs in declining industries) was moved elsewhere, but the underlying problem of how to create 3 per cent growth forever has yet to be resolved (Harvey 2017).

The contemporary landscape of our political economy is now plagued by debt. The withdrawal of the state, stagnation of wages, inflation of assets, and financialization of even the most basic of public services have led to a corresponding increase in debt. The scope and impact of these changes is grand, and we are only now beginning to see its full extent. Those in the younger generations find that their limited prospects lead to correspondingly limited incomes, meaning their capacity to buy property has been frustrated. Inflation and rising rents has driven many back into parental homes (assuming that they can count on such support), even in countries where there is no cultural tradition of such behaviour (Hearne 2017). Some commentary has suggested that the young are at a disadvantage, but will profit eventually by inheriting the property of their parents, who bought before asset inflation grew out of control. I am inclined not to believe such proclamations, primarily because as their parents age, they will likely spend an inordinate amount of money on medical bills and end-of-life care (Debt Collective 2020). If they have a pension, it will likely be exhausted, and then their only option to live with dignity in retirement will be debt leveraged against their assets, which could easily result in the property being repossessed after their death (if they have not sold it already). We borrow for health, for retirement, for rent, for food, for education, and for transport, which would formerly have been provided by (or subsidised by) the state (Langley 2009). We are entrepreneurs of our selves, always improving and optimizing. What else can we do other than borrow and hope for things to change?

Economic theology

What can an economic theology of indebtedness contribute? This is not an exercise in critical sociology, seeking to unveil the 'truth' about the world to the reader, that there is a singular secret explanation which will explain the origins of all things (Boland and Griffin 2021). Rather, economic theology aims to acknowledge the religious and theological influences that impact on the world around us, recognizing that the world is incompletely secularized and that we are bound to our historical traditions (Schwarzkopf 2020). Weber has much to say about this, through his ambivalence about the onset of the iron cage of bureaucracy, ironically brought about by religious innovators who were spurred on to create more specialized and rationalized systems (Boland and Griffin 2020; Palaver 2020). Once such a transformation had taken place, he was concerned that we would lose touch with the religious roots that had made such innovations possible. He may have been correct about that, and yet even if people do not know a full history of debt, they know it is more than a mere economic transaction.

At the most basic level, when we take on a debt, we provide the lender with our promise to repay; if we fail to make good on our promise, we interpolate that we ought to feel guilty. Much of the thinking on the relationship between debt and guilt comes to us from Nietzsche (2014), who was interested in how the Christian conceptualization of guilt had become (within a Western context) almost universalized. To be guilty is to owe something to someone. When a prisoner's sentence ends, we say that they have paid their debt to society; the offence they have caused is forgiven because they have been punished by serving their time. For Nietzsche, guilt is established early on, as parents instil guilt in their children, creating a sense of owing and obligation that will ensure that the children will take care of their parents as they age and become vulnerable. This is then transformed into a general social sense where punishments for breaking laws or social customs are justified because of guilt (Sløk 2020).

When you steal, you do not just damage the person you have stolen from, but in a sense you have also transgressed against society — this makes you guilty and so you must be punished. The emergence of Christianity universalizes guilt by entrapping all humans in a relationship of guilt through the theological device of original sin (Nietzsche 2014). Humans are born in sin, and it is the sacrifice of Jesus Christ that has paid for these sins and has given us a chance of redemption and salvation. The death of Jesus is a payment of sorts to the Devil for the immortal souls of all humanity. Living in a heavily Christianized culture has imbued our social relations with the theological, and in this way the guilt of sin has been applied to the guilt of debt.

Lazzarato (2012) has argued that guilt has been made universal through the creditor–debtor relationship, which has even replaced former Marxian relations of primacy, namely the bourgeoisie–proletariat dyad. Indeed, in reflecting on the financial crisis, an Irish minister used the phrase 'we all partied' to justify the brutal regime of austerity which followed the crash (Coulter and Nagle 2015). In other words, we all sinned by consuming excessively and now it is time for our well-deserved punishment. We are guilty not only as individuals, but also as a society, and so as a society we must perform our penance. The fact that the wealthy partied much more than everyone else is not under consideration because it is a shared burden.

The language of debt is imbued with the language of guilt, either literally or metaphorically. Nietzsche (2014) observed that the German word for guilt ('Schuld') is an etymological root of the word for debts ('Schulden'), while in English our word 'debt' has come to us transitively from the Latin 'Dēbitum', meaning 'owe', 'what is owed', or 'duty' (Lazzarato 2012, 2014). As others have pointed out, the word 'credit' means trust, faith, and/or belief, and of course is also related to the word 'credibility' (Graeber 2011; Lazzarato 2012). To acquire credit means that you are seen as credible by the lender and therefore likely to make your repayments. Attempts to mathematicize credibility through the financial instrument of credit reports has had limited success, and many lenders continue to use in-person meetings as a way to evaluate the credibility of a debtor for large loans (Zelizer 1994; Rock 2014; Wilkis 2018). Debt therefore operates alongside a host of related moral and affective concepts, such as honour, reliability, dependability, trustworthiness, sin, guilt, and shame. As in Howard Garfinkel's breaching experiments, we most easily observe these norms and discourses in the more extreme cases where they are broken. Discourses about indebtedness emerge most strongly in cases of 'bad' debtors who have not paid their debts. In this respect we can also demarcate between those who can't pay, and those who won't pay (Debt Collective 2020). Those in the former category may be seen in a sympathetic light, but those in the latter category who are capable of paying yet choose not to are the subject of derision, or even hatred. Davies et al (2015) have proposed the term 'financial melancholia' to capture the affects created by indebtedness in the contemporary world. Unsurprisingly, guilt, shame, and anxiety feature prominently in this discussion.

Historically, this has given creditors a considerable edge in their relations with debtors. While creditors are rarely seen in a positive light, it is generally debtors who are seen as guilty and in need of accountability and scorn. However, in the recent past we have begun to see the emergence of social movements around debt, such as Strike Debt, which buys bad debts and then forgives them (Debt Collective 2020). This has also extended into debtors creating no-pay campaigns where they decide not to pay as a group, believing that their numbers provide an advantage, since creditors can create huge problems for individual debtors. Yet this becomes increasingly problematic as the number of bad debtors increases. Eventually it could threaten the stability of the entire credit system.

Making sacrifices

Indeed, something which ensures stability is precisely the fact that some debtors who are (or who are at least perceived to be) bad actors are sacrificed (Girard 1965, 1987, 1989, 2013). From the perspective of debtors, it is important that justice is served, especially for those who have sought help and been rejected. The 'bad' debtor becomes a scapegoat of sorts, and any treatment they receive is considered justifiable as long as the debtor's conceptualization of justice is satisfied. A bad debtor is generally one who goes years or even decades without paying, and this is seen to be completely unacceptable. In Chapter 7 this was explored from a Girardian standpoint that debtors are in a mimetic rivalry with one another over their mutual desire to possess property. This leads to suspicion and gossip as the mutual desire transforms first into rivalry and then into hostility. In the Girardian conception, such hostility must be 'released' by a safety valve – a scapegoat must be identified and then sacrificed, which restores a sense of equilibrium to social relations.

The temporalities of indebtedness are also important for a full understanding of the subjectivities created by borrowing. As soon as it is taken on, a debt exists simultaneously in the past, present, and future, and can destroy our ability to even imagine the future because debt drags the future into the present. You must repay the debt in the future, but the only way to make this actionable is by making changes to your behaviours, attitudes, and spending habits in the present. This can risk creating an affective sense that you are perpetually waiting to live your life and, indeed, studies on the subject have revealed this with debtors fantasizing about the 'debt-free day' and characterizing their efforts to become debtless as a journey or quest (Montgomerie 2016; Stanley et al 2016; Boland and Griffin 2020).

Delaying gratification is framed as virtuous and these debtors even enter into contests of a sort where they attempt to spend as little money as possible on a daily basis. This engenders a lifestyle politics of denial and asceticism where debtors are perpetually searching for new ways to cut costs and save money. Every opportunity to spend is simultaneously an opportunity to save. What is remarkable is that these debtors will follow all conventional financial advice, and they are still broke. They grind their own coffee, make their own lunch, buy food at a discount, put a jumper on rather than using their central heating, and so on. Debt is a relation that creates responsible, reflexive, and guilty subjects who exist in an eternal state of apology for their perceived wrongdoing (Karlsen and Villadsen 2020).

Nietzsche (2014) contends that guilt and punishment do not originate in any true sense based on moral transgression or the demarcation between right and wrong. Rather, these emerge from the ancient relationship between creditors and debtors, with punishment emerging as a response to the nonpayment by a debtor. This was not out of any abstract ideal of justice or restitution, but was rather more savage; creditors often accepted that they could not secure their money, so as an alternative, they settled for punishing the debtor. In contrast to our present morality, creditors delighted in their punishments of debtors, and such punishments were seen as a sort of equivalent of the amount owed. A debtor may pay with their flesh, with their wife, with their life, and the ancient Egyptians even permitted the creditor to desecrate the corpse of the debtor, an especially pertinent act in a society so concerned with the afterlife; indeed, many of the societies of antiquity revelled in cruelty and sacrifice.

The limits of transferability

It is important to consider the limitations of research, as no study no matter how grand in scope can possibly apply everywhere. This book is based on a small qualitative ethnographic study conducted in Ireland, and so its results are not generalizable to other statistical contexts. However, in qualitative research it is common to discuss transferability of theory – in other words, that the theoretical framework could be transferable to other countries and settings. Throughout this book I have made frequent comparisons to LMEs that have similar insolvency systems and debt profiles, particularly the UK and the US. In Chapter 5, when I discussed the meeting between insolvency practitioner and debtor, I made the observation that this consultation looks and feels very much like a confession rather than a heavily bureaucratised rule-based meeting with an agenda. I would be willing to bet that similar theoretical patterns emerge in debt relationships in the UK and the US.

This is because concealed within modern debt relief legislation is the requirement to convince a gatekeeper that you are trustworthy, apologetic, and willing to make change, which introduces ambiguity and bias into decision making (Ramsay 2017). This gatekeeper looks a little different in each setting and could be a judge, a lawyer, an insolvency practitioner, and so on. In the US the sheer bureaucratic complexity means that borrowers need a lawyer to help them get through the process, but many lawyers steer borrowers into more expensive programmes (Spooner 2019). Beyond LMEs and the Anglosphere the models of debt relief can be entirely different, and so I make no claims that these findings are transferable to, for example, the French or German settings where things can work quite differently (Heuer 2014; Ramsay 2017).

What is to be done?

This book is a commentary on individual and private struggles, and explores fundamental sociological questions around how agents are created by social structures. However, as observed by C. Wright Mills, personal troubles are often a reflection of public issues, and debt relief on a mass or public scale is a question of growing importance, so I will devote some space here to comment on it. If the theoretical framework I have advanced in this book is correct, then we can assume several things. From the outset, the obstacles to mass debt relief will be significant precisely because it does not rely on individual methods of evaluation. The decision to individualize debt relief rather than pursue a programme of debt abolition in the 20th century was deliberate and ties us to a time-consuming process of evaluating each applicant separately. Next, the greatest obstacle will be moral rather than bureaucratic or procedural; there are no serious opponents to debt relief who suggest that it is literally impossible to do from a legislative standpoint. Instead, they say it is wrong, that it creates a bad precedent, that it is unfair to those who have already repaid, and so on.

The most logical approach is therefore predicated on understanding that the opponents of debt relief will always be against it and always for the same reasons. They will oppose the cancellation of the smallest amount of debt with the same verve that they would for all of it, because the cancellation of any debt will create a precedent, which will lead to future debtors asking for the same treatment. This is what many activists have failed to understand when they are baffled by the rejection of even the most modest demands regarding debt cancellation. The fact that there are historical-theological precedents for debt cancellation means little to lenders today, who have worked for thousands of years to disentangle usury from its theological origins.

The solution is to advocate not for the cancellation of existing debts, but rather for the abolition of those debts which are the most morally defensible. Those who advocate for the abolition of all debts are doomed to fail, not only because our society is so wrapped up in debt that we cannot imagine an alternative way of doing things, but also because each type of debt is perceived to be morally different. Cancelling a payday loan may be seen as a good and virtuous thing, while cancelling a mortgage essentially gives someone a house for free. As this book closes, we will consider the two broad options open to us: a jubilee (mass cancellation of debt) or a reform of the insolvency system as I have described it.

A new jubilee

We live in tumultuous times. The austere aftermath of 2008 featured a brutal foreclosure crisis where subprime borrowers were evicted en masse

(McClanahan 2018) and consumer debt loads decreased – at least for a time. That trend has ended: assets continue to inflate (Adkins et al 2020) and in some cases have even eclipsed the previous high of the last boom. Borrowing for survival is on the rise (Soederberg 2014) and repeated crises (energy costs, a global pandemic, and rent costs) are driving debt up and up. The hardships brought about by these renewed larger debt loads have invigorated dialogues about debt relief and even the possibility of mass debt cancellation through a new jubilee (Montgomerie 2019; Debt Collective 2020). David Graeber noted in his book *Debt: The First 5,000 Years* that the great public conversation we had all been expecting after the financial crisis never actually happened (Graeber 2011, p 15). I believe this conversation is taking place now.

Dialogues around debt cancellation, mass debt relief, or even debt abolition have grown in strength over the past decade and are now the subject of surprisingly resilient social movements. Most notably, this includes the Strike Debt movement, an offshoot of Occupy Wall Street that buys the longstanding debts of delinquent debtors and then forgives them (Debt Collective 2020). This has been a source of untold relief for many thousands of people, with those in the direst of situations having had their debt sold down the chain to increasingly hostile debt collectors who are not afraid to use doorstepping and other threatening actions to get what they want (Soederberg 2014; Debt Collective 2020).

During the COVID-19 pandemic, one of the most impactful decisions was the pausing of student loan payments in the US, which eased the hardship of younger people much more than the comparatively tiny one-off pandemic payments. This pause has now expired, and payments resumed as of October 2023 (Haverstock 2023). The results of this will be disastrous during a cost-of-living crisis where energy prices are increasing anywhere from 10 to 20 per cent (Ogletree and Whatley 2023). These judgements are always refracted through a moral lens. The movement around student loan cancellation in the US is strong precisely because there is widespread belief that the debt is illegitimate. This is rooted in conversations around the neoliberal privatization and commodification of education, and a wish to recapture education as a critical institution of enlightenment over a job training academy where students are advised to calculate the likely returns on their degree (Zaloom 2021). On its own terms, the system is perfectly rational: if you must pay a small fortune to graduate, then it is reasonable to consider what you will gain by spending such a vast sum of money. Yet this overlooks the fact that education should not cost money to begin with, and obscures the vast inequalities and exclusions that have been created by this system.

The obstacles to a new jubilee are very strong. Even modest proposals produce scathing criticism that morality will wither and die if a single cent of debt is cancelled. I have often found it intriguing that debt relief is perceived to be hideous and evil in the abstract, but becomes more acceptable as we add context. The recent struggle over student loan forgiveness in the US is an interesting case study in this respect. A 2023 Ipsos poll found that only 29 per cent of Americans support forgiving all student loan debt regardless of income. However, this number increases to 39 per cent when respondents were asked if they would forgive debt for people earning under $125,000 a year, and further increases to 47 per cent when forgiveness is limited to $20,000 of those with Pell Grants (federal loan subsidies for low-income students). Those with student debt generally support forgiveness twice as much as the average person, as we might expect. The rise of indebtedness created by neoliberalism is simultaneously the creation of the conditions necessary for mass debt cancellation. By creating so many guilty debtors, there is more knowledge and empathy for the problems faced by debtors than ever before, which can be leveraged to create social change.

The discourse of fairness has a hold on our collective imaginations, and government cannot even proceed without considering it. Rather than simply cancelling the debt for all eligible debtors, US President Biden's Department of Education means-tested the cancellation, at a cost of almost $100 million (White House 2022). To spend $100 million just on means-testing should seem absurd, and yet it was done to exclude 'wealthy' borrowers from relief. This obsession with technocracy and bureaucracy is part of our governance and administration procedures, but has become irrational (Debt Collective 2020). The opponents of debt relief will not be satisfied that a means-testing process was implemented; they reject the very relations as illegitimate. Some people cannot be brought over to your side and convinced with reason and dialogue, they are simply your adversaries, and you should oppose them with the same energy with which they oppose you.

Reforming insolvency: from debtfare to welfare

A new debt jubilee would be a positive step forward; however, the obstacles to mass debt cancellation or abolition are significant. I believe that while we should advocate for a new jubilee, we must also advocate for reforms of the prevailing systems of insolvency (including bankruptcy). The first and perhaps most important shift is that insolvency must be seen as a form of welfare protection and as disconnected from its stigmatizing roots. Our culture has, in essence, gradually destigmatized indebtedness, but has failed to do the same for debt relief. Debt is the new normal: it is expected, people use it to pay bills or go to college, and the old inclination to borrow only for luxuries is long gone. This means that many of the excluded forms of debt must be included if reform is to be meaningful. Much suffering would be averted if Americans could discharge student loans in bankruptcy. This would achieve many of the aims of the jubilee by stealth.

I generally support relief from any debt arising from monies lent rather than, for example, fines which build up on unpaid taxes or child support. Further, debt relief must shift its perspective and become exclusively about the discharge of debt rather than a technique for creditors to strip the last remaining assets from the debtor (Spooner 2019). Some assets could be sold to service a debt in this scheme, but it should be reasonable rather than retributive. The current system bankrupts people, strips them of their assets, and then leaves them bereft and rudderless, creating the conditions for repeat bankrupts (Foohey et al 2018) – the very thing the stigma is supposed to discourage. As I have argued throughout this book, people run into difficulty because of reasons that are entirely understandable and recognizable to us. Divorce, ill health, accidents, cost of living increases, unemployment – these things must be taken into consideration when a person is bankrupted and we consider what assets they should be left with at the end. Taking a car from someone in the process seems likely to cause repeat bankruptcy as the person will struggle to get to work; on the other hand, if the person has five cars, it makes more sense to take one or more.

Susanne Soederberg (2014) made a distinction between soft and hard laws in her book on *Debtfare*. Creditors generally enjoy the protections of hard law, meaning that there are strict and unambiguous legal practices which enable them to strip assets from the debtor in their quest to get what is owed to them. They can seek restitution in court and can impose real material consequences on the borrower. Debtors, by contrast, can only expect the protections of soft law. Governments hand down frameworks, guidelines, or best-practice documents on how the creditor should interact with the debtor. Signing up to these is usually optional for the creditor, but even if it is not, enforcement is so loose that the borrower essentially has to rely on the goodwill of their lender. The Code of Conduct on Mortgage Arrears and the Mortgage Arrears Resolution Process are examples of this in Ireland.

This dichotomy even taints insolvency practice. Debtors must convince their insolvency practitioner (a total stranger) of their sincerity and legitimacy, where every decision they have ever made is put under the microscope and subjected to harsh judgement. Even if they succeed, creditors can simply look at the proposed insolvency arrangement and vote 'no', which stops the arrangement dead in its tracks. Debtors can appeal to the courts for an independent assessment, but few take this step, and I echo Spooner (2019), who found that debtors are loath to challenge a decision, even if they believe that the decision is illegal or wrong.

If nothing else moves, this is one element of the contemporary process that must change: debtors need the protections of hard law. Not agreements, frameworks, charters, or codes of conduct, but real material legal protections which are equivalent to those enjoyed by creditors. Having hard legal protections means that insolvency applications must skip the first step, bypassing insolvency practitioners and going directly to the courts. Indeed, Ramsay (2017) and Spooner (2019) have lauded this aspect of the US system, which places decision making and repayment programme design in the hands of judges. Judges are less susceptible to influence than the UK and Irish models, which has essentially privatized the delivery of insolvency protection by delegating authority to legal professionals who are incentivized to establish pre-existing arrangements with creditors to gain any chance of success. The debtor likely has no idea that the framework of their insolvency application has been mapped out before they have ever stepped through the door of the practitioner's office, and they have no data to make comparisons, so they often simply trust that the practitioner has their best interests at heart. This is not to say that the US system is perfect: the 2005 reform represents a huge step backwards (Ramsay 2017; Spooner 2019), particularly its greater complexity, additional paperwork, and its requirement to take two mandatory financial literacy classes regardless of personal circumstances.

I agree with Spooner (2019), who has persuasively argued that we need a single-portal application system rather than the current setup which discourages applicants due to its complexity. This was one of the biggest obstacles my participants related to me as they attempted to get started: how is a debt relief order different from a debt settlement agreement from a personal insolvency arrangement from bankruptcy? Choice paralysis is not helped by the sheer volume of legal jargon and acronyms, which is why under the current system, the insolvency practitioner plays the crucial role of explaining the language to the debtor. Applications should take the form of something similar to the current prescribed financial statement – you list your assets, debts, and the efforts you have made to pay – and anyone experiencing serious hardship for more than two years (a long struggler) should be seen immediately (Foohey et al 2018).

Financial literacy is another element of the process that must change, as it usually amounts to nothing more than a legalized humiliation ritual. It should be offered on an optional basis to those who want it, and classes should be designed to teach meaningful skills rather than to talk down to the applicant. They are already being bankrupted and hardly need another institution to punch down at them. Perhaps an acceptable compromise would be for the judge overseeing the case to determine if the applicant needs financial counselling. This, of course, would introduce another confessional element into the equation where the debtor would have to advocate for themselves. However, the belief in financial literacy among hegemonic actors is very strong, so I see few futures where it does not exist in some form.

My next point is a simple one: programmes must be shorter. In Ireland a PIA can last up to six years, with the possibility of a one-year extension. The life expectancy of an Irish person is now 82 years, meaning that you could spend 8 per cent of your total time alive in an insolvency arrangement on a strict budget, and even then you may fail your programme and lose your house anyway. Bankruptcy restrictions should last no more than a year and insolvency no more than three years. Part of the requirement to join an insolvency programme is that there is no foreseeable return to solvency within the next five years; it is irrational, bordering on obscene, to force people to remain impoverished all this time. It teaches a lesson that insolvency is a form of retribution, feeding the purgatorial logic of Chapters 4 and 7 that debtors deserve to be punished.

Some may suggest that these changes are unlikely or impossible, but I believe that indications of hope lie in the lessons learned from the COVID-19 pandemic, where many impossible things were done. Ireland offered the Pandemic Unemployment Payment to those who were displaced from work by lockdowns. This took the form of a €350 per week welfare payment which featured a one-page application and incredibly light means-testing. It was delivered at a much lower cost than expected and gave Ireland a temporary form of a universal basic income, in defiance of the active labour market policies that have characterized all Irish welfare reforms for the last decade. In the US, student loans were paused, giving many borrowers breathing space and dramatically improving their wellbeing and mental health. Foreclosure and eviction bans across a variety of countries ensured that the over-indebted could remain in their homes, slowing down homelessness, which has been steadily rising in LMEs for a decade or more (Hearne 2022). The changes I have suggested are not only possible, they are also necessary, and by comparison to the jubilee will deliver less of a system shock to our overly financialized economy.

One purported consequence of greater debt relief (either through a jubilee or a reform of bankruptcy) is that it would undermine morality and teach young people that it is acceptable to borrow money and then not pay it back. These moral hazard arguments are exhausting by their frequency and lack of logic, because surely it is the lender who evidences moral hazard. US banks lend large amounts of money to young people with no proven employment or credit history, at high rates of interest, which cannot be discharged in bankruptcy. They then price this into their future lending strategies and have an infinitely replenishing supply of new entrants into the system which keeps it stable regardless of the harm done to those who have come before. Enabling the discharge of all kinds of debt in bankruptcy would encourage lenders to be more responsible.

Yet the greatest success in this vein will always be found by taking a stance of generosity and forgiveness. It is better to espouse the virtue of forgiveness and clemency than it is to attack creditors, as the people who must be convinced are the public and politicians. We should not deny that the money is owed, or that a contract was signed, but rather should follow the moral logic to its conclusion and shift the conversation away from bureaucracy and towards fairness, equity, and justice. With the prevailing socioeconomic and sociomedical crises (Brexit, inflation, cost of living, war, a pandemic) hammering us alongside wage stagnation, the question is not can we afford to forgive debts, but rather can we afford not to?

Notes

Chapter 1
[1] Biological metaphors have often been repeated in sociological research, such as the idea that humans are cells relative to the overall body of society (Levine 1995).

Chapter 3
[1] The most rigorous piece of research in this regard is a 2013 survey/study conducted by Civic Consulting on behalf of the European Union (EU). It is a wide-ranging survey featuring the incorporation of data from other EU research work, such as the Survey on Income and Living Conditions (SILC), with individual authors from each EU Member State writing a report on their country's conditions along with a general commentary. The results show conclusively that macroeconomic crises, rises in the cost of living, and the type of debt taken on are better predictors of debt crisis than individual financial literacy and decision making. The usual methodological problems inherent in such research apply, such as establishing comparability between countries because questions are asked in the local language, which inevitably brings about some loss of specificity. Nevertheless, it remains a hugely comprehensive piece of work.

Bibliography

Adam, S. and Monaghan, R. (2014) 'Fuel poverty: what it means for young parents and their families', available at: https://www.ncb.org.uk/sites/default/files/uploads/documents/ncb_fuel_poverty_report.pdf [accessed 3 December 2016].

Adams, G. (2022) 'Mortgage repayment worries growing: MetLife', available at: https://www.mortgagestrategy.co.uk/news/mortgage-repayment-worries-growing-metlife/ [accessed 28 November 2022].

Adams, R. (2000) 'Loving mimesis and Girard's "scapegoat of the text": a creative reassessment of mimetic desire', in W. Swartley (ed.), *Violence Renounced: Rene Girard, Biblical Studies and Peacemaking*, New York: Pandora Press, pp 30–54.

Adkins, L. (2020) 'Debt, complexity and the sociological imagination', in M. Featherstone (ed.), *The Sociology of Debt*, Bristol: Policy Press, pp 27–48.

Adkins, L., Cooper, M., and Konings, M. (2020) *The Asset Economy*, Cambridge: Polity Press.

Allen, K. (2015) 'Interpretations of the Irish economic crash', in C. Coulter and A. Nagle (eds), *Ireland under Austerity: Neoliberal Crisis, Neoliberal Solutions*, Manchester: Manchester University Press, pp 66–85.

Allon, F. (2015) 'Everyday leverage, or leveraging the everyday', *Cultural Studies*, 29(5–6), 687–706, available at: http://www.tandfonline.com/doi/full/10.1080/09502386.2015.1017140 [accessed 4 August 2018].

ANZ (2022) *COVID-19 Home Loan Deferral Scheme Ends*, available at: https://news.anz.com/new-zealand/posts/2021/03/home-loan-deferral-scheme-ends#:~:text=On%2031%20March%20the%20Government's,of%20defaulting%20on%20their%20loans [accessed 20 February 2022].

Arnold, M. (2023) 'ECB dove says inflation battle can be won without more interest rate rises', *Financial Times*, 3 August, available at: https://www.ft.com/content/f361bc7c-35ee-497c-b59b-f0f5329a9132 [accessed 8 October 2023].

Arrese, Á. and Vara-Miguel, A. (2015) 'A comparative study of metaphors in press reporting of the Euro crisis', *Discourse & Society*, 27(2), 133–155. doi: 10.1177/0957926515611552.

Atfield, G. and Orton, M. (2013) *The Long-Term Impact of Debt Advice on Low Income Households: Year 3 Report*, Warwick: Warwick Institute for Employment Research.

Atfield, G., Lindley, R., and Orton, M. (2016) *Living with Debt after Advice: A Longitudinal Study of People on Low Incomes*, Warwick: Warwick Institute for Employment Research.

Attree, P. (2005) 'Low-income mothers, nutrition and health: a systematic review of qualitative evidence', *Maternal and Child Nutrition*, 1(4), 227–240.

Atwood, M. (2012) *Payback: Debt and the Shadow Side of Wealth*, London: Bloomsbury.

Babb, S. (2005) 'The social consequences of structural adjustment: recent evidence and current debates', *Annual Review of Sociology*, 31(1), 199–222, available at: http://www.annualreviews.org/doi/10.1146/annurev.soc.31.041304.122258 [accessed 19 October 2017].

Bagwell, L.S. and Bernheim, D.B. (1996) 'Veblen effects in a theory of conspicuous consumption', *American Economic Review*, 86(3), 349–373, available at: http://www.jstor.org/stable/2118201 [accessed 12 November 2022].

Balcerowicz, L., Rzonca, A., Kalina, L., and Laszek A. (2013) *Economic Growth in the European Union*, Lisbon Council, available at: https://lisboncouncil.net/growth/documents/LISBON_COUNCIL_Economic_Growth_in_the_EU%20(1).pdf [accessed 22 January 2016].

Bauman, Z. (2000) *Liquid Modernity*, New York: Polity Press.

Bell, D.M. (2020) 'Justification and Salvation', in S. Schwarzkopf (ed.), *The Routledge Handbook of Economic Theology*, Abingdon: Routledge, pp 64–72.

Benefits.gov (2022) *What Is Hope for Homeowners?*, available at: https://www.benefits.gov/benefit/4589#:~:text=What%20is%20Hope%20for%20Homeowners,mortgage%20that%20you%20can%20afford [accessed 14 March 2022].

Ben-Galim, D. and Lanning, T. (2010) *Strength against the Shocks: Low Income Families and Debt*, London: Institute for Public Policy Research.

Bergeron, K. (2016) 'Tricks to win the fight against debt', *Quicken + Simplifi Blog*, 2 June, available at: https://www.quicken.com/blog/tricks-win-fight-against-debt/ [accessed 8 October 2023].

Berlant, L. (2006) 'Cruel optimism', *Differences: A Journal of Feminist Studies*, 17(3), 20–36. doi: 10.1215/10407391-2006-009.

Berlant, L. (2011). *Cruel Optimism*, Durham, NC: Duke University Press.

Bivens, J. and Mishel, L. (2015) *Understanding the Historic Divergence between Productivity and a Typical Worker's Pay: Why It Matters and Why It's Real*, New York: Economic Policy Institute, available at: https://www.epi.org/publication/understanding-the-historic-divergence-between-productivity-and-a-typical-workers-pay-why-it-matters-and-why-its-real/ [accessed 12 June 2017].

Blackwell, N. (2012) ' It's not enough to help people in debt. We must look at the big picture', *The Journal*, 16 March, available at: http://www.thejournal.ie/readme/columnit% E2%80%99s-not-enough-to-help-people-in-debt-we-must-look-at-the-big-picture-385637-Mar2012/ [accessed November 2015].

Boland, T. and Griffin, R. (2015) *The Sociology of Unemployment*, Manchester: Manchester University Press.

Boland, T. and Griffin, R. (2018) 'The purgatorial ethic and the spirit of welfare', *Journal of Classical Sociology*, 18(2), available at: http://journals.sagepub.com/doi/abs/10.1177/1468795X17722079 [accessed 22 August 2018].

Boland, T., and Griffin, R. (2020) 'Purgatory', in S. Schwarzkopf (ed.), *The Routledge Handbook of Economic Theology*, Abingdon: Routledge, pp 47–55.

Boland, T. and Griffin, R. (2021) *The Reformation of Welfare: The New Faith of the Labour Market*, Bristol: Bristol University Press.

Bourdieu, P. (2010) *Distinction: A Social Critique of the Judgement of Taste*, London: Taylor & Francis.

Bourguignon, F. and Scott-Railton, T. (2015). *The Globalization of Inequality*, Princeton: Princeton University Press.

Bowles, J., Lawler, A., and Peigin, D. (2000) *Getting to the Source: Poverty in Ireland*, Dublin: Combat Poverty Agency.

Bramall, R. (2016a) 'Introduction: The Future of Austerity', *New Formations*, 87, 1–10. doi: 10.3898/NEWF.87.INTRODUCTION.2016.

Bramall, R. (2016b) 'Tax justice in austerity: logics, residues and attachments', *New Formations*, 87, 29–46. doi: 10.3898/NEWF.87.2.2016.

Bramall, R., Gilbert, J., and Meadway, J. (2016) 'What is austerity?', *New Formations*, 87, 119–140. doi: 10.3898/NEWF.87.7.2016.

Braucher, J., Cohen, D., and Lawless, R. M. (2012) 'Race, attorney influence, and bankruptcy chapter choice', *Journal of Empirical Legal Studies*, 9(3), 393–429, available at: https://onlinelibrary.wiley.com/doi/abs/10.1111/j.1740-1461.2012.01264.x.

Braverman, R., Holkar, M., and Evans, K. (2018) *Informal Borrowing and Mental Health Problems*, Money and Mental Health Policy Institute, available at: https://www.moneyandmentalhealth.org/wp-content/uploads/2018/05/Money-and-Mental-Health-Informal-borrowing-report.pdf [accessed 1 September 2018].

Breaking News (2018) 'Irish mortgage holders pay highest interest rates in the Eurozone, new figures show', *Breaking News*, 13 July, available at: https://www.breakingnews.ie/business/irish-mortgage-holders-pay-highest-interest-rates-in-the-eurozone-new-figures-show-855074.html [accessed 20 August 2018].

Brennan, C. (2015) 'It's costing banks €100,000 a go to reject insolvency applications…', *The Journal,* 14 April, available at: http://www.thejournal.ie/banks-insolvency-rejection-2047578-Apr2015/ [accessed 5 January 2016].

Brennan, J. and Bardon, S. (2018) 'Insolvency service investigated 300 cases of suspected hidden assets in 2017', *Irish Times,* 5 July, available at: https://www.irishtimes.com/business/financial-services/insolvency-service-investigated-300-cases-of-suspected-hidden-assets-in-2017-1.3554212?mode=sample&auth-failed=1&pw-origin=https%3A%2F%2Fwww.irishtimes.com%2Fbusiness%2Ffinancial-services%2Finsolvency-service-investigated-300-cases-of-suspected-hidden-assets-in-2017-1.3554212 [accessed 22 July 2017].

Broadsheet (2017) 'Judgements in favour of vulture funds will explode in 2017', 10 January, available at: https://www.broadsheet.ie/2017/01/10/judgements-in-favour-of-vulture-funds-will-explode-in-2017/ [accessed 20 January 2017].

Brown, G.W. and Harris, T.O. (1978) *The Social Origins of Depression*, New York: Free Press.

Browne, V. (2011) 'Let's own up to our part in the burst bubble', *Irish Times*, 6 April, available at: https://www.irishtimes.com/opinion/let-s-own-up-to-our-part-in-the-burst-bubble-1.564844?mode=sample&auth-failed=1&pw-origin=https%3A%2F%2Fwww.irishtimes.com%2Fopinion%2Flet-s-own-up-to-our-part-in-the-burst-bubble-1.564844%3Fvia%3Dmr [accessed 1 May 2016].

Brubaker, R., Lawless, R.M., and Tabb, C.J. (2012) *A Debtor World: Interdisciplinary Perspectives on Debt*, Oxford: Oxford Scholarship Online.

Bryman, A. (2004) *Social Research Methods*, 2nd edn, Oxford: Oxford University Press.

Bullock, M. (2018) 'Household debt and mortgage stress' [speech], 20 February, Sydney, Australia, available at: https://www.bis.org/review/r180226e.pdf [accessed 20 March 2018].

Burchell, G., Gordon, C., and Miller, P. (eds) (1991) *The Foucault Effect: Studies in Government*, Chicago: University of Chicago Press.

The Business Post (2013) 'Insolvency service to pursue strategic defaulters, says chief', 14 May, available at: https://www.businesspost.ie/legacy/insolvency-service-to-pursue-strategic-defaulters-says-chief-195214 [accessed 22 February 2016].

Byrne, D. (1999) *Social Exclusion*, Buckingham: Open University Press.

Byrne, M. and Norris, M. (2017) 'Pro-cyclical social housing and the crisis of Irish housing policy: marketization, social housing and the property boom and bust', *Housing Policy Debate*, 28(1), 50–63, available at: https://www.tandfonline.com/doi/abs/10.1080/10511482.2016.1257999 [accessed 23 November 2018].

Caju, P.D., Rycx, F., and Tojerow, I. (2016) 'Unemployment risk and over-indebtedness: a micro-economic perspective', European Central Bank Working Paper No. 1908, available at: https://www.ecb.europa.eu/pub/pdf/scpwps/ecbwp1908.en.pdf [accessed 2 March 2017].

Caporaso, J.A. and Madeira, M.A. (2011) *Globalization, Institutions and Governance*, London: Sage.

Carcasson, M. (2006) 'Ending welfare as we know it: President Clinton and the rhetorical transformation of the anti-welfare culture', *Rhetoric and Public Affairs*, 9(4), 655–692, available at: https://www.jstor.org/stable/41940106?seq=1#page_scan_tab_contents [accessed 29 August 2016].

Carr, J. (2015). *Experiences of Islamophobia: Living with Racism in the Neoliberal Era*, Abingdon: Routledge.

Carruthers, B.G. and Kim, J.-G. (2011) 'The sociology of finance', *Annual Review of Sociology*, 37(1), 239–259, available at: https://www.annualreviews.org/doi/abs/10.1146/annurev-soc-081309-150129 [accessed 3 April 2018].

Central Bank of Ireland (2012) *Residential Mortgage Arrears and Repossession Statistics: Q2 2012*.

Central Bank of Ireland (2016) *Residential Mortgage Arrears and Repossession Statistics: Q2 2016*, available at: https://www.centralbank.ie/polstats/stats/mortgagearrears/Documents/2016q2_ie_mortgage_arrears_statistics.pdf [accessed 2 August 2016].

Central Bank of Ireland (2017a) *Residential Mortgage Arrears and Repossessions Statistics: Q1 2017*, Dublin, Central Bank of Ireland, available at: https://www.centralbank.ie/docs/default-source/statistics/data-and-analysis/credit-and-banking-statistics/mortgage-arrears/2017q1_ie_mortgage_arrears_statisticse2a9c5134644629bacc1ff0000269695.pdf?sfvrsn=8 [accessed 12 June 2017].

Central Bank of Ireland (2017b) 'Research on non-performing loans in the Irish mortgage market [press release], 6 December, available at: https://www.centralbank.ie/news-media/press-releases/research-on-non-performing-loans-in-irish-mortgage-market-06-Dec-2017 [accessed 22 January 2018].

Central Bank of Ireland (2018) *Residential Mortgage Arrears and Repossessions Statistics: Q1 2018*, Dublin, Central Bank of Ireland, available at: https://www.centralbank.ie/docs/default-source/statistics/data-and-analysis/credit-and-banking-statistics/mortgage-arrears/2018q1_ie_mortgage_arrears_statistics.pdf?sfvrsn=11 [accessed 25 July 2018].

Central Bank of Ireland (2021) 'Forbearance during the COVID-19 crisis in 2021', available at: https://www.centralbank.ie/statistics/statistical-publications/behind-the-data/forbearance-during-the-covid-19-crisis-in-2021 [accessed 10 October 2023].

Central Bank of Ireland (2023) *Residential Mortgage Arrears & Repossession Statistics – Q1 2023*, available at: https://www.centralbank.ie/docs/default-source/statistics/data-and-analysis/credit-and-banking-statistics/mortgage-arrears/2023q1_ie_mortgage_arrears_statistics.pdf?sfvrsn=d9dd9e1d_3 [accessed 10 October 2023].

Central Statistics Office (2012) 'Survey on income and living conditions (2010)', available at: https://www.cso.ie/en/media/csoie/releasespublications/documents/silc/2011/silc_2011.pdf [accessed 25 April 2017].

Citizens Advice UK (2022) 'Schemes that can help if you can't pay your mortgage', available at: https://www.citizensadvice.org.uk/scotland/debt-and-money/mortgage-problems/how-to-sort-out-your-mortgage-problems-s/schemes-that-can-help-if-you-cant-pay-your-mortgage-s/ [accessed 15 March 2022].

Civic Consulting (2013) *The Over-indebtedness of European Households: Updated Mapping of the Situation, Nature and Causes, Effects and Initiatives for Alleviating Its Impact – Part 1: Synthesis of Findings*, Final Report, available at: http://www.ecri.eu/system/tdf/part_1_synthesis_of_findings_en.pdf?file=1&type=node&id=97&force=0 [accessed 15 March 2022].

Clarke, A.E. (2005) *Situational Analysis: Grounded Theory after the Postmodern Turn*, Thousand Oaks, CA: Sage.

Cohen, L. (2022) 'White House calls out Republicans who criticized student loan cancellation but had thousands in PPP loans forgiven', *CBS News*, 26 August, available at: https://www.cbsnews.com/news/white-house-republican-critics-student-loan-cancellation-ppp-loan-forgiveness/ [accessed 27 November 2022].

Coleman, R. (2016) 'Austerity futures: debt, temporality and (hopeful) pessimism', *New Formations*, 87, 83–101. doi: 10.3898/NEWF.87.5.2016.

Collins, J.M., Lam, K., and Herbert, C. (2008) 'State mortgage foreclosure policies and lender interventions: impacts on borrower behaviour in default', *Policy Analysis Management*, 30(2), 216–232, available at: https://www.jstor.org/stable/23018981?seq=1#page_scan_tab_contents [accessed 3 March 2017].

Collins, P.H. (1990) *Black Feminist Thought: Knowledge, Consciousness and the Politics of Empowerment*, Boston: Unwin Hyman.

Combat Poverty Agency (2009) *A Policy Framework for Addressing Over-indebtedness*, Dublin: Combat Poverty Agency.

Cook, F.L. (1979) *Who Should Be Helped? Public Support for Social Services*, Beverly Hills, CA: Sage.

Cooke, H. (2022) 'Pizza on buy now pay later raises debt concerns', *Financial Times*, 20 January, available at: https://www.ft.com/content/c4da9b2f-5187-4956-931d-0554d4268d4e [accessed 8 October 2023].

Cooper, M. (2010). *Who Really Runs Ireland? The Story of the Elite Who Led Ireland from Bust to Boom … and Back Again*, London: Penguin.

Copeland, C. (2015) 'Debt of the elderly and near elderly, 1992–2013', *Employee Benefit Research Institute*, 1(36), available at: https: https://papers.ssrn.com/sol3/papers.cfm?abstract_id=2222193 [accessed 15 December 2015].

Corbin, J. and Strauss, A. (2008) *Basics of Qualitative Research*, 3rd edn, London: Sage.

Corrigan, P.W., Watson, A.C., and Miller, F.E. (2006) 'The impact of mental illness and drug dependence stigma on family members', *Journal of Family Psychology*, 20(2), 239–246.

Coulter, C. (2015) 'Ireland under austerity: an introduction to the book', in C. Coulter and A. Nagle (eds), *Ireland under Austerity: Neoliberal Crisis, Neoliberal Solutions*, Manchester: Manchester University Press, pp 1–44.

Coulter, C. and Nagle, A. (eds) (2015). *Ireland under Austerity: Neoliberal Crisis, Neoliberal Solutions*, Manchester: Manchester University Press.

Crenshaw, K. (1989) 'Demarginalizing the intersection of race and sex: a Black feminist critique of antidiscrimination doctrine, feminist theory and antiracist politics', *University of Chicago Legal Forum*, 1(8), 139–167, available at: https://chicagounbound.uchicago.edu/cgi/viewcontent.cgi?article=1052&context=uclf [accessed 2 March 2018].

Creswell, J. (2007) *Qualitative Inquiry and Research Design: Choosing among Five Approaches*, London: Sage.

Creswell, J. (2012) *Qualitative Inquiry and Research Design: Choosing among Five Approaches*, 2nd edn, London: Sage.

Croffey, A. (2013) 'PIP apologises for comments about "bigger houses" for professionals', *The Journal*, 10 September, available at: http://www.thejournal.ie/jim-stafford-pip-1077165-Sep2013/ [accessed 24 September 2015].

Cronin, M. (2015) 'Ireland's disappeared: suicide, violence and austerity', in C. Coulter and A. Nagle (eds), *Ireland under Austerity: Neoliberal Crisis, Neoliberal Solutions*, Manchester: Manchester University Press, pp 133–150.

Crouch, C. (2011) 'What will follow the demise of privatised Keynesianism?', *Political Quarterly*, 80(1), available at: https://onlinelibrary.wiley.com/doi/10.1111/j.1467-923X.2009.02195.x.

Dante, A. (2013) *Dante's Inferno*, CreateSpace Independent Publishing Platform: Amazon.

Das, S. (2006) *Traders, Guns and Money: Knowns and Unknowns in the Dazzling World of Derivatives*, New York: Financial Times.

Das, S. (2011) *Extreme Money: Masters of the Universe and the Cult of Risk*, New York: Financial Times.

Davies, W., Montgomerie, J., and Wallin, S. (2015) *Financial Melancholia: Mental Health and Indebtedness*, Political Economy Research Centre, available at: https://research.gold.ac.uk/id/eprint/16269/1/FinancialMelancholiaMentalHealthandIndebtedness.pdf [accessed 24 September 2023].

Davis, M. and Cartwright, L. (2020) '"Deferred lives": money, debt, and the financialised futures of young temporary workers', in M. Featherstone (ed.), *The Sociology of Debt*, Bristol: Policy Press, pp 91–118.

De Visé, D. (2023) 'Americans are hiding their credit card debt', *The Hill*, 27 June, available at: https://thehill.com/homenews/state-watch/4068846-americans-are-hiding-their-credit-card-debt/ [accessed 24 September 2023].

Dean, M. (2012) 'The Signature of Power', *Journal of Political Power*, 5(1), 101–117, available at: https://www.tandfonline.com/doi/abs/10.1080/2158379X.2012.659864 [accessed 12 November 2015].

Dean, M. (2018) 'From governmentality to economic theology', presented at the Economy and Society Summer School 2018, 14–18 May.

Dean, M. and Zamora, D. (2021) *The Last Man Takes LSD: Foucault and the End of Revolution,* New York: Verso.

Debt Collective (2020) *Can't Pay Won't Pay: The Case for Economic Disobedience and Debt Abolition,* Chicago: Haymarket Books.

Debt and Development Coalition Ireland (2014) 'The debt debate', available at: http://www.debtireland.org/issues/ [accessed 5 November 2015].

Debt.org (2018) 'The emotional effects of debt', available at: https://www.debt.org/advice/emotional-effects/ [accessed 2 August 2018].

Dempsey, M.T. (2020) 'Providence', in S. Schwarzkopf (ed.), *The Routledge Handbook of Economic Theology*, Abingdon: Routledge, pp 19–28.

Denzin, N.K. and Lincoln, Y.S. (2017) *The Sage Handbook of Qualitative Research,* London: Sage.

Devaney, E. (2017) 'Governing families: state discourses and professional practices in the making of Irish drug policy 1971–2016', unpublished PhD thesis, University of Limerick.

Devereux, E. (2013) *Understanding the Media*, 3rd edn, London: Sage.

Deville, J. (2015) *Lived Economies of Default: Consumer Credit, Debt Collection and the Capture of Affect*, Abingdon: Routledge.

Deville, J. (2020) 'Digital subprime: tracking the credit trackers', in M. Featherstone (ed.), *The Sociology of Debt*, Bristol: Policy Press, pp 145–174.

Dineen, M. (2013) 'Bankruptcy cases to flood new insolvency service', *Irish Independent*, 14 January, available at: https://www.independent.ie/business/irish/bankruptcy-cases-to-flood-new-insolvency-service-28958021.html [accessed 2 October 2016].

Dixon, J.A. and Macarov, D. (1998) *Poverty: A Persistent Global Reality*, Abingdon: Routledge.

Dobbie, W. and Song, J. (2015) 'Debt relief and debtor outcomes: measuring the effects of consumer bankruptcy protection', *American Economic Review*, 105(3), 1272–1311, available at: https://www.jstor.org/stable/43495417 [accessed 1 May 2023].

Donovan, D. (2016) 'The IMF's role in Ireland', Working Paper, No. 16–02/04, available at: http://www.ieo-imf.org/ieo/files/completedevaluations/EAC__BP_16-02_04__The_IMF_s_Role_in_Ireland%20v5.PDF [accessed 1 May 2016].

Donzelot, J. (1991) 'Pleasure in work', in G. Burchell, C. Gordon and P. Miller (eds), *The Foucault Effect: Studies in Governmentality*, Chicago: University of Chicago Press, pp 169–181.

Dorling, D. (2015) *Injustice: Why Social Inequality Still Persists*, Bristol: Policy Press.

Dorling, D. (2014) *Inequality and the 1%*, London: Verso.

Downing, J. (2019) 'Ireland has lowest rate of home-ownership in almost 50 years – Dáil told', *Independent.ie*, 3 July, available at: https://www.independent.ie/irish-news/ireland-has-lowest-rate-of-home-ownership-in-almost-50-years-dail-told/38278560.html [accessed 8 October 2023].

Drudy, P. and Punch, M. (2005) *Out of Reach: Inequalities in the Irish Housing System*, Dublin: TASC, available at: http://www.d1054313.blacknight.com/upload/file/PDF%20documents/First%20chapter.pdf [accessed 22 November 2018].

Dubois, H., Klára, F., Ethan, K. and Anderson, R. (2020) *Addressing Household Over-indebtedness*, available at: https://www.eurofound.europa.eu/publications/report/2020/addressing-household-over-indebtedness [accessed 8 October 2023].

Durkheim, E. (2007) *On Suicide*, London: Penguin.

Dwyer, P.J. (1995) 'Foucault, docile bodies and post-compulsory education in Australia', *British Journal of Sociology of Education*, 16(4), 467–477, available at: https://www-jstor-org.proxy.lib.ul.ie/stable/1393414?seq=1#metadata_info_tab_contents [accessed 10 July 2018].

Economic Policy Institute (2022) 'The productivity-pay gap', available at: https://www.epi.org/productivity-pay-gap/ [accessed 8 October 2023].

Epsing-Andersen, G. (1990) *The Three Worlds of Welfare Capitalism*, Princeton: Princeton University Press.

Ewald, F. (1991) 'Insurance and risk', in G. Burchell, C. Gordon and P. Miller (eds), *The Foucault Effect: Studies in Governmentality*, Chicago: University of Chicago Press, pp 197–210.

Fahy, D., O'Brien, M., and Poti, V. (2010) 'From boom to bust: a post-Celtic Tiger analysis of the norms, values and roles of Irish financial journalists', *Irish Communication Review*, 12(1), available at: https://arrow.dit.ie/cgi/viewcontent.cgi?referer=https://www.google.ie/&httpsredir=1&article=1118&context=icr [accessed 11 January 2016].

Featherstone, M. (ed.) (2020) *The Sociology of Debt*, Bristol: Policy Press.

Fegan, J. (2018) 'Protests as family farm put up for sale by vulture fund', *Irish Examiner*, 16 September, available at: https://www.irishexaminer.com/breakingnews/ireland/protests-as-family-farm-put-up-for-sale-by-vulture-fund-869139.html [accessed 16 September 2018].

Fine Gael (2016) *General Election Manifesto: Let's Keep the Recovery Going*, available at: http://michaelpidgeon.com/manifestos/docs/fg/Fine%20Gael%20GE%202016.pdf [accessed 23 January 2016].

Finn, C. (2018) '"Mary" is recovering from cancer and her mortgage – in 29k arrears – has been sold to a vulture fund', *The Journal*, 18 August, available at: http://www.thejournal.ie/ptsb-cancer-mortgage-sold-4181772-Aug2018/ [accessed 5 September 2018].

Finn, D. (2015) 'Ireland, the left and the European Union', in C. Coulter and A. Nagle (eds), *Ireland under Austerity: Neoliberal Crisis, Neoliberal Solutions*, Manchester: Manchester University Press, pp 241–259.

Flick, U. (2009) *An Introduction to Qualitative Research*, 4th edn, London: Sage.

Foohey, P., Lawless, R.M., Porter, K., and Thorne, D. (2018) 'Life in the sweatbox', *Notre Dame Law Review*, 94(1), available at: https://scholarship.law.nd.edu/ndlr/vol94/iss1/4/.

Forkert, K. (2016) 'Austere creativity and volunteer-run public services: the case of Lewisham's libraries', *New Formations*, 87, 11–28. doi: 10.3898/NEWF.87.1.2016.

Foucault, M. (1979) 'On governmentality', *Ideology and Consciousness*, 6(1), 5–21.

Foucault, M. (1989). *Madness and Civilization*, Abingdon: Routledge.

Foucault, M. (1991a) 'Politics and the study of discourse', in G. Burchell, C. Gordon and P. Miller (eds), *The Foucault Effect: Studies in Governmentality*, Chicago: University of Chicago Press pp 53–73.

Foucault, M. (1991b) 'Questions of method', in G. Burchell, C. Gordon and P. Miller (eds), *The Foucault Effect: Studies in Governmentality*, Chicago: University of Chicago Press, pp 74–87.

Foucault, M. (1995). *Discipline and Punish: The Birth of the Prison*, New York: Random House.

Foucault, M. (1996) *The Birth of the Clinic: An Archeology of Medical Perception*, New York: Random House.

Foucault, M. (1997) *Ethics, Subjectivity and Truth: The Essential Works of Michel Foucault, 1954–1984, Volume One*, P. Rabinow (ed.), New York: The New Press.

Foucault, M. (2000) 'The subject and power', in J.D. Faubion (ed.), *Power: Essential Works of Foucault 1954–1984*, Vol. 3, London: Penguin, pp 326–49.

Foucault, M. (2015) *The History of Sexuality: Will to Knowledge*, London: Penguin.

Foucault, M. and Lotringer, S. (1996) *Collected Interviews 1961–1984*, New York: Semiotext(e).

Foucault, M. and Macey, D. (2003) *Society Must Be Defended: Lectures at the Collège de France 1975–76*, London: Pan Macmillan.

Foucault, M. and Rabinow, P. (1984). *The Foucault Reader*, New York: Pantheon Books.

Foucault, M. and Senellart, M. (2008). *The Birth of Biopolitics: Lectures at the Collège de France 1978–1979*, Basingstoke: Palgrave Macmillan.

Foucault, M., Burchell, G., Gordon, C. and Miller, P. (1991). *The Foucault Effect: Studies in Governmentality*, Chicago: University of Chicago Press.

Foucault, M., Senellart, M., Ewald, F., and Fontana, A. (2009). *Security, Territory, Population: Lectures at the Collège de France, 1977–1978*, New York: Palgrave Macmillan.

Fourcade, M. and Healy, K. (2013) 'Classification situations: life-chances in the neoliberal era', *Accounting, Organizations and Society*, 38(8), 559–572, available at: https://kieranhealy.org/files/papers/classification-situations.pdf [accessed 5 January 2016].

Frank, R. (2007) *Falling Behind: How Rising Inequality Harms the Middle Class*. Berkeley: University of California Press.

Free Legal Advice Centre (2015) *Owner-Occupier Mortgage Arrears: What Progress Has Been Made towards Resolution?* Dublin: Free Legal Advice Centre.

Freud, S. and Gay, P. (1995) *The Freud Reader*, London: Random House.

Fukuyama, F. (2012) *The End of History and the Last Man*, London: Penguin.

Gallagher, A. (2014) 'The "caring entrepreneur"? Childcare policy and private provision in an enterprising age', *Environment and Planning A: Economy and Space*, 46(5), available at: http://journals.sagepub.com/doi/10.1068/a46235 [accessed 14 June 2018].

Gane, N. (2012) 'The governmentalities of neoliberalism: panopticism, post-panopticism and beyond', *Differences: A Journal of Feminist Studies*, 60(4). doi: 10.1111/j.1467-954X.2012.02126.x.

Garthwaite, K. (2016) *Hunger Pains: Life inside Foodbank Britain*, London: Policy Press.

Gartland, F. (2013) 'Insolvency service receives 78 applications from potential personal insolvency practitioners and intermediaries', *Irish Times*, 15 July, available at: http://www.irishtimes.com/news/crime-and-law/insolvency-service-receives-78-applicationsfrom-potential-personal-insolvency-practitioners-and-intermediaries-1.1463519 [accessed 12 December 2015].

Gayman, C. (2011) 'Politicizing the personal: thinking about the feminist subject with Michel Foucault and John Dewey', *Foucault Studies*, 11(1), available at: https://rauli.cbs.dk/index.php/foucault-studies/article/download/3206/3400 [accessed 14 November 2015].

Gazso, A. (2009) 'Gendering the "responsible risk taker": citizenship relationships with gender-neutral social assistance policy', *Citizenship Studies*, 13(1), 45–63.

Geertz, C. (1973) *The Interpretation of Cultures*, New York: Basic Books.

Geisst, C.R. (2013) *Beggar Thy Neighbour: A History of Usury and Debt*, Philadelphia: University of Pennsylvania Press.

Germain, R. (1997) *The International Organization of Credit: States and Global Finance in the World-Economy*, Cambridge: Cambridge University Press.

Gershon, I. (2018) 'Employing the CEO of Me, Inc.: US corporate hiring in a neoliberal age', 45(2), 173–185, available at: https://anthrosource.onlinelibrary.wiley.com/doi/abs/10.1111/amet.12630 [accessed 13 February 2021].

Ghate, D. and Hazel, N. (2002) *Parenting in Poor Environments*, London: Jessica Kingsley.

Gielens, E., Roosma, F., and Achterberg, P. (2019) 'Deservingness in the eye of the beholder', *International Journal of Social Welfare*, 28(4), 442–453, available at: https://pure.uvt.nl/ws/portalfiles/portal/32018480/SOC_Gielens_deservingness_in_the_eye_IJoSW_2019.pdf.

Girard, R. (1965) *Deceit, Desire and the Novel: Self and Other in Literary Structure,* Baltimore: Johns Hopkins University Press.

Girard, R. (1987) *Things Hidden since the Foundation of the World*, Palo Alto: Stanford University Press.

Girard, R. (1989) *The Scapegoat*, Baltimore: Johns Hopkins University Press.

Girard, R. (2013) *Violence and the Sacred*, London: Bloomsbury.

Gleeson, C. (2017) 'Almost 100,000 mortgages adjusted since economic crash', *Irish Times*, 6 December, available at: https://www.irishtimes.com/business/financial-services/almost-100-000-mortgages-adjusted-since-economic-crash-1.3317588 [accessed 8 September 2018].

Goffman, E. (1951) 'Symbols of class status', *British Journal of Sociology*, 2(4), 294–304, available at: https://www.jstor.org/stable/588083?origin=crossref&seq=1#page_scan_tab_contents [accessed 4 March 2016].

Goffman, E. (1963) *Stigma: Notes on the Management of Spoiled Identity*, London: Touchstone.

Golding, P. and Middleton, S. (1982) *Images of Welfare: Press and Public Attitudes to Poverty*, London: Blackwell.

Goodchild, P. (2020) 'Debt and credit', in S. Schwarzkopf (ed.), *The Routledge Handbook of Economic Theology*, Abingdon: Routledge, pp 96–106.

Goode, J. (2012) 'Feeding the family when the wolf's at the door: the impact of over- indebtedness on contemporary foodways in low-income families in the UK', *Food and Foodways*, 20(1), 8–30.

Gordon, C. (1991) 'Governmental rationality: an introduction', in G. Burchell, C. Gordon and P. Miller (eds), *The Foucault Effect: Studies in Governmentality*, Chicago: University of Chicago Press, pp 1–52.

Gov.uk (2022) 'Support for Mortgage Interest (SMI)', available at: https://www.gov.uk/support-for-mortgage-interest [accessed 17 February 2022].

Graeber, D. (2011). *Debt: The First 5,000 Years*, New York: Melville House Publishing.

Graham, A. and Wise, A. (2023) 'Bank of England hikes interest rates for 14th time in a row', *BreakingNews.ie*, 3 August, available at: https://www.breakingnews.ie/world/bank-of-england-hikes-interest-rates-for-14th-time-in-a-row-1510739.html [accessed 17 February 2022].

Haas, O.J. (2006) 'Over-indebtedness in Germany', Employment Sector Social Finance Program Working Paper No. 44, available at: http://citeserx.ist.psu.edu/viewdoc/download?doi=10.1.1.460.745&rep=rep1&type=pdf [accessed 4 April 2017].

Hacker, J.S. (2002) *The Divided Welfare State: The Battle over Public and Private Social Benefits in the United States*, New York: Cambridge University Press.

Hall, P.A. and Soskice, D. (2001) *Varieties of Capitalism: The Institutional Foundations of Comparative Advantage*, Oxford: Oxford University Press.

Halpin, H. (2017) 'Almost half of people in rural Ireland would conceal a mental health difficulty', *The Journal*, 22 May, available at: http://www.thejournal.ie/almost-half-of-people-in-rural-ireland-would-conceal-a-mental-health-difficulty-3393617-May2017/ [accessed 23 May 2017].

Harman, C. (2009) *Zombie Capitalism: Global Crisis and the Relevance of Marx*, Chicago: Haymarket Books.

Harvey, D. (2007). *A Brief History of Neoliberalism*, Oxford: Oxford University Press.

Harvey, D. (2017) *Marx, Capital and the Madness of Economic Reason*, London: Profile Books.

Harvey, L. and Macdonald, M. (1993) *Doing Sociology: A Practical Introduction*, London: Palgrave Macmillan.

Haverstock, E. (2023) 'When do student loan payments resume?', *NerdWallet*, 24 August, available at: https://www.nerdwallet.com/article/loans/student-loans/federal-student-loan-forbearance-extended-yet-again [accessed 17 February 2022].

Hayes, T.A. (2000) 'Stigmatizing indebtedness: implications for labelling theory', *Symbolic Interaction*, 23(1), available at: https://onlinelibrary.wiley.com/doi/abs/10.1525/si.2000.23.1.29 [accessed 21 April 2016].

Hearne, R. (2017) *A Home or a Wealth Generator? Inequality, Financialization and the Irish Housing Crisis*, Maynooth: TASC, available at: https://www.tasc.ie/download/pdf/a_home_or_a_wealth_generator_inequality_financialisation_and_the_irish_housing_crisis.pdf [accessed 23 November 2018].

Hearne, R. (2022) *Gaffs: Why No One Can Get a House, and What We Can Do about It*, New York: HarperCollins.

Hearne, R. and Murphy, M.P. (2018) *Investing in the Right to a Home: Housing, HAPs and Hubs*, Maynooth: University of Maynooth, available at: https://www.maynoothuniversity.ie/sites/default/files/assets/document/Investing%20in%20the%20Right%20to%20a%20Home%20Full_1.pdf [accessed 23 November 2018].

Hennessey, M. (2007) 'Taoiseach apologises for suicide comments', *Irish Times*, 4 Jul, available at: https://www.irishtimes.com/news/taoiseach-apologises-for-suicide-comments-1.809130 [accessed 25 February 2016].

Hennessy, M. (2018a) '"This is a human crisis": David Hall believes 17,000 families will have homes repossessed', *The Journal,* 17 May, available at: http://www.thejournal.ie/vulture-funds-5-4017879-May2018/ [accessed 30 June 2018].

Hennessy, M. (2018b) '"Bizarre carry-on": criticism of consumer expert who said tracker victims should have faced tougher questioning', *The Journal*, 20 May, available at: http://www.thejournal.ie/tracker-mortgage-scandal-13-4021131-May2018/ [accessed 30 June 2018].

Hennink, M., Hutter, I., and Bailey. A. (2011). *Qualitative Research Methods*, London: Sage.

Heuer, O. (2014) 'Rules and norms of consumer insolvency and debt relief: a comparison and classification of personal bankruptcy systems in 15 economically advanced countries', unpublished PhD thesis, University of Bremen.

Heyes, C.J. (2010) 'Subjectivity and power', in D. Taylor (ed.), *Michel Foucault: Key Concepts*, Slough: Acumen Publishing, pp 159–172.

Hillebrand, B., Kok, R., and Biemand, W. (2001) 'Theory-testing using case studies: a comment on Johnston, Leach, and Liu', *Industrial Marketing Management*, 30, 651–657.

Hills, J. (2014) *Good Times Bad Times: The Welfare Myth of Them and Us*, Bristol: Policy Press.

Himmelstein, D.U., Thorne, D., Warren, E., and Woolhandler, S. (2009) 'Medical bankruptcy in the United States, 2007: results of a national study', *American Journal of Medicine*, 122(8), 741–746, available at: https://www.amjmed.com/article/S0002-9343(09)00404-5/fulltext [accessed 8 October 2023].

Hitchen, E. (2016) 'Living and feeling the austere', *New Formations*, 87, 102–118. doi: 10.3898/NEWF.87.6.2016.

Hodson, R., Dwyer R., and Neilson, L. (2014) 'Credit card blues: the middle class and the hidden costs of easy credit', *Sociological Quarterly*, 55(2), 315–340.

Holland, S. (2010) 'Metaphors flying at Wall Street bankers hearing', *Reuters*, 13 January, available at: https://www.reuters.com/article/us-financial-commission-scene-idUSTRE60C4TY20100113 [accessed 8 October 2023].

Holloway, I. (1997) *Basic Concepts for Qualitative Research*, Oxford: Blackwell.

Honohan, P. (2009) *What Went Wrong in Ireland?* Washington DC: World Bank.

Horgan-Jones, J. (2014) '"Pathetic" Insolvency Service "not fit for purpose" – IMHO', *The Journal*, 15 July, available at: http://www.thejournal.ie/insolvency-service-not-fit-for-purpose-1571897-Jul2014/ [accessed 14 February 2015].

Hourigan, N. (2015) *Rule-Breakers: Why 'Being There' Trumps 'Being Fair', in Ireland*, Dublin: Gill and Macmillan.

Household Finance and Consumption Survey (2013) Central Statistics Office, Cork, available at: https://www.cso.ie/en/media/csoie/releasespublications/documents/socialconditions/2013/hfcs2013.pdf [accessed 8 October 2023].

Household Finance and Consumption Survey (2018) Central Statistics Office, Cork, available at: https://www.cso.ie/en/releasesandpublications/ep/p-hfcs/householdfinanceandconsumptionsurvey2018/ [accessed 8 October 2023].

Household Finance and Consumption Survey (2020) Central Statistics Office, Cork, available at: https://www.cso.ie/en/releasesandpublications/ep/p-hfcs/householdfinanceandconsumptionsurvey2020/ [accessed 8 October 2023].

Housing Policy Review 1990–2002 (2003), Dublin: Stationery Office, available at: https://researchrepository.ucd.ie/bitstream/10197/5325/1/Norris_and_Winston_HPR_2004.pdf [accessed 25 April 2016].

Howard, L. (2023) 'Brits lean on credit cards – but are in the dark about how they work', *Forbes Advisor UK*, 16 January, available at: https://www.forbes.com/uk/advisor/credit-cards/brits-understanding-credit-cards/ [accessed 25 September 2023].

Hoyes, M. (2019) 'Women and bankruptcy study: facing higher risks', available at: https://www.hoyes.com/press/joe-debtor/women-and-bankruptcy/ [accessed 25 September 2023].

Insolvency Service of England (2021) 'About us', available at: https://www.gov.uk/government/organisations/insolvency-service/about [accessed 11 November 2022].

Insolvency Service of Ireland (2013a) Chartered Accountants Leinster Society Luncheon, available at: https://assets.gov.ie/239519/1ced63a1-256d-447b-902e-a45529959f5a.pdf [accessed 25 July 2017].

Insolvency Service of Ireland (2013b) Annual Report 2013, Report 1, available at: https://www.gov.ie/pdf/?file=https://assets.gov.ie/232760/f8222972-ffe6-4f08-a80f-0f4ffeb7cd3e.pdf#page=null [accessed 2 March 2016].

Insolvency Service of Ireland (2014a) *Insolvency Service Launches 'Back on Track' Information Campaign for People in Debt following Research* [press release], 7 October, available at: http://www.isi.gov.ie/en/ISI/Press_Release_07_10_14.pdf/Files/Press_Release_07_10_14.pdf [accessed 1 October 2015].

Insolvency Service of Ireland (2014b) Annual Report 2014, Report 2, available at: https://www.gov.ie/pdf/?file=https://assets.gov.ie/232759/b81b79bc-8ebe-4346-847a-d719fb91579b.pdf#page=nul [accessed 3 March 2016].

Insolvency Service of Ireland (2015a) *Insolvency Service of Ireland (ISI) Q1 Statistics and PIA Protocol Published* [press release], 14 April, available at: https://www.gov.ie/pdf/?file=https://assets.gov.ie/239209/3c98b944-1bc0-4fd1-95ed-a3f316f3d06e.pdf#page=null [accessed 12 June 2017].

Insolvency Service of Ireland (2015b) *ISI Statistics: Quarter 3 2015*, Report 3, Dublin: Department of Justice and Equality.

Insolvency Service of Ireland (2015c) Annual Report 2015, Report 3, available at: https://www.gov.ie/pdf/?file=https://assets.gov.ie/239210/28fea8e0-41ed-4726-9617-98f1ea0bef7f.pdf#page=null [accessed 12 March 2017].

Insolvency Service of Ireland (2016a) *Back on Track: Dealing with Problem Debt*, available at: https://www.isi.gov.ie/en/ISI/Backontrack_Dealing_with_Debt_July_2016.pdf/Files/Backontrack_Dealing_with_Debt_July_2016.pdf [accessed 10 October 2016].

Insolvency Service of Ireland (2016b) *ISI Statistics: Quarter 2 2016*, Report 10, Dublin: Department of Justice and Equality.

Insolvency Service of Ireland (2016c) *Guide to a Personal Insolvency Arrangement*, available at: https://backontrack.ie/pia/ [accessed 22 October 2017].

Insolvency Service of Ireland (2016d) *Annual Report 2016*, Report 4, available at: http://www.isi.gov.ie/en/ISI/Final%20ISI%20Annual%20Report%20&%20Financial%20Statements%202016%20(Eng%20&%20Irish).pdf/Files/Final%20ISI%20Annual%20Report%20&%20Financial%20Statements%202016%20(Eng%20&%20Irish).pdf [accessed 2 June 2018].

Insolvency Service of Ireland (2017a) *ISI Statistics: Quarter 2 2017*, Report 6, Dublin: Department of Justice and Equality.

Insolvency Service of Ireland (2017b) *Annual Report 2017*, Report 5, available at: https://www.gov.ie/pdf/?file=https://assets.gov.ie/232754/f9c347c1-26bf-4351-9961-e63d88a41f7c.pdf#page=null [accessed 1 September 2018].

Insolvency Service of Ireland (2018) *ISI Statistics: Quarter 2 2018*, Report 2, Dublin: Department of Justice and Equality.

Insolvency Service of Ireland (2023a) 'Donna's story', *YouTube*, available at: https://www.youtube.com/watch?v=dZlrIoim2yM&t=2s [accessed 8 October 2023].

Insolvency Service of Ireland (2023b) 'Michael's story', *YouTube*, available at: https://www.youtube.com/watch?v=lU51-bPSODw&t=1s [accessed 8 October 2023].

Insolvency Service of Ireland (2023c) 'Josephine and Damien's story', *YouTube*, available at: https://www.youtube.com/watch?v=JATr4yhGsGo [accessed 8 October 2023].

Ipsos Mori (2022) 'A survey of the American general population (ages 18+), including an oversample of Americans with student loan debt', available at: https://www.ipsos.com/sites/default/files/ct/news/documents/2022-06/NPR%20Student%20Loan%20Debt%20Topline%20%2806.15.2022%29_1.pdf [accessed 8 October 2023].

Ireland, Citizens Information (2016) 'Money Advice and Budgeting Service', available at: http://www.citizensinformation.ie/en/money_and_tax/personal_finance/debt/mabs_service.html [accessed 22 July 2016].

Irish Hotels Federation (2009) *Over-capacity in the Irish Hotel Industry and Required Elements of a Recovery Programme*, Dublin: Irish Hotels Federation, available at: https://www.ihf.ie/documents/HotelStudyFinalReport101109.pdf [accessed 11 February 2016].

Irish Mortgage Holders Organisation (2014a) 'IMHO proposal to the Department of Finance', available at: https://www.mortgageholders.ie/proposal/ [accessed 2 July 2016].

Irish Mortgage Holders Organisation (2014b) 'The Insolvency Service 1 year on – major changes are needed for it to work', available at: https://www.mortgageholders.ie/the-insolvency-service-1-year-on-major-changes-are-needed-for-it-to-work/ [accessed 22 April 2016].

Irish Mortgage Holders Organisation (2018) 'Ulster Bank outsourcing the repossession of thousands of families', available at: https://www.mortgageholders.ie/ulster-bank/ [accessed 22 August 2018].

Jackson, P. (2009) *Changing Families, Changing Food*, Basingstoke: Palgrave Macmillan.

James, D. (2022) 'Owing everyone: debt advice in the UK's time of austerity', *Ethnos*, 87(1), 59–77. doi: 10.1080/00141844.2019.1687544.

Jessop, R. (2012) 'Narratives of crisis and crisis response: perspectives from North and South', in P. Utting, S. Razavi, and R.V. Buchholz (eds), *The Global Crisis and Transformative Change*, Basingstoke: Palgrave Macmillan, pp 23–42.

Jibrin, R. and Salem, S. (2015) 'Revisiting intersectionality: reflections on theory and praxis', *Trans-scripts*, 5(1), available at: https://cpb-us-e2.wpmucdn.com/sites.uci.edu/dist/f/1861/files/2014/10/2015_5_salem.pdf [accessed 22 May 2016].

Johnson, L., Chen, Y., Stylianou, A., and Arnold, A. (2022) 'Examining the impact of economic abuse on survivors of intimate partner violence: a scoping review', *BMC Public Health*, 22(1014). doi: 10.1186/s12889-022-13297-4.

Jones, D. (2003) *Reforming the Morality of Usury: A Study of Differences That Separated the Protestant Reformers*, Lanham: University Press of America.

Jones, O. (2011) *Chavs: The Demonization of the Working Class*, London: Verso.

Kane, S. and Kirby, M. (2003) *Wealth, Poverty and Welfare*, Basingstoke: Palgrave Macmillan.

Kanougiya, S., Daruwalla, N., Gram, L., Gupta, A.D., Sivakami, M., and Osrin, D. (2021) 'Economic abuse and its associations with symptoms of common mental disorders among women in a cross-sectional survey in informal settlements in Mumbai, India', *BMC Public Health*, 21(842). doi: 10.1186/s12889-021-10904-8.

Karlsen, M.P. and Villadsen, K. (2020) 'Confession', in S. Schwarzkopf (ed.), *The Routledge Handbook of Economic Theology*, Abingdon: Routledge, pp 36–46.

Kavanagh, D., Keohane, K., and Kuhling, C. (2011) *Organization in Play*, Witney: Peter Lang.

Kay, S. (2011) *Celtic Revival? The Rise, Fall, and Renewal of Celtic Tiger Ireland*, Lanham: Rowman & Littlefield.

Kearns, G., Meredith, D., and Morrissey, J. (2016) *Spatial Justice and the Irish Crisis*, Dublin: Royal Irish Academy.

Kelly, R., O'Malley, T., and O'Toole, C. (2014) *Do First Time Buyers Default Less? Implications for Macro-prudential Policy*, Report 14, Dublin: Central Bank of Ireland.

Kemeny, J. (1980) 'Home ownership and privatization', *International Journal of Urban and Regional Research*, 4(3), 372–388.

Kennedy, S. (2015) 'A perfect storm: crisis, capitalism and democracy', in C. Coulter and A. Nagle (eds), *Ireland under Austerity: Neoliberal Crisis, Neoliberal Solutions*, Manchester: Manchester University Press, pp 86–109.

Keohane, K. (2009) 'Haunted houses and liminality: from the deserted homes of the faithful departed to the social desert of schizmogenesis', *International Political Anthropology*, 2(1), 27–48.

Keohane, K. and Kuhling, C. (2014). *The Domestic, Moral and Political Economies of Post-Celtic Tiger Ireland: What Rough Beast?* Manchester: Manchester University Press.

Keohane, K. and Petersen, A. (2013) *The Social Pathologies of Contemporary Civilization*, Abingdon: Routledge.

Kerr, D. (1999) 'Beheading the king and enthroning the market: a critique of Foucauldian governmentality', *Science & Society*, 63(2), 173–202, available at: https://www.jstor.org/stable/40404696?seq=1#page_scan_tab_contents [accessed 5 July 2018].

King, A. (2004) 'The prisoner of gender: Foucault and the disciplining of the female body', *Journal of International Women's Studies*, 5(2), 29–39, available at: https://vc.bridgew.edu/cgi/viewcontent.cgi?referer=https://www.google.ie/&httpsredir=1&article=1532&context=jiws [accessed 22 April 2016].

Kirk-Jenkins, A.J. and Hughey, A.W. (2021) 'Abrupt adaption: a review of the Impact of the COVID-19 pandemic on faculty in higher education', *Journal of the Professoriate*, 12(1), 104–121, available at: https://caarpweb.org/wp-content/uploads/2021/04/abrupt_adaption-Jenkins-12-1.pdf.

Kirwan, S. (2018) 'On "those who shout the loudest": debt advice and the work of disrupting attachments', *Geoforum*, 98, 318–326. doi: 10.1016/j.geoforum.2018.05.005.

Kirwan, W., Dawney, L., and Walker, R. (2020) '"Choose your moments": discipline and speculation in the indebted everyday', in M. Featherstone (ed.), *The Sociology of Debt*, Bristol: Policy Press, pp 119–144.

Kiviat, B. (2019) 'The art of deciding with data: evidence from how employers translate credit reports into hiring decisions', *Socio-Economic Review*, 17(2), 283–309. doi: 10.1093/ser/mwx030.

Knapp, M., McDaid, D., and Parsonage, M. (2011) *Mental Health Promotion and Mental Illness Prevention: The Economic Case*, Personal Social Services Research Unit, available at: http://eprints.lse.ac.uk/32311/1/Knapp_et_al__MHPP_The_Economic_Case.pdf [accessed 27 February 2017].

Koch, I. and James, D. (2022) 'The state of the welfare state: advice, governance and care in settings of austerity', *Ethnos*, 87(1), 1–21. doi: 10.1080/00141844.2019.1688371.

Korczak, D. (2004) *The Money Advice and Budgeting Service Ireland: A Service to Help People with Financial Problems and to Tackle Over-indebtedness*, Synthesis Report, Dublin: European Commission of Employment and Social Affairs.

Krier, D. (2017) 'Debt, value and economic theology', *Continental Thought and Theory*, 1(2), 252–268, available at: https://ir.canterbury.ac.nz/bitstream/handle/10092/13076/Krier-CTT-v1-2-2017.pdf?sequence=1 [accessed 12 August 2018].

Krueger, D. and Perri, F. (2006) 'Does income inequality lead to consumption inequality? Evidence and theory', *Review of Economic Studies*, 73(1), 163–193.

Krugman, P. (2012) *End This Depression Now!* New York: W.W. Norton & Company.

Kuhling, C. (2003) *The New Ethic and the Spirit of Postmodernity*, New York: Hampton Press.

Kuhling, C. (2004) *The New Age Ethic and the Spirit of Postmodernity*, New York: Hampton Press.

Kuhling, C. and Keohane, K. (2004) *Collision Culture: Transformations in Everyday Life in Ireland*, Dublin: Liffey Press.

Kuhling, C. and Keohane, K. (2007) *Cosmopolitan Ireland: Globalization and Quality of Life*, London: Pluto Press.

Kuperberg, A. and Mazelis, J.M. (2022), 'Social norms and expectations about student loans and family formation', *Sociological Inquiry*, 92: 90–126. doi: 10.1111/soin.12416.

Kus, B. (2006) 'Neoliberalism, institutional change and the welfare state: the case of Britain and France', *International Journal of Comparative Sociology*, 47(6), 488–525.

Ladson-Billings, G. (2006) 'From the achievement gap to the education debt: understanding achievement in U.S. schools', *Education and Educational Research*, 35(7), available at: http://edr.sagepub.com/content/35/7/3.short [accessed 1 January 2016].

Lajoie, A (2020) *Exploring Household Debt in Ireland: The Burden of Non-Mortgage Debt & Opportunities to Support Low-Income Households*. Dublin: TASC.

Lakoff, G. and Johnson, M. (2008) *Metaphors We Live by*, Chicago: University of Chicago Press.

Langley, P. (2009) *The Everyday Life of Global Finance: Saving and Borrowing in Anglo-America*, Oxford: Oxford University Press.

Last Week Tonight (2021) 'Bankruptcy: Last Week Tonight with John Oliver (HBO)', *YouTube*, available at: https://www.youtube.com/watch?v=GzFG0Cdh8D8 [accessed 15 August 2021].

Law Society of Ireland (2023) 'House-buyer median age up from 33 to 43 in decade', available at: https://www.lawsociety.ie/gazette/top-stories/2023/april/house-buyer-median-age-up-from-33-to-43-in-a-decade [accessed 8 October 2023].

Lawler, S. (2005) 'Disgusted subjects: the making of middle-class identities', *Sociological Review*, 53(3), 429–446, available at: https://onlinelibrary.wiley.com/doi/abs/10.1111/j.1467-954X.2005.00560.x [accessed 22 January 2018].

Lazzarato, M. (2012) *The Making of the Indebted Man: An Essay on the Neoliberal Condition*, Los Angeles: Semiotext(e).

Lazzarato, M. (2014) *Governing by Debt*, Los Angeles: Semiotext(e).

Leicht, K. and Fitzgerald, S. (2014a) *Middle Class Meltdown in America: Causes, Consequences, and Remedies*, New York: Routledge.

Leicht, K. and Fitzgerald, S. (2014b) 'The real reason 60 is the new 30: consumer debt and income insecurity in late middle age', *Sociological Quarterly*, 55(2), 236–260.

Lerner, G. (1986) *The Creation of Patriarchy*, Oxford: Oxford University Press.

Levine, D.M. (1995) 'The organism metaphor in sociology', *Social Research*, 62(2), 239–265, available at: https://www.jstor.org/stable/40971093 [accessed 22 January 2018].

Levitas, R. (2005) *The Inclusive Society: Social Exclusion and New Labour*, Basingstoke: Palgrave Macmillan.

Lincoln, Y. and Guba, E. (1985) *Naturalistic Inquiry*, Thousand Oaks: Sage.

Lister, R. (2004) *Poverty*, Oxford: Polity.

Lister, R. (2013) '"Power, not pity": poverty and human rights', *Ethics & Social Welfare*, 7(2), 109–123, available at: http://search.proquest.com/docview/1373226573/ [accessed 22 January 2018].

Logemann, J. (2008) 'Different paths to mass consumption: consumer credit in the United States and West Germany during the 1950s and 1960s', *Journal of Social History*, 41(3), 525–559.

Lyons, B. (2014) 'Insolvency service statistics suggest it is unfit for purpose', *Irish Times*, 20 October, available at: https://www.irishtimes.com/business/financial-services/insolvency-service-statistics-suggest-it-is-unfit-for-purpose-1.1959333 [accessed 23 September 2015].

Mackay, H. (2014) 'Sociological perspectives on austerity', *Berlin Britain Research Network Meeting September 2014*, Berlin, 25 September.

Managh, R. (2018) 'Couple to lose home after mortgage not paid for five years', *Irish Times*, 23 January, available at: https://www.irishtimes.com/news/crime-and-law/courts/circuit-court/couple-to-lose-home-after-mortgage-not-paid-for-five-years-1.3366054 [accessed 28 January 2018].

Mann, R.J. and Porter, K. (2010) 'Saving up for bankruptcy', *Geo*, 98(1): 289–339, available at: https://scholarship.law.columbia.edu/faculty_scholarship/443/ [accessed 10 October 2023].

Marglin, S. and Schor, J. (eds) (1992). *The Golden Age of Capitalism: Reinterpreting the Postwar Experience*, New York: Clarendon Press.

Marron, D. (2009) *Consumer Credit in the United States: A Sociological Perspective from the 19th Century to the Present*, New York: Palgrave Macmillan.

Martin, G.P. and Waring, J. (2018) 'Realising governmentality: pastoral power, governmental discourse and the (re)constitution of subjectivities', *Sociological Review*, 66(6), 1292–1308. doi: 10.1177/0038026118755616.

Martin, N. (2005) 'The role of history and culture in developing bankruptcy and insolvency systems: the perils of legal transplantation', *Boston College International and Comparative Law Review*, 28(2), available at: https://ssrn.com/abstract=1444531.

Mason, J. (1996) *Qualitative Researching*, London: Sage.

Mason, P. (2010) *Meltdown: The End of an Age of Greed*, New York: Verso.

Mauss, M. (2002) *The Gift*, Abingdon: Routledge.

Mazzucato, M. (2018) *The Value of Everything: Making and Taking in the Global Economy*, London: Penguin.

McCabe, C. (2015) 'False economy: the financialisation of Ireland and the roots of austerity', in C. Coulter and A. Nagle (eds), *Ireland under Austerity: Neoliberal Crisis, Neoliberal Solutions*, Manchester: Manchester University Press, pp 47–65.

McClanahan, A. (2018) *Dead Pledges: Debt, Crisis, and Twenty-First-Century Culture*, Stanford: Stanford University Press.

McDonald, D. (2013) 'Number of people going bankrupt doubles in just a year', *Independent.ie*, 26 December, available at: https://www.independent.ie/irish-news/number-of-people-going-bankrupt-doubles-in-just-a-year/29866894.html [accessed 10 October 2023].

McDonald, H. (2019) 'Sean Quinn's UK bankruptcy blocked', *The Guardian*, 18 December, available at: https://www.theguardian.com/business/2012/jan/10/sean-quinn-uk-bankruptcy-bid-blocked-belfast [accessed 10 October 2023].

McDonough, T. (2018) 'Economic causes and consequences of the Celtic Tiger crash', *Boundary 2*, 45(1), 7–30, available at: https://read.dukeupress.edu/boundary-2/article-abstract/45/1/7/133051/Economic-Causes-and-Consequences-of-the-Celtic?redirectedFrom=PDF [accessed 22 August 2018].

McGoey, L. (2012) 'The logic of strategic ignorance', *British Journal of Sociology*, 63, 533–576.

McGrath, M. (2000) 'Starting from scratch: housing and community welfare services to women who have experienced domestic violence', unpublished MA thesis, University of Limerick.

McIntosh, I. and Wright, W. (2018) 'Exploring what the notion of "lived experience" offers for social policy analysis', *Journal of Social Policy*, 48(3), 449–467. doi: 10.1017/S0047279418000570.

McLeod, J. (2017) 'Reframing responsibility in an era of responsibilisation: education, feminist ethics', *Discourse Studies in the Cultural Politics of Education*, 38(1), 43–56, available at: https://www.tandfonline.com/doi/pdf/10.1080/01596306.2015.1104851 [accessed 23 September 2017].

McWilliams, D. (2018) 'The crash was foreseeable. The rapid recovery wasn't', *Irish Times*, 6 January, available at: https://www.irishtimes.com/opinion/david-mcwilliams-the-crash-was-foreseeable-the-rapid-recovery-wasn-t-1.3339111?mode=sample&auth-failed=1&pw-origin=https%3A%2F%2Fwww.irishtimes.com%2Fopinion%2Fdavid-mcwilliams-the-crash-was-foreseeable-the-rapid-recovery-wasn-t-1.3339111 [accessed 17 August 2018].

Mechtraud, S. (1955) 'Durkheim's concept of solidarity', *Philippine Sociological Review*, 3(3), 23–27, available at: https://www.jstor.org/stable/41853340 [accessed 8 October 2023].

Mental Health Ireland (2018) *Debt*, available at: https://www.mentalhealthireland.ie/a-to-z/debt/ [accessed 22 August 2018].

Miles, M. and Huberman, A. (1994) *Qualitative Data Analysis: A Sourcebook of New Methods*, 2nd edn, Thousand Oaks: Sage.

Miller, P. and Rose, N. (1990) 'Governing economic life', *Economy and Society*, 19(1), 1–31. doi: 10.1080/03085149000000001.

Mills, C.W. (2000) *The Sociological Imagination*, Oxford: Oxford University Press.

Mind (2008) *In the Red: Debt and Mental Health*, London: Mind Mental Health Organisation.

Minihan, M. (2013) 'Kenny attempts to reassure women over insolvency controversy', *Irish Times,* 28 March, available at: https://www.irishtimes.com/news/social-affairs/kenny-attempts-to-reassure-women-over-insolvency-controversy-1.1341084 [accessed 21 November 2015].

Money Advice Budgeting Service (2015) *101+ Square Meals Cookbook*, available at: https://www.mabs.ie/downloads/publications/101_Square_Meals_Cookbook_Feb_2015.pdf [accessed 2 March 2016].

Money Advice Budgeting Service (2016a) *Weekly Spending Booklet*, available at: https://www.mabs.ie/downloads/publications/Final_MABS_Weekly_Spending_Booklet_v8_27.1.12.pdf [accessed 2 March 2016].

Money Advice Budgeting Service (2016b) *Managing Your Bills*, available at: https://www.mabs.ie/downloads/publications/factsheets/Managing_your_Bills.pdf [accessed 2 September 2016].

Money Advice Budgeting Service (2022) *Abhaile*, available at: https://mabs.ie/abhaile/ [accessed 2 February 2022].

Montgomerie, J. (2007) 'The logic of neo-liberalism and the political economy of consumer debt-led growth', in S. Lee and S. McBride (eds), *Neoliberalism: State Power and Global Governance*, Dordrecht: Springer, pp 157–172.

Montgomerie, J. (2009) 'The pursuit of (past) happiness? Middle-class indebtedness and American financialisation', *New Political Economy*, 14(1), 1–24.

Montgomerie, J. (2013) 'America's debt safety-net', *Public Administration*, 91(4), 871–888.

Montgomerie, J. (2016) 'Austerity and the household: the politics of economic storytelling', *British Politics*, 11(4), 418–437, available at: https://link.springer.com/article/10.1057/s41293-016-0039-z [accessed December 2016].

Montgomerie, J. (2019) *Should We Abolish Household Debts?* Cambridge: Polity Press.

Montgomerie, J. and Tepe-Belfrage, D. (2016) 'Caring for debts: how the household economy exposes the limits of financialisation', *Critical Sociology*, 43(4–5), available at: https://journals.sagepub.com/doi/10.1177/0896920516664962 [accessed 9 July 2018].

Moral Foundations of Economy and Society Research Centre (2015), available at: http://www.moraleconomy.eu/ [accessed 1 September 2017].

Moran, C. (2018) 'Farmers among those most likely to die by suicide', *Irish Independent*, 20 March, available at: https://www.independent.ie/business/farming/rural-life/farmers-among-those-most-likely-to-die-by-suicide-36723840.html [accessed 22 May 2018].

Morrison, A. (2014) 'Hegemony through responsibilisation: getting working-class students into higher education in the United Kingdom', *Power and Education*, 6(2), 1–27, available at: http://shura.shu.ac.uk/9727/4/Morrison_Hegemony_through_responsibilisation.pdf [accessed 22 September 2016].

Mortgage Brokers (2013) 'Let's take the emotion out of strategic default', available at: https://www.mortgagebrokers.ie/debt-reduction/lets-take-the-emotion-out-of-strategic-default/ [accessed 12 June 2017].

Mouffe, C. (2005) *On the Political*, New York: Routledge.

Mudge, S. (2008) 'What is neo-liberalism?', *Socio-Economic Review*, 6(4), 703–731.

Munday, R. (1994) '*Bentham's Prison: A Study of the Panopticon Penitentiary*. By Janet Semple. [Oxford: Clarendon Press. 1993. 328 (select bibliography) 7 and (index) 8pp. Illustrated. Hardback £40·00 net. ISBN 0-19-827387-8.],' *Cambridge Law Journal*, 53(1), 167–169. doi: 10.1017/S000819730009694X.

Murray, N. (2010) 'No, minister we didn't all "party" in the boom', *Irish Examiner*, 6 December, available at: https://www.irishexaminer.com/ireland/politics/no-minister-we-didnt-all-party-in-the-boom-138578.html [accessed 22 January 2017].

Murray, S. (2018a) 'How many mortgage holders have banks taken to court so far this year?', *The Journal*, 9 April, available at: http://www.thejournal.ie/mortgage-banks-legal-action-3939390-Apr2018/ [accessed 22 July 2018].

Murray, S. (2018b) 'The average first time buyer in Ireland is 34 years old and needs at least a €50,000 deposit', *The Journal*, 25 May, available at: http://www.thejournal.ie/central-bank-mortgage-3408011-May2017/ [accessed 30 May 2018].

Nagle, A. (2015) 'Ireland and the new economy', in C. Coulter and A. Nagle (eds), *Ireland under Austerity: Neoliberal Crisis, Neoliberal Solutions*, Manchester: Manchester University Press, pp 110–130.

National Homeownership Strategy (1995) *The National Homeownership Strategy: Partners in the American Dream*, available at: https://www.globalurban.org/National_Homeownership_Strategy.pdf [accessed 22 September 2016].

National Women's Council of Ireland (2013) 'NWCI cautiously welcomes changes to draft Insolvency Guidelines', available at: https://www.nwci.ie/index.php/learn/article/nwci_cautiously_welcomes_changes_to_draft_insolvency_guidelines [accessed 21 November 2015].

Nelson, M.C., Lust, K., Story, M., and Ehlinger, E. (2008) 'Credit card debt, stress and key health risk behaviours among college students', *American Journal of Health Promotion*, 22(6), 400–407, available at: http://journals.sagepub.com/doi/10.4278/ajhp.22.6.400 [accessed 3 August 2018].

New York Federal Reserve (2023), *Household Debt and Credit Report*, available at: https://www.newyorkfed.org/microeconomics/hhdc [accessed 8 October 2023].

Niemi-Kiesiläinen, J. (2003) 'Collective or individual? Constructions of debtors and creditors in consumer bankruptcy', in J. Niemi-Kiesiläinen, I. Ramsay and W. Whitford (eds), *Consumer Bankruptcy in Global Perspective*, Oxford: Hart Publishing, pp 41–60.

Nietzsche, F. (2014) *On the Genealogy of Morals*, London: Penguin.

Norris, M. (2013) 'Property-led urban, town and rural regeneration in Ireland: positive and perverse outcomes in different implementation contexts', Geary Working Paper, No. 11, available at: http://www.ucd.ie/geary/static/publications/workingpapers/gearywp201311.pdf [accessed 22 May 2016].

Norris, M. and Winston, N. (2011) 'Home-ownership, housing regimes and income inequalities in Western Europe', *International Journal of Social Welfare*, 21(2), 127–138, available at: https://onlinelibrary.wiley.com/doi/pdf/10.1111/j.1468-2397.2011.00811.x [accessed 23 November 2015].

O'Brien, C., Willoughby, T. and Levy, R. (2014) *The Money Advice Service Debt Advice Review, 2013/2014 Report*, Dublin: Optisma Research.

O'Callaghan, C., Boyle, M., and Kitchin, R. (2014) 'Post-politics, crisis, and Ireland's "ghost estates"', *Political Geography*, 42(1), 121–133, available at: http://eprints.maynoothuniversity.ie/7269/1/RK_Pol%20Geog%202014.pdf [accessed 12 August 2018].

O'Callaghan, C., Kelly, S., Boyle, M., and Kitchin, R. (2015) 'Topologies and topographies of Ireland's neoliberal crisis'. *Space and Polity*, 19(1), 31–46, available at: https://www.tandfonline.com/doi/abs/10.1080/13562576.2014.991120 [accessed 24 November 2018].

O'Connor, B. (2007) 'The smart, ballsy guys are buying up property right now', *Irish Independent*, 29 July, available at: https://www.independent.ie/opinion/analysis/the-smart-ballsy-guys-are-buying-up-property-right-now-26307728.html [accessed 14 September 2016].

O'Donovan, D. (2013) 'AIB crackdown on strategic defaulters', *Irish Independent*, 2 August, available at: http://www.independent.ie/business/personal-finance/property-mortgages/aib-crackdown-on-strategic-defaulters-29466902.html [accessed 13 March 2017].

O'Flynn, M., Monaghan, L., and Power, M.J. (2014) 'Scapegoating during a time of crisis: a critique of post-Celtic Tiger Ireland', *Sociology*, 48(5), 921–937, available at: http://journals.sagepub.com/doi/pdf/10.1177/0038038514539059 [accessed 28 May 2016].

O'Halloran, M. (2017) 'Loophole lets firms earning millions pay €250 tax, Dáil told', *Irish Times*, 6 July, available at: https://www.irishtimes.com/news/politics/oireachtas/loophole-lets-firms-earning-millions-pay-250-tax-d%C3%A1il-told-1.3145769?mode=sample&auth-failed=1&pw-origin=https%3A%2F%2Fwww.irishtimes.com%2Fnews%2Fpolitics%2Foireachtas%2Floophole-lets-firms-earning-millions-pay-250-tax-d%25C3%25A1il-told-1.3145769 [accessed 12 July 2017].

O'Regan, E. (2022) 'More than 6,000 HSE workers are absent at any given time as nearly 100,000 children are on some form of waiting list', *Irish Independent*, 14 November, available at: https://www.independent.ie/irish-news/health/more-than-6000-hse-workers-are-absent-at-any-given-time-as-nearly-100000-children-are-on-some-form-of-waiting-list-42141954.html [accessed 17 November 2022].

O'Toole, F. (2009) *Ship of Fools: How Stupidity and Corruption Sank the Celtic Tiger*, London: Faber & Faber.

OECD (2023) 'Household debt (indicator)'. doi: 10.1787/f03b6469-en.

Office of the Superintendent of Canada (2016) *Ten-Year Insolvency Trends in Canada 2007–2016*, available at: https://ised-isde.canada.ca/site/office-superintendent-bankruptcy/en/statistics-and-research/ten-year-insolvency-trends-canada-2007-2016 [accessed 20 February 2021].

Ogletree, A. and Whatley, H. (2023) 'Will energy prices increase in 2023?', *SaveOnEnergy*, available at: https://www.saveonenergy.com/resources/energy-price-trends/ [accessed 8 October 2023].

Oireachtas (2013) *EU Regulations on Insolvency Proceedings: Motion*, Dublin: Joint Committee on Justice, Defence and Equality.

Oireachtas (2015a) *Witness Statement of Mr. Bertie Ahern to Oireachtas Committee of Inquiry into the Banking Crisis*, Dublin: Oireachtas Committee of Inquiry into the Banking Crisis.

Oireachtas (2015b) *Witness Statement of Brien Cowen*, Dublin: Oireachtas Committee of Inquiry into the Banking Crisis.

Oireachtas (2017) *Mortgage Arrears Resolution (Family Home) Bill 2017: Discussion*, Dublin: Joint Committee on Justice, Defence and Equality.

Oireachtas (2023) *Home Ownership: Motion [Private Members]*, Dublin: Dáil Debate.

Oxford Dictionary of Psychology (1995), 2nd edn, Oxford: Oxford University Press.

Oxford Dictionary of Sociology (2009), 3rd edn, Oxford: Oxford University Press.

Palaver, W. (2020) 'Faith and trust', in S. Schwarzkopf (ed.), *The Routledge Handbook of Economic Theology*, Abingdon: Routledge, pp 55–63.

Parkin, F. (2002) *Max Weber*, Abingdon: Routledge.

Paul, M. (2018) 'Moral panic on vultures delays end of arrears crisis', *Irish Times,* 2 March, available at: https://www.irishtimes.com/business/economy/moral-panic-on-vultures-delays-end-of-arrears-crisis-1.3411377?mode=sample&auth-failed=1&pw-origin=https%3A%2F%2Fwww.irishtimes.com%2Fbusiness%2Feconomy%2Fmoral-panic-on-vultures-delays-end-of-arrears-crisis-1.3411377 [accessed 9 September 2018].

Penguin Dictionary of Sociology (2006), 5th edn, London: Penguin.

Personal Insolvency Act 2012, Dublin: Stationery Office, available at: http://www.irishstatutebook.ie/eli/2012/act/44/enacted/en/html [accessed 25 September 2015].

Pettifor, A. (2017) *The Production of Money: How to Break the Power of Bankers*, London: Verso.

Phelan, C. (2023) 'Leo Varadkar "alarmed" at Ireland's low home-ownership rates', *Irish Examiner*, 15 February, available at: https://www.irishexaminer.com/news/politics/arid-41072558.html [accessed 10 October 2023].

Pickford, J. (2016) 'Men and women go bankrupt for different reasons', *Financial Times,* 17 June, available at: https://www.ft.com/content/70ef225c-347d-11e6-ad39-3fee5ffe5b5b [accessed 10 October 2023].

Pitcher, B. (2016) 'Race, debt and the welfare state', *New Formations*, 87, 47–63. doi: 10.3898/NEWF.87.3.2016.

Pleasence, P., Buck, A., Balmer, N.J. and Williams, K. (2007) *A Helping Hand: The Impact Problems: Research and Evaluation of Outreach Services for Financially Excluded People*, London: Sage.

Pope, C. (2021) 'Half of Ireland's tenants spend more than 30% of pay on rent, research shows', *Irish Times*, 14 July, available at: https://www.irishtimes.com/news/ireland/irish-news/half-of-ireland-s-tenants-spend-more-than-30-of-pay-on-rent-research-shows-1.4619762 [accessed 8 October 2023].

Porter, K. and Thorne, D. (2006) 'The failure of bankruptcy's fresh start', *Cornell Law Review*, 92(1), 67–128, available at: http://scholarship.law.cornell.edu/clr/vol92/iss1/2.

Postmus, J.L., Hoge, G.L., Breckenridge, J., Sharp-Jeffs, N., and Chung, D. (2020) 'Economic abuse as an invisible form of domestic violence: a multicountry review', *Trauma, Violence, & Abuse*, 21(2). doi: 10.1177/1524838018764160.

Power, J. (2018) 'Masked men and angle grinders: how not to repossess a property', *Irish Times*, 15 September, available at: https://www.irishtimes.com/news/social-affairs/masked-men-and-angle-grinders-how-not-to-repossess-a-property-1.3629157?mode=sample&auth-failed=1&pw-origin=https%3A%2F%2Fwww.irishtimes.com%2Fnews%2Fsocial-affairs%2Fmasked-men-and-angle-grinders-how-not-to-repossess-a-property-1.3629157 [accessed 22 November 2018].

Power, M. (2009) 'Outwitting the gatekeepers of the purse: the impact of micro-level interactions in determining access to the Back to Education Allowance Welfare to Education Programme', *International Review of Modern Sociology*, 35(1), 25–42.

Power, M. (2010) 'You can only get a degree! Theoretically situating the alterations to the Back to Education Allowance Welfare to Education Programme of 2003/2004', *Policy Futures in Education*, (8)5, 499–512.

Power, M., Haynes, A., and Devereux, E. (2016) 'Reasonable people vs. the sinister fringe: interrogating the framing of Ireland's water charge protestors through the media politics of dissent', *Critical Discourse Studies*, 13(3), 261–277, available at: https://www.tandfonline.com/doi/full/10.1080/17405904.2016.1141694 [accessed 28 September 2016].

Prasad, M. (2012) *The Land of Too Much: American Abundance and the Paradox of Poverty*, Cambridge, MA: Harvard University Press.

Pressman, S. and Scott, R. (2009) 'Consumer debt and the measurement of poverty and inequality in the US', *Review of Social Economy*, 67(2), 127–148.

Prügl, E. (2015) 'Neoliberalising feminism', *New Political Economy*, 20(4), 614–631. doi: 10.1080/13563467.2014.951614.

Quinn, E. (2018) 'Mortgage arrears deals fail at "very high" rate', *Irish Examiner*, 8 September, available at: https://www.irishexaminer.com/breakingnews/business/mortgage-arrears-deals-fail-at-very-high-rate-867586.html [accessed 9 September 2018].

Quinn, T. (2018) 'Relatives of gambling addicts would prefer them to be hooked on heroin instead, expert claims', *Irish Mirror*, 23 April, available at: https://www.irishmirror.ie/news/irish-news/relatives-gambling-addicts-would-prefer-12409068 [accessed 25 May 2018].

Ramsay, I. (2012) 'A tale of two debtors: responding to the shock of over-indebtedness in England and France – a story from the Trente Piteuses', *Modern Law Review*, 75(2), 212–248.

Ramsay, I. (2017) *Personal Insolvency in the 21st Century: A Comparative Analysis of the US and Europe*, Oxford: Hart Publishing.

Reddan, F. (2017) 'Too many buyers, too few homes: what's the story?', *Irish Times,* 4 April, available at: https://www.irishtimes.com/life-and-style/homes-and-property/too-many-buyers-too-few-homes-what-s-the-story-1.3035522?mode=sample&auth-failed=1&pw-origin=https%3A%2F%2Fwww.irishtimes.com%2Flife-and-style%2Fhomes-and-property%2Ftoo-many-buyers-too-few-homes-what-s-the-story-1.3035522 [accessed 15 December 2017].

Reddan, F. (2018) 'Dublin rents to rise to €2,500 before they start to slow', *Irish Times*, 13 February, available at: https://www.irishtimes.com/business/economy/dublin-rents-to-rise-to-2-500-before-they-start-to-slow-1.3389643?mode=sample&auth-failed=1&pw-origin=https%3A%2F%2Fwww.irishtimes.com%2Fbusiness%2Feconomy%2Fdublin-rents-to-rise-to-2-500-before-they-start-to-slow-1.3389643 [accessed 4 March 2018].

Reinhart, C. and Rogoff, K. (2010) 'Growth in a time of debt', *American Economic Review*, NBER Working Paper, No. 15639, available at: http://www.nber.org/papers/w15639 [accessed 18 January 2016].

Rent Café (2023) 'Average rent in the U.S. and rent prices by state', available at: https://www.rentcafe.com/average-rent-market-trends/us/ [accessed 8 October 2023].

Residential Tenancies Board (2021) 'The RTB publish findings from their Rental Sector Survey 2020 reports', 14 July, available at: https://www.rtb.ie/news/the-rtb-publish-findings-from-their-rental-sector-survey-2020-reports#:~:text=Affordability%20remains%20a%20significant%20issue,their%20net%20income%20on%20rent [accessed 8 October 2023].

Roche, Z. (2012) 'A qualitative analysis of debt, truth production and value among Irish urban middle class professionals', unpublished BA thesis, Waterford Institute of Technology.

Roche, Z. (2019) 'Life after debt: a critical analysis of the engagement/non-engagement of debtors with the Insolvency Service of Ireland', unpublished PhD thesis, University of Limerick.

Rock, P. (2014) *Making People Pay*, Abingdon: Routledge.

Rodriguez, G.J. (1999) 'Commentary: generalisability and validity in qualitative research', *British Medical Journal*, available at: https://go.gale.com/ps/i.do?p=AONE&u=googlescholar&id=GALE|A55670112&v=2.1&it=r&sid=AONE&asid=9c300c76 [accessed 15 August 2016].

Rose, N. (1991). *Powers of Freedom: Reframing Political Thought*, Cambridge: Cambridge University Press.

Rose, N. (1998) 'Governing risky individuals: the role of psychiatry in new regimens of control', *Psychiatry, Psychology and Law*, 5(2), 177–195.

Rose, N. (1999) *Governing the Soul: The Shaping of the Private Self*, 2nd edn, London: Free Association Books.

Rose, N. (2000) 'Community, citizenship, and the third way', *American Behavioral Scientist*, 43(9), 1395–1411.

RTE (2015) 'Bertie Ahern admits mistakes, but defends legacy', *RTE*, 17 July, available at: https://www.rte.ie/news/2015/0716/715090-banking-inquiry/ [accessed 24 February 2016].

Russell, H., Maitre, B., and Donnelly, N. (2011) *Financial Exclusion and Over-Indebtedness in Irish Households, Social Inclusion Report 1*, Dublin: Department of Community, Equality and Gaeltacht Affairs.

Russell, H., Maitre, B., and Whelan, C.T. (2013) 'Economic vulnerability and severity of debt problems: an analysis of EU-SILC 2008', *European Sociological Review*, 29(4), 695–706, available at: https://academic.oup.com/esr/article-abstract/29/4/695/540267?redirectedFrom=fulltext [accessed 22 October 2015].

Ryan, N. (2015) 'The banks weren't showing compassion, they were waiting for an increase in property prices', *The Journal*, 9 May, available at: http://www.thejournal.ie/repossessions-figures-grow-1980701-Mar2015/?utm_source=businessetc [accessed 15 August 2016].

Ryan, O. (2016) 'Many people in mortgage arrears are contemplating suicide', *The Journal*, 20 March, available at: http://www.thejournal.ie/mortgage-arrears-suicide-2670570-Mar2016/ [accessed 25 October 2017].

Safe Food (2012) 'Food poverty indicator: three key food deprivation factors', available at: https://www.safefood.net/getmedia/1ed61304-31c0-4684-8b0f-49efe4a8d278/Final-G6056_Safefood_Report_FoodPoverty Ireland_V21.aspx?ext=.pdf [accessed 21 March 2016].

Saldana, J. and Omasta, M. (2017) *Qualitative Research: Analyzing Life*, New York: Sage.

Sayer, A. (2005) *The Moral Significance of Class,* Cambridge: Cambridge University Press.

Schwandt, T. (2007) *The Sage Dictionary of Qualitative Inquiry*, 3rd edn, London: Sage.

Schwartz, B. (2022) 'Inhabiting debt(un)worthiness: encounters between people with problem debt and state institutions', unpublished PhD thesis, Roskilde University.

Schwarzkopf, S. (2018) 'Cosmos, excess and surveillance: an account of the economic theology of data', presented at the Economy and Society Summer School, 14–18 May.

Schwarzkopf, S. (ed.) (2020) *The Routledge Handbook of Economic Theology*, Abingdon: Routledge.

Sernau, S. (2016) *Social Inequality in a Global Age*, London: Sage.

Sheehy, C. (2013) 'Flood of 20,000 to go for controversial debt relief service in first year', *The Herald*, 19 April, available at: https://www.herald.ie/news/flood-of-20000-to-go-for-controversial-debt-relief-service-in-the-first-year-29207899.html [accessed 23 March 2016].

Shildrick, T. (2013) *Poverty and Insecurity: Life in Low-Pay, No-Pay Britain*, Bristol: Policy Press.

Shipman-Roberts, P. (2022) *Excessive Debt Is a Disease That Can Be Cured: 5 Steps to Debt Freedom*, Gaithersburg: Roberts Target Financials LLC.

Silverman, D. (1993) *Interpreting Qualitative Data: Methods for Analysing Talk, Text, and Interaction*, London: Sage.

Silverman, D. (2005) *Doing Qualitative Research*, 2nd edn, London: Sage.

Singletary, M. (2023) 'Credit card debt tops $1 trillion, trapping even six-figure earners', *Washington Post*, 9 August, available at: https://www.washingtonpost.com/business/2023/08/08/credit-card-debt-1-trillion-high-earners/ [accessed 8 October 2023].

Skeggs, B. (1997) *Formations of Class and Gender*, London: Sage.

Skidelsky, R. and Skidelsky. (2012). *How Much is Enough? The Love of Money and the Case for the Good Life*, London: Penguin.

Sløk, C. (2020) 'Guilt', in S. Schwarzkopf (ed.), *The Routledge Handbook of Economic Theology*, Abingdon: Routledge, pp 72–80.

Smiles, S. (2009) *Character*, Colorado: Serenity Publishers.

Society of Saint Vincent de Paul (2013) *Submission to Amárach Research and the Central Bank of Ireland on Money Lending in Ireland*, Dublin: SVP Social Justice and Policy Team.

Soederberg, S. (2014) *Debtfare: States and the Poverty Industry: Money, Discipline and the Surplus Population*, New York: Routledge.

Sousa, M. (2013) 'Just punch my bankruptcy ticket: a qualitative study of mandatory debtor financial education', *Marquette Law Review*, 97(2), 391–467, available at: http://scholarship.law.marquette.edu/mulr/vol97/iss2/6 [accessed 8 October 2023].

Sousa, M. (2017) 'Debt stigma and socioeconomic class', University of Denver Legal Studies Research Paper, No. 17–16, available at: https://papers.ssrn.com/sol3/papers.cfm?abstract_id=2966310 [accessed 1 May 2018].

Spooner, J. (2012) 'Long overdue: what the belated reform of Irish personal insolvency law tells us about comparative consumer bankruptcy', *American Bankruptcy Law Journal*, 86(2), 243–304, available at: https://heinonline.org/HOL/LandingPage?handle=hein.journals/ambank86&div=14&id=&page=.

Spooner, J. (2018) 'The quiet-loud-quiet politics of post-crisis consumer bankruptcy law: the case of Ireland and the Troika', *Modern Law Review*, 81(5), 790–824. doi: 10.1111/1468-2230.12365.

Spooner, J. (2019) *Bankruptcy: The Case for Relief in an Economy of Debt*, Cambridge: Cambridge University Press.

Springer, S. (2016) *The Discourse of Neoliberalism: An Anatomy of a Powerful Idea*, Baltimore: Rowman & Littlefield.

Stake, R. (1995) *The Art of Case Study Research*, Thousand Oaks: Sage.

Stamp, S. (2009) *To No One's Credit? A Study of the Debtor's Experience of Instalment and Committal Orders in the Irish Legal System*, Dublin: Free Legal Advice Centre.

Stamp, S. (2012a) *The Over-indebtedness in European Households: Updated Mapping of the Situation, Nature and Causes, Effects and Initiatives for Alleviating Its Impact: Irish Country Report*, available at: https://www.mabs.ie/downloads/reports_submissions/part_2_synthesis_of_findings_en.pdf [accessed October 1 2015].

Stamp, S. (2012b) 'The impact of debt advice as a response to financial difficulties in Ireland', *Social Policy and Society*, 11(1), 93–104. doi: 10.1017/S1474746411000443.

Stamp, S. (2013) 'Socializing the loss, personalizing the responsibility and privatizing the response – the Irish policy approach to personal debt post 2008', available at: http://www.birmingham.ac.uk/Documents/college-social-sciences/socialpolicy/ CHASM/briefing-papers/2013/irish-policy-approach-to-personal-debt-post-2008.pdf.

Stamp, S. (2016) 'Personal finance: financial services, access to credit and debt management', in M.P. Murphy, and F. Dukelow (eds), *The Irish Welfare State in the Twenty-First Century*, London: Palgrave Macmillan, pp 119–139.

Stamp, S. (2017) 'Left behind in the cold? Fuel poverty, money management and financial difficulty among Dublin 10 and 20 clients', available at: https://www.mabs.ie/downloads/reports_submissions/Left_Behind_in_the_Cold_Dublin_10_and_20_MABS_Report.pdf [accessed 20 May 2018].

Stanley, L., Deville, J. and Montgomerie, J. (2016) 'Digital debt management: the everyday life of austerity', *New Formations*, 87, 64–82. doi: 10.3898/NEWF.87.4.2016.

Stiglitz, J. (2012) *The Price of Inequality*, New York: W.W. Norton & Company.

Streeck, W. (2011) 'The crises of democratic capitalism', *New Left Review*, 71(1), 5–29, available at: http://pubman.mpdl.mpg.de/pubman/item/escidoc:1231852/component/escidoc:1827359/NLR_71_2011_Streeck.pdf [accessed 4 November 2015].

Stuber, J. and Schlesinger, M. (2006) 'Sources of stigma for means-tested government programs', *Social Science and Medicine*, 63, 933–945.

Surviving Economic Abuse (2020) 'What is economic abuse?', available at: https://survivingeconomicabuse.org/what-is-economic-abuse/ [accessed 22 March 2021].

Sylvia, W. (2010) 'A social science research agenda on the financial crisis', *21st Century Society: Journal of the Academy of Social Sciences*, 5(1), 19–31.

Szakolczai, A. (2014) 'Permanent (trickster) liminality: the reasons of the heart and of the mind', presented at *ESF Exploratory Workshop, Affectivity and liminality: Conceptualising the dynamics of suspended transition*, Brighton, 17–19 November.

Tanguay, L. (2015) 'Governmentality in crisis: debt and the illusion of liberalism', *Symploke*, 23(1), 459–468, available at: https://muse.jhu.edu/article/605683/pdf [accessed 21 February 2016].

Tansel, C.B. (2017) *States of Discipline: Authoritarian Neoliberalism and the Contested Reproduction of Capitalist Order*, Lanham: Rowman & Littlefield.

Taylor, B.K. (1990) *Imagine No Possessions: Towards a Sociology of Poverty*, New York: Harvester Wheatsheaf.

Taylor, C. (2015) 'Ireland still among top countries to do business – Forbes', *Irish Times*, 18 December, available at: https://www.irishtimes.com/business/economy/ireland-still-among-top-countries-to-do-business-forbes-1.2471015 [accessed 23 January 2016].

Thomassen, B. (2009) 'The uses and meanings of liminality', *International Political Anthropology*, 2(1), available at: https://forskning.ruc.dk/en/publications/the-uses-and-meaning-of-liminality [accessed 2 June 2016].

Thompson, E.P. (1971) 'The moral economy of the English crowd in the eighteenth century', *Past & Present*, 50(1), 76–136, available at: https://www.jstor.org/stable/pdf/650244.pdf [accessed 8 October 2023].

Thornton, L. (2014) 'Direct provision: the beginning of the end?', *Human Rights in Ireland*, 6 August, available at: https://liamthornton.ie/2014/08/06/direct-provision-the-beginning-of-the-end/ [accessed 1 June 2018].

Thornton, L. and Ni Raghallaigh, M. (2014) '#Direct provision at 14: no place to call home', available at: http://irserver.ucd.ie/handle/10197/5707 [accessed 12 November 2015].

Titley, G. (2015) 'All aboard the migration nation', in C. Coulter and A. Nagle (eds), *Ireland under Austerity: Neoliberal Crisis, Neoliberal Solutions*, Manchester: Manchester University Press, pp 192–216.

Turner, V. (1967). *The Ritual Process: Structure and Anti-structure*, Piscataway: Aldine Transaction.

Tyler, I. (2008) '"Chav mum chav scum"', *Feminist Media Studies*, 8(1), 17–34, available at: https://www.tandfonline.com/doi/abs/10.1080/14680770701824779 [accessed 8 January 2018].

UK Land Registry (2023) 'UK House Price Index', available at: https://landregistry.data.gov.uk/app/ukhpi/browse?from=1990-01-01&location=http%3A%2F%2Flandregistry.data.gov.uk%2Fid%2Fregion%2Funited-kingdom&to=2020-12-01&lang=en [accessed January 5 2023].

US Courts (2022a) 'Bankruptcy', available at: https://www.uscourts.gov/services-forms/bankruptcy [accessed 11 November 2022].

US Courts (2022b) 'Caseload data statistics tables', available at: https://www.uscourts.gov/statistics-reports/caseload-statistics-data-tables [accessed 19 October 2022].

Van Oorschot, W. (2000) 'Who should get what, and why? On deservingness criteria and the conditionality of solidarity among the public', *Policy & Politics*, 28(1), 33–48. doi: 10.1332/0305573002500811.

Veblen, T. (2005) *Conspicuous Consumption: Unproductive Consumption of Goods Is Honourable*, London: Penguin.

Viala-Gaudefroy, J. (2019) 'Neoliberal metaphors in presidential discourse from Ronald Reagan to Donald Trump', *Angles: New Perspectives in the Anglophone World*, 8(1), available at: https://journals.openedition.org/angles/625 [accessed 8 October 2023].

Wahlbeck, K. and McDaid, D. (2012) 'Actions to alleviate the mental health impacts of the economic crisis', *World Psychiatry*, 11(3), 139–145, available at: https://www.ncbi.nlm.nih.gov/pmc/articles/PMC3449359/ [accessed 5 November 2016].

Walby, S. (2009) *Globalization and Inequalities: Complexity and Contested Modernities*, London: Sage.

Waldron, R. (2016) 'The "unrevealed casualties" of the Irish mortgage crisis: analysing the broader impacts of mortgage market financialisation', *Geoforum*, 69(1), 53–66. doi: 10.1016/j.geoforum.2015.11.005.

Waldron, R. and Redmond, D. (2015) 'Stress in suburbia: counting the costs of Ireland's property crash and the mortgage arrears crisis', *Tijdschrift voor economische en sociale geografie*, 107(4), 484–501. doi: 10.1111/tesg.12170.

Waldron, R. and Redmond, D. (2016) '"We're just existing, not living!" Mortgage stress and the concealed costs of coping with crisis', *Housing Studies*, 10(1), 584–612. doi: 10.1080/02673037.2016.1224323.

Walker, C. (2011) 'Personal debt, cognitive delinquency and techniques of governmentality: neoliberal constructions of financial inadequacy in the UK', *Journal of Community & Applied Psychology*, 22(6), 533–538. doi: 10.1002/casp.1127.

Waring, J. and Latif, A. (2018) 'Of shepherds, sheep and sheepdogs? Governing the adherent self through complementary and competing "pastorates"', *Sociology*, 52(5). doi: 10.1177/0038038517690680.

Waring, J. and Martin, G. (2016) 'Network leadership as pastoral power: the governance of quality improvement communities in the English National Health Service', in M. Bevir (ed.), *Governmentality after Neoliberalism*. Abingdon: Routledge, pp 135–151.

Watts, G. (2021) 'Are you a neoliberal subject? On the uses and abuses of a concept', *European Journal of Social Theory*, 25(3), 458–476. doi: 10.1177/13684310211037205.

Weston, C. (2012) 'Bank agrees to write off €110k mortgage debt', *Irish Independent*, 6 November, available at: https://www.pressreader.com/ireland/irish-independent/20121106/281694022044373 [accessed 26 February 2017].

Weston, C. (2018) 'Thousands of homeowners "paid nothing on loan for years"', *Irish Independent*, 22 February, available at: https://www.independent.ie/business/personal-finance/property-mortgages/thousands-of-homeowners-paid-nothing-on-loan-for-years-36630688.html [accessed 23 March 2018].

Weston, C. (2022) 'Mortgage misery for thousands as Start and county councils hike interest rates', *Irish Independent*, 26 November, available at: https://www.independent.ie/business/personal-finance/property-mortgages/mortgage-misery-for-thousands-as-start-and-county-councils-hike-interest-rates-42175036.html [accessed 27 November 2022].

Whelan, J. (2022) *Hidden Voices: Lived Experiences in the Irish Welfare Space*, Bristol: Policy Press.

White, A. (2022) 'Americans have an average of 4 credit cards – is that too many?', *CNBC*, 10 May, available at: https://www.cnbc.com/select/how-many-credit-cards-does-the-average-american-have/ [accessed 27 November 2022].

White, B.T. (2010) 'Underwater and not walking away: shame, fear, and the social management of the housing crisis', *Wake Forest Law Review*, 45(1), available at: https://papers.ssrn.com/sol3/papers.cfm?abstract_id=1494467 [accessed 14 July 2017].

White House (2022) 'Fact sheet: President Biden announces student loan relief for borrowers who need it most' available at: https://www.whitehouse.gov/briefing-room/statements-releases/2022/08/24/fact-sheet-president-biden-announces-student-loan-relief-for-borrowers-who-need-it-most/ [accessed 27 August 2022].

Wilde, O. (1891) *The Soul of Man under Socialism*, available at: https://www.marxists.org/reference/archive/wilde-oscar/soul-man/ [accessed 27 August 2022].

Wilkis, A. (2017) *The Moral Power of Money: Morality and Economy in the Life of the Poor*, Stanford: Stanford University Press.

Williams, B. (2005) *Debt for Sale: A Social History of the Credit Trap*, Philadelphia: University of Pennsylvania Press.

Williams, B. (2008) 'The precipice of debt', in J. Collins, M. Leonardo and B. Williams (eds), *New Landscapes of Inequality: Neoliberalism and the Erosion of Democracy in America*, Santa Fe: School for Advanced Research Press, pp 65–90.

Women's Aid (2020) 'What is economic abuse?', available at: https://www.womensaid.ie/what-is-abuse/types-of-abuse/economic-abuse/#:~:text=Economic%20abuse%20is%20when%20your%20partner%20or%20ex%2Dpartner%3A&text=Denies%20you%20access%20to%20joint,Refuses%20to%20pay%20child [accessed 25 March 2021].

Women's Health Council (2007) Women, Debt and Health, Dublin: A Joint Report of the Women's Health Council and MABS, available at: https://www.lenus.ie/bitstream/handle/10147/45715/8730.pdf?sequence=1&isAllowed=y [accessed 2 March 2018].

Wood, J.D.G. (2016) 'The effects of the distribution of mortgage credit on the wage share: varieties of residential capitalism compared', *Comparative European Politics*, 15, 819–847. doi: 10.1057/s41295-016-0006-5.

Wray, M. (2006) *Not Quite White: White Trash and the Boundaries of Whiteness*, Durham, NC: Duke University Press.

Wright, C.W. (2000) *The Sociological Imagination*, Oxford: Oxford University Press.

Zaloom, C. (2021) *Indebted: How Families Make College Work at Any Cost*, Princeton: Princeton University Press.

Zelizer, V.A. (1994) *The Social Meaning of Money: Pin Money, Paychecks, Poor Relief, and Other Currencies*, Princeton: Princeton University Press.

Zelizer, V.A. (2011) *Economic Lives: How Culture Shapes the Economy*, Princeton: Princeton University Press.

Žitko, M. (2018) 'Governmentality versus moral economy: notes on the debt crisis', *Innovation: The European Journal of Social Science Research*, 31(1), 68–82, available at: https://www.tandfonline.com/doi/abs/10.1080/13511610.2018.1429897 [accessed 22 February 2018].

Žižek, S. (2015) *Trouble in Paradise: From the End of History to the End of Capitalism*, Brooklyn: Melville House.

Index

References to endnotes show both the page number and the note number (231n3).

A

Adams, R. 124
addiction 71, 83, 84, 111
Adkins et al 18
Aristotle 32
asceticism 138
asset economy 17–19
attachment 121, 122

B

bad debt 22, 24, 139, 146
bad debtors 54, 115, 127, 147
bankruptcy 1
  alternatives to 20–21
  consumer-oriented approach 24
  definition 4
  delaying 26
  experience of 5
  fees for 26
  overrepresentation of groups 25–27
  reasons for 25–27
  reforms 20–22
    application of debtors 21
    insolvency 20–21
    reduced restrictions 21
    reduction in period of 20
Bankruptcy Abuse Prevention and Consumer Protection Act (BAPCPA, 2005) 26
bankruptcy tourism 20
banks 126, 129–130
  inflation control 42
  new money creation 14
  stockpiles 14
  see also central banks
Bauman, Z. 124
Bell, D.M. 96
Berlant, Lauren 32–33, 121, 134, 135
  see also good life
Biden, Joe 23
Boland, T. and Griffin, R. 51, 109

borrowers, cognitive biases of 31
  see also debtors
borrowing 129, 147
  reasons for 144
  see also debt
Bourdieu, P. 82, 84
Braucher et al 26
budgeting 45–46, 53, 59

C

capitalism 133
  desire 121
  economic theology and 95–97
  gospel of liberty 96
  poverty and 95, 142
  problem-solving 16
  purchasing decisions 96
  stagflation 16
  see also neoliberalism
caring debts 78, 79, 86–87
cash in hand 132
Catholicism 108
Celtic Tiger 124, 126
central banks 16, 42
Chapter 7 liquidation bankruptcy 4, 11, 26
Chapter 13 bankruptcy 4, 11, 20, 26–27, 106
charity 53
Christianity 145
Civic Consulting survey (2013) 156n1
class 82–89
clean slate 108
  definition 94
  legendary reputation 94
  origins of 94
  see also insolvency programmes; PCs (Protective Certificates)
Code of Conduct on Mortgage Arrears 152
coerced debt 38
confessional churches 82
confessions in insolvency 71, 74–92, 92, 139
  absolution 81–82
  appeal of 75–76

INDEX

class and gender 82–89
common features of 77–78
contrition 74–75, 76–77, 80, 92–93
cooperation 77
guilt 82
moral storytelling 78, 92
morally convincing 143
penance 74, 80–81, 93, 112
quantities of debt 77
self-advocacy 143
truthfulness 77
understanding behaviour of PIPs 89–92
Connolly, Christine 100
conspicuous consumption 79, 96
consumerism 71, 85, 137
cost of living 42–44
COVID-19 pandemic 35, 150, 154
cramdown 11
credit 2, 146
credit card debt 28
credit reports 101–102, 103
credit sanctioning 102
credit scores 102, 103
creditors 10, 55–57, 61
  assessing debtors' legitimacy 131
  communication from debtors 47–48
  cooperativeness of debtors 104–105
  dealings with PIPs 103–104
  debt advisors and 61
  delinquent debtors and 142
  exercising restraint 130–131
  pastoral care 57
  PCs (Protective Certificates) 98, 101–106
  power to veto 25, 90, 101, 101–106, 112
  preferential treatment 24–25
  punishment of debtors 148
  restructuring and negotiation 11
  setting debtors up to fail 106
  strategic defaulters 131–132
  threats and aggression by 56–57
  tools of 58
  toxic debts 142
  in the US 106
cruel optimism 120–123, 131, 134, 135
cultural capital 82

D

Davies et al 108, 122, 131, 146
debt
  in America 13
  deluge of 8–9, 13–30
  discourse on 137
  excess of 140–143
  feminization of 88–89
  guilt and 145, 146
  in Ireland 17
  language of guilt and sin 142, 146
  moral and social considerations 141
  promise to pay 145

sources of problems 31–32
stigma of 8
temporality and 52
theories and metaphors of 8–9
types of 9
debt abolition 149, 150
debt advice 54, 57–62
debt advisors 58
  functions of 60
  role of 58–59
  siding with debtors 61
  training and qualifications 60
debt cancellation 149, 150, 151
debt collectors 10, 56
debt crisis 37
debt distress 1, 28, 46, 49, 118
debt forgiveness 97
debt relief 1–2
  case for 9–12
  characterization by neoliberalism 69
  conditionalized 28
  goal of 27–30
  goal of reform of 142
  inability to pay 142, 143, 146
  lessening of stigma 22–25
  liberalization of lending 13
  means-testing of 151
  modernizing 19–30
  older systems of 19–20
  opponents of 149, 151
  policy approach 141
  process of purification 137
  punitive conditions 141
  reimagining of 119
  salvific and miraculous 142
  stabilizing mechanism 142
  unwillingness to pay 142, 143, 146
debt resolution process 58
debtfare 28
debtors 36–46
  accepting guilt and shame 138–139
  accessing expertise 139
  applying for bankruptcy *see* bankruptcy
  attachment to homes 122
  background of 83–84
  bad 54, 115, 127, 147
  becoming 37
  'borrowing from Peter to pay Paul' 41–42
  characterization of 22–23
  confessions of *see* confessions in insolvency
  creditors and 9, 61–62
  cruel optimism 120–123, 131, 134, 135
  debt-free day 147
  deviancy, feeling of 52
  disadvantages in negotiations 141
  economic confessions 143
  fictitious 'other' 122
  financial literacy classes 23–24
  Foucault's pastor metaphor 50

governmentality 120–121, 122
guilt of 146–147
hatred of other debtors 114–115
impact on relationships 37–40
inaction of 138
independence 60
individualization of 120
insolvency practitioners and 61–62
ISI (Insolvency Service of Ireland)
  critique of application process 116
  reconstruction of 119
  refusing to return to 115–116, 127–128
  rejection by 115–123
  scapegoating other debtors 117–119
  unfairness of 117
lazy 116, 122, 125, 127
pawning of valuables 53
processing 140
professional debt advisors 54
reform through suffering 52–54
rising cost of living 42–44
sacrifices of 54, 67, 115, 123–124, 126, 147–148
salvific language of 9, 63
sincerity of 81
stereotyping of 68, 82–89, 115, 127
stories in newspapers 119
subjectivity 37
symbolic gestures 44–46, 47, 67, 138, 139
taking control 131–132
unemployment 40–42
views on PIPs 90–91
see also insolvency: debtors; PIPs (Personal Insolvency Practitioners): debtors; purgatorial sweatbox
delinquent debt 21
deluge metaphor 8–9, 13–30
Dempsey, M.T. 96
deregulation 15
desire 124
  cruel optimism 120–121
  good life 47, 121
  triangular relationship 124
  unfulfilled and irrational 32
  see also mimetic desire
deviancy 83
Deville, J. 11, 56
digital subprime 11
dirty starts 28, 29
disciplinary power 37
disidentification 84, 85, 86
displacement theory 118, 122, 123
distinction 96, 97
Durkheim, Émile 8

E

economic abuse 38
economic capital 82
economic confessions 143
economic drag 1, 4, 9–10

economic storytelling 78
economic theology 2, 9, 70, 95–97, 145–148
  contribution of 145
  making sacrifices 147–148
economics 95–96
education 33, 150
efficiency 96, 97
entrepreneurs 14
Epicurus 32
equitability rhetoric 24–25
European Economic Community (EEC) 95

F

fairness 151
family life 122
fantasy 121
feudalism 133
finance 15–16
financial advice 58
financial incompetence 85–86
financial literacy 23–24, 43, 46, 53
  courses in 94
  new standards of 141
  reform of 153
financial melancholia 122, 146
financialization 11, 16, 144
food poverty 88, 122
food riots 133
Foohey et al 51
Foucault, Michel 37, 50, 81
  confession 75–76
  pastoral power 50, 54–69, 139
free time
  employed people 109, 142
  unemployed people 40–41, 109, 142
freedom 15–16, 108
fresh starts 27–28, 29

G

Garfinkel, Howard 146
Geertz, Clifford 5
gender 82–89
GFC (Global Financial Crisis) 1, 29, 36, 40, 144
Girard, R. 124, 125, 147
Girardian mimetic rivalry 115, 123, 124, 125, 127, 147
Goffman, E. 22
good faith 2, 20, 105, 106
good life 32–36, 39, 47, 121, 122, 134
  consequences of failure 38–39, 47, 122
  education 33
  expense of 35, 47
  fantasy/dream of 114–115, 121
  ideal family 33, 35
  imaginary of 35
  milestones 36–37, 134
  neoliberal ideal of 123
  owning a home 33, 34, 35
  pervasive narrative of 121
  philosophical considerations 32–33

INDEX

seductiveness of 34
socialization 34
as a story 33
under attack 34–36
work 33
good work 33
governmentality
  acceptance of 122
  governing through freedom 66
  of indebtedness 120, 123
  neoliberal 66, 68–69, 73, 120
  relays 66
  respect and cooperation of debtors 120–121, 122
  responsibilization and normalization 67–68, 120
Graeber, D. 141, 150
Greeks 125
Greene, Marjorie Taylor 23
guilt
  Christianity and 145
  confessions 82
  debt and 145, 146
  of debtors 146–147
  language of 142, 146
  universalism of 146

H

hard laws 152
Harvey, David 16
Hayek, Friedrich 15
help-to-buy scheme 19
heteronormativity 35
hidden debt 38–39
homeownership 17–18, 47, 134–135
  borrowing for 19
  evictions 126
  falling rates of 19
  fantasy of 114
  mimetic desire for 124
  qualitative properties of 125
  repossessions 57, 128
  see also mortgages
hourly compensation 16–17
houses see homeownership
housing, median price of 19

I

indebted subjectivity 128–129
indebtedness 48, 60
  coerced debt 37–38
  economic theology of 142
  experts in 62
  governmentality of 120
  in Ireland 12
  moral economy of 142
  purgatory of 52, 54, 58, 98, 114
  stigmatization of 86
  stress of 10
  subjectivity of 47, 61, 132

temporalities of 147
unemployment 41
women 87
see also over-indebtedness
Individual Voluntary Arrangements see IVAs (Individual Voluntary Arrangements)
infinite repayments 11
inflation 42
insolvency 10, 62–69
  alternatives to bankruptcy 20–21
  application criteria 25
  applications process of 91–92
  clearing the market 21–22
  debtors
    confessions of see confessions in insolvency
    disidentification 84, 85, 86
    documents 71–72
    interviews at homes of PIPs 71–73
    invisible curriculum 71
    middle-class 71, 79, 82, 84
    women 71, 85–88
    working-class 71, 83, 84–85
  definition 4
  discriminatory practices in 27
  legislation 27–28
  reforming 151–155
  see also confessions in insolvency; ISI (Insolvency Service of Ireland); PCs (Protective Certificates); PIPs (Personal Insolvency Practitioners)
insolvency practitioners 11, 139
  see also PIPs (Personal Insolvency Practitioners)
insolvency programmes 20, 20–21, 23–24, 87
  annual reviews 109–111
  benefits of 107, 108–109
  conditions on debtors 109
  duration of 153–154
  infractions 111
  see also confessions in insolvency
insolvency relations 139
Insolvency Service of England 24, 26
Insolvency Service of Ireland (ISI) 26
interest rates 1
  low 16, 42
  raising of 16, 43
investing 141
Ireland
  Celtic Tiger 12
  housing policy 79
  rent crisis 126
  scapegoating 125–126
  two-tier health service 36
ISI (Insolvency Service of Ireland) 26, 27, 51
  accessibility of 127–128
  agreement of creditors 105
  avoidance of 115–116, 127–128
  concerns about 63
  debtors' experience of 116–117
  development of 107

expectations of 62–63
funding, lack of 66
gender discrimination 89
guidelines for RLEs 99–100
insolvency applications 107
optimism towards 63
perception of 111
political work 100
rejection of debtors 115–123
structure of 65
uncertainty about 62–63, 63–64
IVAs (Individual Voluntary Arrangements) 4, 11, 20

J

jargon 60–61
Jesus 145
jubilee 149–151
just prices 133
justification 60, 68
  concept of 107–108

K

Keynes, John Maynard 96
Kiviat, B. 78

L

Lagarde, Christine 12
language 83–84
lazy debtors 116, 122, 125, 127
Lazzarato, M. 125, 128–129, 146
leisure debts 78, 79, 85, 87, 118
lenders
  credit reports 102
  data on debtors 102
  face-to-face meetings 102
liberal market economies *see* LMEs (liberal market economies)
liberty 96, 97
life trajectory 121
lived experience 83
  of bankruptcy 5
  definition 5
  participant profiles 6–7
LMEs (liberal market economies) 10, 148
  debt relief in 20–22
  welfare 28
loans for wages 2, 10, 16–17
London Gazette 21

M

MABS (Money Advice and Budgeting Service) 58
market prices 133
markets
  complexity of 15
  conditions for flourishing 69
  efficiency of 96
  innovation 35–36

neoliberalism 15
  reducing influence of state in 15, 66, 69, 139, 141, 142, 144
  regulation 15
  see also LMEs (liberal market economies)
Martin, G.P. and Waring, J. 55
mass debt forgiveness 140
mass evictions 140
Mauss, M. 124
McClanahan, A. 10, 129
mental health 79–80
metaphors 8, 14
  see also purgatorial sweatbox
Mills, C. Wright 148
mimesis 123–128
  scapegoats 125
  seductiveness of 124–125
  theories of 124
mimetic desire 123, 124, 125
mimetic relationships 124–125
mimetic rivalry 115, 123, 124, 125, 127, 147
minimum wage 10
  in Ireland 17
  in the US 17
money
  dead money 18
  moral and social meanings 9, 44–45, 47
  status and class 96, 97
Money Advice and Budgeting Service (MABS) 58
money management funds 123–124, 128
Montgomerie, J. 78
moral economy 133
moral hazard 2, 25, 63, 128, 154
moral storytelling 78, 92
morality 136–138
Mortgage Arrears Resolution Process 77, 130, 152
mortgages
  accessibility of 18
  arrears in 57
  cost of 126–127
  fixed-rate 43
  median cost of 19, 30
  repossessions 57, 128
  restructuring of 57
  switching 43–44
  symbolism of success 36–37
  variable rate 43
mortgagors
  concerns of 42–43
  median age of 19
  see also homeownership
Murray, S. 126

N

nanny state 15
National Assets Management Agency (NAMA) 100

INDEX

negative status debts 79
neoliberal governmentality 66, 68–69, 73, 120
neoliberalism 13, 14–19, 55, 96
  creating exclusion 69
  definition 15
  financial deregulation 141
  flourishing markets 141
  resistance to 128–134
  theoretical forms of 14
  see also capitalism
NHS (National Health Service) 36
Nietzsche, Friedrich 32, 129, 148
  guilt, theory of 145
NINA debtors 11
nixers 117
nonmortgage loans 17
normalization 67, 68, 120

O

O'Connor, Lorcan 24, 25
Official Receiver 26
O'Mahony, Larry 100
optimism 120–123
optimism bias 31
outsourced jobs 16
over-indebtedness 8, 47
  definitions 3
  experience of 52
  literature about 31
  living through 137–140
  macroeconomic causes 31, 47
  rising cost of living 42
  unending punishment of 142
  women 71, 87

P

Pandemic Unemployment Payment 154
passive income 19
pastoral power 50, 54–69, 139
  creditors 55–57
  debt advice 57–62
  investigating insolvency 62–69
  problem solving 55
  see also debt advisors
Paycheck Protection Program (PPP) loans 23
payday loans 23, 28, 136
  rates of interest 42
paying bills 44–45
PCs (Protective Certificates) 97–106, 107
  application to courts 97–98
  benefits of 98
  convincing creditors 98, 101–106
  court reviews 105
  international comparisons 106
  reasonable living expenses (RLEs) 98–101
peasantry 133
Pell Grants 151
Personal Insolvency Act (2012) 20
Personal Insolvency Arrangements *see* PIAs (Personal Insolvency Arrangements)
Personal Insolvency Practitioners *see* PIPs (Personal Insolvency Practitioners)
PFSs (Prescribed Financial Statements) 72, 97, 107
PIAs (Personal Insolvency Arrangements) 4, 11, 20, 107
PIPs (Personal Insolvency Practitioners) 4, 29, 64–65
  background of 83
  championing debtors 104
  common themes 65–66
  complaints of 90
  confessions of debtors *see* confessions in insolvency
  debtors
    characterizing and stereotyping of 68, 71, 82–89
    face-to-face meetings 76
    ignoring documents of 89–90
    inconsistencies in stories of 78–79
    interviewing 71–73
    power to veto 90
    procedure for insolvency applications 89–90
    sacrifices demanded of 67, 68
    untrustworthiness of 74–75, 90
    women 84, 86–89
    working-class 83–85
  discretionary powers of 65–66
  fees and income 65, 66–67, 100–101
  independence of 72
  language of 83–84
  limited resources of 109–110
  middle-class character of 83
  neoliberal governmentality 68
  processing of PCs *see* PCs (Protective Certificates)
  rejection of PFSs 107
  views on debtors
    abusers of system 68
    checking up on 109–110
    dishonesty of 67
    lack of knowledge or training 90
    passing judgement on 78–79, 90
    power to veto 90
    sacrifices demanded of 67
    sad stories of 91
    understanding 'unable' criterion 66
    untrustworthiness of 75, 90
    women debtors 87–88
    working-class debtors 83–84
Plato 32
political economy of obligations 143–144
Porter, K. and Thorne, D. 28
positive mimesis 124
postwar era 16, 19, 33, 35
poverty 53, 88–89

power 64
Prescribed Financial Statements *see* PFSs (Prescribed Financial Statements)
privatization 35–36
privatized Keynesianism 17
productivity 16–17
professional debtors 102, 137
profitability 11
property developers 19
Protective Certificates *see* PCs (Protective Certificates)
Protestant Ethic (Weber) 96, 138
Protestantism 108
Prügl, Elisabeth 14
purgatorial sweatbox 49, 50–51, 70
  pastoral power 54–69
  reform through suffering 52–54
  time and anxiety 51–52
purgatory 49, 51–52, 70, 109
  ultimate goal of 53

Q

qualitative research 5
Quinn, Seán 20
quitters 116, 119, 128

R

Ramsay, I. 11, 153
Reagan, Ronald 15
reasonable living expenses *see* RLEs (Reasonable Living Expenses)
rejection 115–123, 129
relationships 37–40
relays 66
rent
  dead money 18
  increases in 10, 17, 18
Residential Tenancies Board (RTB) 91
responsibilization 67–68, 120, 129
retirement savings 16
rivalry, in society 124
RLEs (Reasonable Living Expenses) 94, 98–101, 112
Rock, P. 97, 129
Rose, Nikolas 15, 81–82, 96
RTB (Residential Tenancies Board) 91

S

sacrifices
  of debtors 54, 67, 115, 123–124, 126, 147–148
  of homeownership 122
  sacredness of 127
  sacrificial subjects 127
  of scapegoats 68, 123–124, 126
salvation 96, 109–112
scapegoats/scapegoating 50, 125–126, 133, 147
  Greeks 125
  historic origins of 125
  in Ireland 125–126
  in Irish public policy 68
  of other debtors 114–115, 117, 118, 123–128
  positive mimesis 124
  sacrifices of 68, 123–124, 126
  strategic defaulters 123, 126, 127
secondary deviance 129
sin 54, 70, 80, 145
Skeggs, Beverly 84, 130
Smiles, Samuel 22
smoking 46
social capital 82
social care 60
social exclusion 88, 122
Social Meaning of Money, The (Zelizer) 44
social welfare 69, 142
socialization 33–34, 35
socially bankrupt 86
Soederberg, Susanne 11, 28, 152
soft laws 152
Spooner, J. 29, 152, 153
stagflation 16, 42
Stamp, Stuart 3
Start Mortgages 43
state, the 17
  discretionary powers of PIPs 66
  thriftiness 66
  withdrawal from markets 15, 66, 69, 139, 141, 142, 144
status debts 78, 79, 118
status symbols 121
stereotyping
  of bad debtors 115, 127
  of debtors 68, 82–89
  fictitious 'others' 122
  of women 71, 84, 88
stigma 22–25, 26, 27
  definition 22
strategic default 119, 120, 134
strategic defaulters 126, 127, 128, 131–132, 133–134
  embracing identity of 129–130
  informal networks 132–133
  moral storytelling 133
Strike Debt movement 146, 150
student loans 4, 13, 17, 36
  cancellation of 150
  forgiveness of 23, 151
  pausing of 150, 154
Student Universal Support Ireland (SUSI) grant 36
subjectivity 37
surplus population 11
survival debts 42, 78, 87, 118
sweatbox of bankruptcy 10, 26, 49
  longer periods 50–51
  see also purgatorial sweatbox
symbolic gestures 44–46, 47, 67, 138, 139

INDEX

T

Thatcher, Margaret 15
thick description 5
Thompson, E.P. 133
time inconsistency 31
torture 81
transferability of theory 148
true love 33

U

unemployment 31–32, 40–42, 109
United States of America (USA)
　anti-debt social movements 106
　debt 13–14
　debt resolution process 91
　debtors
　　race of 26–27
　　women 27
　insolvency arrangements 106
unsecured debt 13

V

Veblen, T. 79
virtues 32
vulture funds 123–124, 126, 127, 128

W

water metaphors 14
Watts, G. 14

Weber, Max 53, 92, 138, 145
welfare fraud 117
welfare provision/state 23, 57, 121
　comparative frameworks 28
　conditionality 28
　in LMEs 28, 29
　reform 151–155
　sanctioning 28
　social problems in absence of 142
　stigma 28, 59
　withdrawal of 10
　see also debt relief; social welfare
women
　caring debts 71, 86
　characterization by PIPs 87–88
　consumerism characterization 71, 84
　debt relief 27
　economic vulnerability 87
　emotional strain on mothers 88–89
　indebtedness 87
　managing household budgets 86, 87–88
　responsibility for household tasks 35, 86, 87
　stereotyping of 71, 84, 88
work 96–97
workhouses 53

Z

Zelizer, Viviana 9, 44, 59, 86
Žižek, Slavoj 108

www.ingramcontent.com/pod-product-compliance
Lightning Source LLC
LaVergne TN
LVHW050048200525
811683LV00004B/60